ANNA AKHMATOVA
AND HER CIRCLE

D1603528

Анна Ахматова
и её окруже́ние

Progress Publishers 1991

ANNA AKHMATOVA AND HER CIRCLE

Compilation and notes by

KONSTANTIN POLIVANOV

Translated from the Russian by

PATRICIA BERIOZKINA

THE UNIVERSITY OF ARKANSAS PRESS

Fayetteville

1994

Originally published by Progress Publishers, Moscow, as

Анна Ахматова
и её окружёние

English edition copyright 1994 by the Board of Trustees of the University of Arkansas

98   97   96   95   94   5   4   3   2   1

Designed by Gail Carter

Silhouette of Akhmatova drawn by Elizaveta Kruglinova.

The paper used in this publication meets the minimum requirements of the
American National Standard for Permanence of Paper for Printed Library Materials
Z39.48-1984. ♾

Library of Congress Cataloging-in-Publication Data

Anna Akhmatova i eë okruzhenie. English
    Anna Akhmatova and her circle / compilation and notes by Konstantin Polivanov;
translated from the Russian by Patricia Beriozkina.
      p.   cm.
    ISBN 1-55728-308-7. — ISBN 1-55728-309-5 (pbk.)
    1. Akhmatova, Anna Andreevna, 1889-1966—Biography.   2. Akhmatova, Anna
Andreevna, 1889-1966—Contemporaries.   3. Poets, Russian—20th century—
Biography.   I. Polivanov, Konstantin.   II. Beriozkina, Patricia.   III. Title
PG3476.A324Z538133   1993
891.71'42—dc20   93-34633
[B]   CIP

CONTENTS

POETS' CIRCLE: ON AKHMATOVA'S FRIENDS

APPENDIX

PREFACE TO THE ENGLISH EDITION

Russians do not commonly use courtesy titles comparable to Mr., Mrs., Miss, and Ms. and often do not refer to one another or address one another by a single given name. These facts, together with the relatively spare use of personal pronouns, may have a Russian addressing Anna Andreyevna Akhmatova repeatedly as Anna Andreyevna or referring to the poet Nikolai Vladimirovich Nedobrovo two or three times in a short passage as Nikolai Vladimirovich. This is the polite use of the "name" and "patronymic," but the form is commonly used even among good friends in certain situations and in the writing of a work of this nature.

Another characteristic of the language involving names is the use of suffixes to create pet names, names special to the family or circle of friends, or to serve the purpose of "Mrs." in English. What might be called intimate names are, for example, Tata from Ekaterina and Tanya from Tatyana; Mrs. Punin is Irina Punina.

The use of names has not been Anglicized, because to do so would have lost even more of the Russian mind than translation inevitably does.

A couple of other notes on the text may prove helpful.

Because Akhmatova's friends and colleagues recorded their reminiscences apart from one another and at different times, and because the author of one piece will be one of the subjects of another, the same incident is sometimes described in two or three of the memoirs. The point of view is never the same, of course, and the repetitions have been left in place as an enrichment of the biography of Anna Akhmatova which all the reminiscences add up to.

English translations of the poetry from which quotes are occasionally offered in the text have been drawn from various translators. In some cases they will serve mainly to convey the content of the poems.

Throughout, a footnote not designated as editorial or identifying a translator of quoted poetry is by the author.

Parentheses are the authors'; brackets are the translators' or editors' additions.

Most individuals referred to in the text, as well as many of the literary works, institutions, and geographical locations, are identified in alphabetical order in the appendix.

Every effort has been made to ensure that no inclusion of poetry or prose in this book conflicts with rights held by others. There are difficulties in making such a determination with a collection compiled in Moscow shortly before the breakup of the Soviet Union. We will appreciate hearing from anyone who can help us to correct an oversight.

Very special thanks is due Professor Janet Tucker of the foreign language department of the University of Arkansas for invaluable help to the English editors in clarifying more than a few references to Russian and Soviet history and the contemporary culture.

FOREWORD

Anatoly Naiman
LESSONS OF A POET

In *Pages of a Diary,*[*] Akhmatova wrote the following about Pushkin's verse "In early life I remember school . . .":

"The marble compasses and lyres—everything . . . all my life it has seemed to me that Pushkin was speaking about Tsarskoye Selo. . . ."

In 1916, several decades before she wrote this, at the end of his critique on *Almanac of the Muses,* Mandelshtam referred to the same verse:

> Akhmatova's recent poetry reflects a change toward gravity, religious simplicity, and solemnity. I would put it like this: the woman has given way to the *wife*. To recall a line [by Pushkin]: "Modest and poorly dressed, but with the appearance of a majestic wife." The voice of renunciation is heard more and more in Akhmatova's verse. At present her poetry is increasingly becoming one of the symbols of Russia's greatness.

The "pages" of Akhmatova's "diary," which she wrote in the final years of her life, are as unlike a writer's diary—describing ordinary daily life—as her life—filled with losses and despair, on the verge of ruin and homelessness—was unlike what is customarily called a writer's life. Mandelshtam wrote, inscribing his first book for her: "bursts of consciousness in the noise of the times." And during these bursts she caught momentary snatches of events that formed her memories of him and became the essence of her later poetry. *Pages of a Diary* reveals the light of

---

[*] Akhmatova's reminiscences on Osip Mandelshtam (see p. 236).—ed.

time passing through a prism of pain and then collected once again in the prism of memory. It was in connection with her recollections of Mandelshtam that she reread his critique of her and later, no doubt, the Pushkin *terza rima*.

I first spoke with Akhmatova in the autumn of 1959. I was seated opposite her in the Leningrad apartment on Krasnaya Konnitsa Street. A short time later three other members of our poetic circle met her: Dmitri Bobyshev, Joseph Brodsky, and Yevgeny Rein. Akhmatova was the first to begin calling us a poetry group; we had common, or at least similar, viewpoints and opinions, but primarily we were united simply in friendship. After a time the four of us became Akhmatova's students. But the word "student" is somewhat misleading, implying learning the skills of the master, which was not really the case with us. Still, Akhmatova did teach, not only the art of poetry, but also the art of resisting the base instincts, inhumanity and disbelief in fate; she taught the art of genuineness and the integrity of believing in destiny; she taught the beauty of destiny. At that time, shunning her lessons and reproaches, I wrongly understood the idea of honest conversations. Today, a quarter of a century later, her lessons are more clear, and I can make an effort to more or less precisely formulate them.

I

Today, the Khrushchev thaw of the late 1950s to early 1960s* is described as being practically the sister of *perestroika*. Although outwardly similar, the differences are significant. In the late 1950s and early 1960s, the country and the people were being liberated not from the inconveniences of everyday living, but from camp zones and prison cells. In the face of those who lived through ten, twenty, thirty years of penal servitude, no one would dream of complaining that the head of state had yelled at him or that he was banished to the countryside for a few months. Also, at that time it was still risky to speak of one's opposition to the regime: those who

---

* After the Twentieth Party Congress, between the years of 1956 and 1964, Krushchev took the first steps to disclose the heinous crimes of Stalin and his circle. Millions of prisoners were freed from the camps and exile; most were posthumously rehabilitated. Literature was revived: the works of many writers who were repressed or, like Akhmatova, declared to be ideologically apart from the Communist regime, were now published.—ed.

were only "internal emigrants" strongly rejected this honor, for close on the heels of the "internal emigrant"★ was the "enemy of the people."★ Though she sincerely and deeply sympathized with Pasternak for the persecution he suffered for writing *Doctor Zhivago,* Akhmatova called the campaign against him a "butterfly fight" and also said that Brodsky's trial was "molding" his biography. She could not compare the disruption of ordinary life, much less the loss of a literary fund, country house, and the right to travel abroad, with the shooting of Gumilev and the death of Mandelshtam in a prison camp in the Far East. Akhmatova's awareness of what was happening to the people around her and to herself as well—the arrests, torture, loss of close friends, humiliation (i.e., the real tragedies rather than the unpleasantries of life)—combined with her strength of character, served to determine her rare, insightful, and masterful talent and to shape her independent and honest behavior.

Akhmatova created an astonishing impression with her substantive ideas, her gestures, facial expressions, and her character, as well as her aloofness and at the same time her deep involvement in her surroundings, through the ordinary presentation of such an extraordinary thing as her poetry. She never demonstrated in any other way whatsoever that she was a poet. She never exploited her position, her influence, or her mission. In conversation, her remarks were grave, irrefutable, irrevocable, and aphoristic, but she never spoke in aphorisms. Having an acute and accurate understanding of the workings of literary politics, she detested literary politics. It was beneath her to show up at the right place at the right time, or to take precautionary measures, much less to settle the score with others or to become involved in intrigues. She did not try to make a pretty package of her verse or her actions, and her writing style was a little disordered. Her method of composition—to be more precise, her recording of the humming noise, the singing, that came to her—was devoid of the need to consider commercial appeal. Quite the opposite: she knew how to capture her poetry's natural sound, like the blind man's violin that so enchanted Mozart. Akhmatova's most rigid construction of verse was the sonnet. Yet "The West spoke slander" or "All here shall, when I am gone, remain"

★ Political charges devised in the 1920s and used against Soviet citizens suspected of being unsympathetic to the Communist cause, in the first instance, or of having committed crimes against the State, in the second.

reflect the almost imperceptible changes she wrought in the stultified and typical modern sonnet.

Finally, she wrote verse; she did not describe a subject in verse. From the very beginning, critics noted the "novella style" of her short poems—the exposition of drama within the space of a few lines. But even intentionally informative poems, like "Biblical Verse," for example, never became illustrations of something already known by the reader and thus an imitation of poetry. Deeply reflecting a world's culture, her verse was not secondary to it. Her writing was always an act of *creativity* not of *composition*.

II

Possessing a "mysterious gift of song," Akhmatova used it wisely and carefully. She did not rely, like the majority of young poets, on "inner" talent. She put her talent into action, relating and comparing her first experiences with the vast body of poetry—of all art—accumulated in different languages and over many centuries. She nourished her own creativity with the creative energy of her predecessors and shared her skills and achievements with her contemporaries. Throughout her life she enriched her poetry by supplementing her voice with the echo of the voices of others. She devised an extremely complicated system of poetic mirrors in which each element of her poetry and all of poetry as a whole reflected a new universe, a universe that was remarkably made visible by art. Her fathomless verse compels us to forget her illusiveness.

Akhmatova always kept close at hand those books, often read and partially memorized, that she used frequently in her work—the Bible, Dante, Shakespeare, Pushkin, Baudelaire, and other ancient texts, especially Horace. There is a mysterious attraction in the quatrain often quoted by Akhmatova scholars; the attraction is greater than the thought itself:

> Do not repeat what someone else has said,
> Use your own words and imagination.
> But it may be that poetry itself
> Is simply one magnificent quotation.*

Beginning with a reference to Baratynsky ("Do not repeat: the inspiration is unique . . .") the verse unexpectedly becomes a *rubai* and thus

---

* Tr. by Olga Shartse.

gives an impression of "Oriental wisdom"; that is, something timeless and anonymous. And it attains this goal in a subtle, unpredictable way: the final word, the key "quotation," which repeats the first two rhymes, refutes the first word, the semantic beginning. The very construction of the quatrain is an example of Akhmatova's skillful and constantly employed practice of borrowing, referring, reflecting, and echoing.

Akhmatova made a myth of her fate, but it was her fate, the myths that she lived. She did not rent for wear the clothing of erudition. She claims that it was her meeting in autumn 1945 with the well-known English philosopher and philologist Isaiah Berlin (officially, of course, suspected of all the sins inherent in a foreigner) that resulted in the Central Committee resolution of 1946[*] and also the cold war between the East and West. One of the central poems in the cycle is dedicated to this man. "You demand my verses outright" begins with a carefully veiled quote from Dante (*Purgatory,* Canto XXX. 46–48). In turn, the last line of this Dante *terza rima* is a translation of Dido's words from Virgil's *Aeneid* (IV. 23), which brings the reader back to the previous poem in Akhmatova's cycle, "Dido speaks." Usually, reference to Dante in Akhmatova's poetry is a sign of persecution, banishment, or solitude. But the use of the Dido-Aeneas myth somehow gives the theme a new dimension. Aeneas, who prefers action, no matter how unimportant, to love, the only meaning of life, was for Akhmatova (who had been deserted in 1917 by a man[**] who sailed to England) a symbol not only of male perfidy but of the inevitability of it. "There was no Romeo, but there was, of course, Aeneas." These words, used occasionally in conversation, Akhmatova had originally set as an epigraph to the cycle "Dido speaks." Abandonment and desertion were linked with the English theme already in her early poetry, and this link would continue throughout the entire body of her work, especially through references to *Hamlet, Macbeth,* and other Shakespearean dramas. So in this poem as well. "Rome was built" is a typical Akhmatova reference to antiquity—that is, to time and not to place—while "The hordes of fleet are sailing" refers to place: England, "the mistress of the seas."

---

[*] On 14 August 1946 the Central Committee of the CPSU(B) issued a resolution, "On the magazines *Zvezda* and *Leningrad,*" in which the works of Akhmatova and the writer Mikhail Zoshchenko (1895–1958) were declared to be inimical to the policy of the Soviet state and to have a corrupting influence on Soviet youth.—ed.

[**] Boris Anrep (see his reminiscence later in the book).—ed.

Akhmatova said that she had never in her life met anyone who did not remember the day of the 1946 Central Committee resolution. In her view of the world, this was the day the cold war was declared. Perhaps there is some exaggeration in this interpretation of her role in what occurred, but there is no romantic fancy. Her verse was written by her fate, which she recognized as being one in common with Dido. Like many of the heroes of her poems and like herself, Dido was not a character in an ancient fable but a real person whose existence was documented by Virgil, Dante, and Akhmatova.

III

Akhmatova accepted her whole life as fate, first of all, as something preordained from above—Divine Will requiring an honorable and humble obedience—and secondly, as something integral and valuable, important in all its manifestations and excluding any element of chance. Its mission was to resolve two centuries of Petersburg and, in a broader sense, several centuries of Russian culture. The revolution defined the criteria, values, and achievements that this culture had accumulated throughout a diverse history of almost a thousand years. Though the history held its own contradictions, it was supported by a common foundation and direction. Akhmatova entered a new era being already a mature individual; she never changed her morals, principles, or tastes. She had much more in common with the author of "The Lay of Igor's Host" than with the poets and writers twenty to thirty years younger. She learned Russian culture from her family, relatives, friends, and predecessors. They transmitted its true legacy to Akhmatova gradually, carefully, and completely, not hurriedly, carelessly, and in pieces as in the 1950s and 1960s, when our generation tried to repair the "link of time."

The letters and early poetry (before *Evening*) of Anna Gorenko* paint an image of a provincial girl similar to Chekhov's heroines who fought against a stifling, cheerless existence among people spiritually alien to her. But already by 1910 she had become Anna Akhmatova, not to be confused with anyone else and remaining true to herself until the end. A few semi-bohemian years gave her fame, inculcated a high standard of artistic value,

* Akhmatova is a pseudonym. Before her marriage to Nikolai Gumilev she had the surname Gorenko.—ed.

and determined the direction of her life. The first day of World War I stripped away all the scenery once and for all and left her on a bare stage. From that day on she felt each blow of that cruel time. She saw people most dear to her taken away to be tortured in prison camps and to be shot; she stood in prison lines;* she suffered poverty, homelessness, public oppro-brium, surveillance, and abuse—all this she accepted and endured without concession, without despair, without losing her sanity. She never stopped writing poetry. For those who lived at that time, she became an example and the personification of stoicism, a living symbol of victory over inhu-manity. To those who were weak and near despair, she gave strength by her very survival and her refusal to give up. Her own weakness, her com-position under political pressure of the poems in *Glory to Peace,*** only evoked kindness and sympathy and made her more understandable and acceptable than a flawless heroine. She lived a long life that coincided with the first half of the twentieth century; an age was personified in her. She managed to escape only prison, though it loomed over her shoulder for decades. But if one tries to paint a portrait of the "average" Russian fate of that period, adding together all fates without exception and dividing by the number of people, Akhmatova's life would be characteristic. Its foundation was tragedy. She was a tragic figure even before the beginning of the new epoch ("It was terrible to live in that house . . . ," etc.), but the epoch was incredibly magnanimous in providing her with all the components of tragedy: bloodshed, inconsolable grief, innumerable graves. The valiant manner in which she endured her fate justified her writing:

. . . No, no alien wings protected me.
I was with my people, I was ever
Where my people had the ill luck to be.

* From the early 1920s until the mid-1950s, whenever they wanted to give a food or clothes parcel or simply to find out the location of a prisoner, relatives were forced to stand in line for hours. This was because the number of prisoners was so great and because the penal authorities, in accordance with the spirit of state policy, deliberately tried to complicate matters. Akhmatova describes such lines in *Requiem.*—ed.

** In 1949 Akhmatova's son, Lev Gumilev, was arrested for the third time. In the hope of easing his plight, she wrote a cycle of poems—*Glory to Peace*—praising Stalin's regime and socialist construction. The poems were published in 1950 in the magazine *Ogonyok*. Up until that time and after the 1946 Central Committee resolution "On the magazines *Zvezda* and *Leningrad*" her name was mentioned in print only in the context of grave political censure. The publication of this cycle had not the slight-est effect on the fate of her son. Lev Gumilev was not released until 1956, after the Twentieth Party Congress.—ed.

and also, "I am happy that I lived during those years and witnessed events unlike any others."

In early 1942, a quarter of a century after the drastic and irrevocable changes in her life, and the lives of all Russians, and a quarter of a century before her own death, Akhmatova published the poem "Courage." It was written during the war and, as would have been said in the old days, "on the occasion of the war." It was customarily cited whenever there arose a need to praise the poet and to juxtapose her patriotism with her many faults.

> We know that our fate in the balance is cast
> And we are the history makers.
> The hour for courage has sounded at last
> And courage has never forsaken us.
> We do not fear death where the wild bullets screech.
> Nor weep over homes that are gutted,
> For we shall preserve you our own Russian speech,
> The glorious language of Russia!
> Your free and pure utterance we shall convey
> To new generations, unshackled you'll stay
> Forever!*

In no way rejecting the "war" aspect of the verse, I read the poem in a broader and also stricter sense. Despite the catastrophic situation at the time, and despite the threat of enslavement by the enemy, there was no talk of the destruction of the Russian language; Russian speech was beyond any danger. The poem speaks of the courage demanded of the poet in order to resist the destruction of the great Russian culture by new times— both before and after the war—in order to preserve the free and pure Russian poetry of Gumilev, who was shot; of Tsvetayeva, who was hanged; of Mandelshtam, who disappeared behind barbed wire; and dozens of others who made up the list of dead. Akhmatova, by her courage, gave poetry to our grandchildren and saved it from being imprisoned by lies. With hope and some audacity, I presume to say that she has saved it forever.

* Tr. by Peter Tempest.

AKHMATOVA
ON AKHMATOVA

Akhmatova's autobiographical prose is for the most part fragmented and of varying degrees of completion and length. Exceptions are a few auto-biographical notes intended for publication in the form of prefaces to col-lections of her later verse and her remembrances of contemporary poets Alexandr Blok and Osip Mandelshtam (the latter is to be found in this book). The notes were written in her later life, for the most part scattered in notebooks among bits of verse, routine, and diary entries. Akhmatova was concerned about how subsequent generations would consider the cir-cumstances of her own life and fate and that of her closest literary circle. Many of her comments reflect her dispute with unkind writers of mem-oirs. She would often speak in detail about what was written about her to her younger friends: in the 1920s, to poet Pavel Liknitsky, who wrote a biography on Nikolai Gumilev; in the 1930s, to Lydia Chukovskaya, author of Notes on Anna Akhmatova, *and in the 1950s and 1960s, to philologist Vyacheslav Ivanov, poet Anatoly Naiman, and many others. This is why many of the remembrances of Akhmatova's contemporaries are filled with meaningful and thoughtful illustrations taken from Akhmatova's very words. Therefore, reminiscences about Akhmatova are a supplement and a continuation of the poet's own fundamental creative position, not only in prose, but also in poetry.*

Autobiographical Prose
SKETCHES, NOTES, DIARY ENTRIES, AND LECTURES

A LITTLE ABOUT MY LIFE

I was born on 11 (23)* June 1889 near Odessa (Bolshoi Fontan). At that time my father was a retired naval mechanical engineer. When I was a year old, we moved to the north—to Tsarskoye Selo—where I lived until I was sixteen.

My first reminiscences are of Tsarskoye Selo: the green, damp magnificence of the parks and pasture where my nanny would bring me for outings, the hippodrome where small, mottled ponies cantered, the old train station, and other things that were later described in *Ode to Tsarskoye Selo*.

I spent each summer near Sevastopol, on the coast of Streletskaya Bay. And it was there I learned to love the sea. The strongest memory I have of these years is of a place we lived close to—Chersonesus.

I learned to read from Lev Tolstoy's ABC-book. At the age of five, listening to the teacher of the older children, I also learned to speak French.

I wrote my first poem when I was eleven. For me poetry did not begin with Pushkin or Lermontov but with Derzhavin (*On the Birth of Portphyrogene Child*) and Nekrasov (*Father Frost the Red Nose*). My mother knew these poems by heart.

I studied at the Tsarskoye Selo women's gymnasium**—badly at first, later quite well, but always grudgingly.

In 1905 my parents separated, and my mother took the children south. We lived a whole year in Yevpatoria, where I completed the course of the next to final year of the gymnasium at home. I missed Tsarskoye Selo and wrote a great number of bad poems. The muffled echoes of the 1905 Revolution reached the isolation of Yevpatoria. I completed the last course of my studies in Kiev at the Fundukleyev Gymnasium and graduated in 1907.

---

* By the Gregorian calendar, adopted February 1918.—ed.

** School.—ed.

I enrolled in the law curriculum of the Higher Women's Courses in Kiev. I was happy studying the history of law and, especially, Latin. But I lost interest when the subjects were only about law itself.

In 1910 (25 April, Old Style)★ I married Nikolai Gumilev. We left for Paris and spent a month there.

The process of paving the living body of Paris with new boulevards (as Zola described it) was not quite complete (Raspail Boulevard). Werner, a friend of Edison, pointed out two tables in Taaverne Pantheon and said: "These are your social democrats. Here are the Bolsheviks and over there the Mensheviks." With sporadic success, women were trying to wear trousers (*jupes-culottes*) or practically swaddling their legs (*jupes-entravées*). Poetry was completely neglected and only the vignettes of more or less famous artists were being bought. I realized even then that Parisian fine art had swallowed French poetry.

Moving to St. Petersburg, I studied history and literature under Rayev at the Higher Women's Institute. At that time I was writing the poems that would later make up my first book.

I was amazed when I saw the proofs of Innokenty Annensky's *Cypress Casket*. Reading it, I forgot about everything else.

In 1910 symbolism was experiencing an evident crisis, and beginning poets were no longer joining this movement. Some went into futurism,★★ others into acmeism. I, along with my friends from the First Poets' Workshop—Mandelshtam, Zenkevich, and Narbut—became acmeists.

I spent the spring of 1911 in Paris, where I witnessed the first triumph of the Russian ballet. In 1912 I traveled around northern Italy (Genoa, Pisa, Florence, Bologna, Padova, Venice). I was enormously impressed by Italian painting and architecture: it's like a dream one remembers an entire lifetime.

My first collection of poems—*Evening*—came out in 1912. Only three hundred copies were printed. The reviews were favorable.

On October 1, 1912, my only son, Lev,† was born.

In March 1914 my second book—*The Rosary*—came out. It was destined to exist only six weeks. In early May the Petersburg season began to

---

★ Julian Calendar.—ed.

★★ Other poets in this movement were Boris Pasternak, Vladimir Mayakovsky, David Burlyuk, and Valimir Khlebnikov.—ed.

† Lev Gumilev is now a well-known historian and ethnographer.—ed.

fade: everyone gradually departed. This time it turned out that we were leaving Petersburg for good. We returned not to St. Petersburg but to Petrograd,* having moved immediately from the nineteenth century into the twentieth. Everything had changed, including the appearance of the city. It would appear that a small book of love lyrics by a beginning author should have drowned in world events. But time deemed otherwise.

I spent each summer in the former Tver province, fifteen versts** from Bezhetsk. This is not a very picturesque place: a hilly field marked by even, plowed squares, mills, bogs, drained marshes, and cornfields everywhere. This is where I wrote many of the poems in *Rosary* and *A Flock of White Birds*. *A Flock of White Birds* was published in September 1917.

Readers and critics have been unjust to this book. For some reason they believe it was less successful than *Rosary*. It appeared under considerably more threatening circumstances. Transportation was at a standstill, and it was impossible to send the book even to Moscow. All the copies were distributed in Petrograd. Magazines and newspapers were shutting down, so, unlike *Rosary, A Flock of White Birds* had little publicity. Famine and dislocation increased with every day. These circumstances are strangely ignored today.

After the October Revolution I worked in the library of the Agronomy Institute. In 1921 my collection *The Plantain* was published, and in 1922 my book *Anno Domini*.

Sometime in the mid-twenties I began with great diligence my study of the architecture of old St. Petersburg and the works of Pushkin. The study of Pushkin resulted in three works—on "The Golden Cockerel," on Benjamin Constant's "Adolphe," and on "The Stone Guest." All were published eventually. "Alexandrina," "Pushkin and the Nevan Coast," and "Pushkin in 1828," works on which I have spent almost the last twenty years of my life, will probably be included in a book to be called *On the Death of Pushkin*.

In the mid-twenties my new poems were almost unpublished and my old ones were not being reprinted.

I was in Leningrad when the Patriotic War of 1941 began. In late

---

* The name was changed in 1914, at the start of the war with Germany.—ed.

** A verst is approximately equal to seven-tenths of a mile.—ed.

September, after the blockade had already started,* I left Leningrad and flew to Moscow.

Until May 1944 I lived in Tashkent, hungrily grasping for any news about Leningrad and the front. Like other poets, I often gave recitals in hospitals, reading my verse to wounded soldiers. It was in Tashkent that I first realized what the shade of a tree and the sound of water meant in the scorching heat. I also discovered human kindness: I suffered many serious illnesses in Tashkent.

In May 1944 I flew back to the Moscow spring. The city was filled with joyful hopes and expectations of the approaching victory. In June I returned to Leningrad.

I was so appalled at the specter my city had become that I described my return in prose. I wrote essays—"Three Lilacs" and "Visiting with Death," the latter about reciting verse at the front in Terioki. I have always found prose mysterious and intriguing. I knew everything about poetry right from the start, but I never knew anything about prose. Everyone praised my first attempt, but of course I didn't believe them. I called in Zoshchenko. He told me to omit a few things and that he agreed with the rest. I was happy. Later, after my son was arrested,** I burned it along with all my archives.

I have long had an interest in literary translation. In the years after the war I translated a great deal and continue to do so now.

In 1962 I finished *Poem Without a Hero,* on which I had worked for twenty-two years.

Last winter, on the eve of Dante's Year, I once again heard the sounds of Italian speech—I visited Rome and Sicily. In the spring of 1955 I traveled to the land of Shakespeare,† saw the British sky and the Atlantic, saw some old friends and met new ones, and once again visited Paris.

I did not stop writing verse. For me poetry is a link with time, with the new life of my people. When I was writing, I lived under the same

---

* For nine hundred days, beginning in September of 1941, Leningrad was surrounded by German and Finnish troops, and contact with the outside world (especially during the first six months) was virtually cut off.—ed.

** In 1949 Lev Gumilev was arrested a third time.—ed.

† In 1964 Akhmatova was invited to visit Catania, Sicily, where she was awarded a literary prize, and in 1965 she traveled to Oxford, where she was awarded the honorary degree of doctor at Oxford University.—ed.

rhythm that sounded during the heroic past of my country. I am happy to have lived during those years and to have been witness to such incomparable events.   1965

THE HUT

I was born the same year as Charlie Chaplin, Tolstoy's "The Kreutzer Sonata," the Eiffel Tower, and, it seems, Eliot. That summer—1889—Paris celebrated the centennial of the fall of the Bastille. Midsummer Night was and still is celebrated on the night I was born—23 June. I was named Anna after my grandmother Anna Yegorovna Motovilova. Her mother— the Tatar princess Akhmatova (whose surname I took as my pen name, having no idea that I wanted to be a Russian poet)—was descended from Genghiz Khan. I was born at the Sarakini summer cottage (Bolshoi Fontan, 11th railway station) near Odessa. This summer cottage (actually, it was more like a hut) stood at the bottom of a narrow and downward-sloping piece of land next to the post office. The seacoast there is very steep, and the rails lie along the very edge.

Once when I was fifteen and we were living at the summer cottage in Lustdorf we happened to pass by this particular area, and my mother suggested I get out and look at the Sarakini cottage, which I had never seen before. At the door of the hut, I said, "One day there will be a memorial plaque here." I was not being vain; it was just a silly joke. Mama was upset: "Lord! How badly I have raised you."   1957

· · ·

No one in my large family wrote poetry. But the first Russian woman poet, Anna Bunina, was the aunt of my grandfather Erasm Ivanovich Stogov. The Stogovs were modest landowners in the Mozhaisk region of the Moscow province. They were moved here after the insurrection during the time of Posadnitsa* Marfa. In Novgorod they had been a wealthier and more distinguished family.

Khan Akhmat, my ancestor, was killed one night in his tent by a Russian killer-for-hire. Karamzin tells us that this marked the end of the

---

* *Posadnik*—governor of a medieval Russian city-state; *posadnitsa*—wife of a *posadnik*. See appendix for Marfa.—ed.

Mongol yoke on Russia. On that day, to commemorate the happy occasion, a religious procession marched from Sretensky (The Feast of Purification) Monastery in Moscow. It was well known that this Akhmat was a descendant of Genghiz Khan.

In the eighteenth century, one of the Akhmatov princesses—Praskovya Yegorovna—married the rich and famous Simbirsk landowner Motovilov. Yegor Motovilov was my great-grandfather; his daughter, Anna Yegorovna, was my grandmother. She died when my mother was nine years old, and I was named in her honor. Several diamond rings and one with an emerald were made from her brooch. Though my fingers are thin, still her thimble didn't fit me.

THE SHUKHARDINA HOUSE

The house was a hundred years old. It belonged to the merchant widow Yevdokia Ivanovna Shukhardina, who looked like a lynx and whose strange clothes I used to admire as a child. The house stood on the corner of Shirokaya Street and Bezymyanny Lane (the second from the train station). They say that before the railroad was built, there was a kind of tavern or roadside inn here at the entrance to the city. I tore the wallpaper (layer by layer) from my yellow room. The last layer was a wonderful, bright red color. "This is the wallpaper that was in the tavern," I thought to myself. The shoemaker B. Nevolin lived in the cellar. Today this would be a still from a historical movie.

I remember this house better than any other in the world. This was where I spent my childhood (on the ground floor) and my youth (on the upper floor). About half my dreams take place there. We left in the spring of 1905. Later it was renovated and lost its old look. It has been gone for a long time. On this spot now there is a railway station park or something of the sort. (I was last in Tsarskoye Selo in June 1944.) Gone as well is the Tur cottage ("Joy" or "New Chersonesus")—three versts from Sevastopol—where I spent each summer with my family up to the age of thirteen and earned the nickname "wild girl." Nor does the Slepnyovo remain, where we lived from 1911 to 1917. The only thing that remains is the word itself used in my poems *A Flock of White Birds* and *The Plantain*. But, no doubt, this is as it should be.   1957

• • •

Sometimes a funeral procession of incredible magnificence would pass down Shirokaya Street either to or from the train station. A boy's choir sang with the voices of angels, and the coffin was concealed under live plants and flowers dying in the frost. People carried lit lanterns, the priests burned incense, and the horses with blinders stepped slowly and ceremoniously. Behind the coffin walked officers of the Guard (who always brought to mind Vronsky's brother,*—in other words, "having drunk, open faces"), and gentlemen in top hats. Important old women with their entourages sat in carriages that followed the hearse. They seemed to be waiting for their own turn, and everything resembled the funeral described in "Queen of Spades."**

Later (when I recalled these scenes) it always seemed to me they were a part of the grand funerals of the entire nineteenth century. This was how they buried Pushkin's youngest contemporaries in the nineties. With the blinding snow and bright Tsarskoye Selo sun, it was a magnificent sight. The yellow light and heavy darkness that fell from all around made it frightening and even a little infernal.

I was ten years old and we lived (one winter) in the Daudel house (on the corner of Srednaya and Leontyevskaya streets in Tsarskoye Selo). A Hussar officer who lived somewhere close by would leave in his red and terrifying automobile. After a block or two, the car would break down. It would then be hauled home in shame. At that time no one really believed in the possibilities of the automobile, much less those of air travel.

•   •   •

I was eleven years old when I first began writing my autobiography in my mother's red-lined household account book (1900). When I showed my notes to my elders, they said I remembered almost back to the time when I was two years old (Pavlovsk Park, the puppy Ralph, etc.).

•   •   •

The smells of Pavlovsk Railway Station . . . Like a deaf-mute, I am doomed to remember them my entire life. First, the smoke from the

---

* A character in Tolstoy's *Anna Karenina*.—ed.
** A story by Pushkin.—ed.

ancient steam locomotive that brought me to Tyarlevo, the park and *salon de musique* (which we called salty *muzhik*★); second, the polished parquet and a barbershop smell; third, strawberries in the railway station store (Pavlovsk); fourth, the mignonettes and roses (coolness in oppressive heat), the fresh roses sold in the flower kiosk (to the left), and the cigars and greasy food from the restaurant. And also the ghost of Nastasia Filippovna.★★ Tsarskoye was everyday, because it was home; Pavlovsk was always a holiday, because one had to travel to get there, because it was far from home.

• • •

People of my generation are not threatened by sad returns—we have nowhere to return to. . . . Sometimes it seems to me that it would be possible to take a car and travel on the days when Pavlovsk station is opened (when the parks are so deserted and fragrant) to those spots where the "inconsolable shadow searches for me." But then I begin to understand that this is impossible, that one should not delve into the mansions of the memory (especially while traveling in a metal box propelled by gasoline), that I will see nothing and in trying will erase what I see so clearly now.

AN IMAGINARY BIOGRAPHY

Winters were at Tsarskoye, summers in the Crimea (at the Tur cottage). But it is impossible to convince anyone of this, because they all believe I am Ukrainian. First, because the surname of my father is Gorenko; second, because I was born in Odessa and graduated from the Fundukleyev Gymnasium; third, and most important, because N. S. Gumilev wrote:

> What I took from the serpent's nest,
> the serpent's nest in Kiev,
> was a witch, not a wife.
> (1910)

Yet I lived less in Kiev than I did in Tashkent (1941–44, during the evacuation)—one winter, when I was finishing at the Fundukleyev Gymnasium, and two winters when I was studying in the Higher Women's

---

★ "pickled peasant."—ed.
★★ The heroine in Dostoyevsky's *The Idiot*, set in Petersburg and Pavlovsk.—ed.

Courses. But there is no limit to the lack of consideration people show each other. And the reader of this book must learn to realize that everything did not happen the way, at the time, nor at the place as might have been thought. It is sad to say this, but people see only what they want to see and hear only what they want to hear. They speak primarily to themselves and almost always answer themselves, not listening to the persons they are supposed to be conversing with. Ninety percent of the incredible rumors, false reputations, and sacredly guarded gossip is based on this failing of the human character. (We still preserve Poletika's venomous remarks about Pushkin!) I only ask those who don't agree with me to recall what they have heard said about themselves.

THE WILD GIRL

A pagan childhood. In the vicinity of this cottage ("Joy," the Streletskaya Bay, Chersonesus), I earned the nickname "Wild Girl" because I went barefoot, did not wear a hat, etc., because I jumped from a boat into the open sea and swam during storms, and because I was in the sun so much my skin peeled. All these things shocked the provincial Sevastopol nobility.

• • •

My childhood was as unique and wonderful as that of all children in the world. . . .

It is both easy and difficult to speak of childhood. Because it's fixed in time, it is very easy to describe. But too often this description reflects a sentimentality that is totally alien to such an important and profound period of life as childhood. Moreover, some wish to portray themselves as too unhappy in childhood, others as too happy. Both are usually nonsense. Children have nothing with which to make comparisons, and they simply don't know if they are happy or not. As soon as consciousness appears the individual finds himself in a completely prepared and static world, and it is only natural to believe that this world was never any different. This initial picture remains in the person's soul, and there are people who believe only in it, somehow trying to conceal this strangeness. Others, on the contrary, have no faith whatsoever in this picture and rather awkwardly ask: "Was that really me?"

Somewhere around the age of fifty we return to our early life. This explains some of my 1940 poems ("Willow," "Arms of a Fifteen-year-old . . ."), which, as is known, evoked reproaches that I was living in the past.

. . .

Anna's* room: the window facing Bezymyanny Lane . . . which in winter was deeply snowbound and in summer was overgrown with weeds—luxuriant nettles and giant burdocks. . . . A bed, a desk for preparing lessons, a bookshelf. A candle in a brass candlestick (there was no electricity yet). An icon in the corner. No attempt was made to brighten the austerity of the surroundings with knick-knacks, embroidery, or postcards.

. . .

In Tsarskoye Selo she did everything expected of a well-brought-up young lady of that time. She knew how to hold her hands in the proper way, how to curtsey, how to answer politely and concisely in French the question of an elderly lady, and how to fast during Passion Week in the gymnasium church. Sometimes, but not often, her father would take her to the opera (in her gymnasium uniform) at Mariinsky Theater (in the box). She visited the hermitage and the Alexander III Museum. In spring and summer she listened to music in Pavlovsk Station, and went to museums and art exhibitions. In winter she frequently skated in the park.

In the parks of Tsarskoye Selo there is also antiquity, but it is quite different (statues). She read a good deal. She was (in my opinion) greatly influenced by the master of charisma at the time, Knut Hamsun (*Enigmas and Mystery*); *Pan* and *Victoria* to a lesser degree. Another dominant influence was Ibsen. . . . She was a bad pupil in the lower grades, but later a good one. She always attended the gymnasium grudgingly (she had few friends).

. . .

I wrote my first poem when I was eleven (it was horrible), but for some reason my father called me a "decadent poetess" even earlier. . . .

---

* Akhmatova wrote this and the following excerpt in the third person, as planned inserts in the reminiscences of Valeria Sreznevskaya, whom she met in the gymnasium and who remained a friend for life.—ed.

I graduated not from the Tsarskoye Selo Gymnasium (because my family moved south) but from the Kiev (Fundukleyev Gymnasium), where I studied only one year. Later I studied two years at the Kiev Higher Women's Courses. . . . All this time (with considerable lapses) I continued to write poems, for some unknown reason numbering them. As a matter of interest I might relate that judging from extant manuscripts, "Song of a Last Meeting" was my two-hundredth poem.

• • •

I returned north in June 1910. After Paris, Tsarskoye seemed quite dead to me. This was not surprising. But where had my Tsarskoye Selo life disappeared to in those five years? I did not find one classmate from the gymnasium and did not cross the threshold of one Tsarskoye Selo home. Then the new life in St. Petersburg began. In September Nikolai Gumilev left for Africa.* During the 1910–11 winter I wrote the poems that comprised my book *Evening*. On 25 March Gumilev returned from Africa and I showed him my poetry. . . .

• • •

For some reason these meager poems of an exceptionally frivolous young girl were reprinted thirteen times (if I saw all the counterfeit publications). They also appeared in several foreign languages. The young girl herself (as far as I recall) had not foreseen such an outcome and, "to avoid becoming upset," hid under sofa cushions the magazines where they were first printed. Distressed that *Evening* had appeared, she left for Italy (spring 1912). Sitting in a tram, she looked at the people and thought: "They are happy; they have no books being published."

SLEPNYOVO

At that time I wore a green malachite necklace and a bonnet made of fine lace. In the north end of my room hung an icon—Christ in the dungeon. The narrow sofa was so hard that I would wake up at night and sit for a long time in order to rest. . . . Above the sofa hung a small portrait

---

* Gumilev made two ethnographic expeditions to Africa in the 1910s.—ed.

of Nikolai I. I did not consider it an exotic object, as did the snobs in St. Petersburg, but simply and seriously as Onegin* did ("the portrait of Czars on the wall"). I don't know if there was a mirror in the room, I've forgotten. In the cupboard were the remnants of an old library, including *Northern Flowers,*** Baron Brambeum, and Rousseau. I was there when the war began in 1914, and it was there that I spent the last summer (1917).

In 1911 I came to Slepnyovo directly from Paris. Though she had known everyone in Slepnyovo for ages, the hunched-back servant in the women's room at the railway station in Bezhetsk refused to recognize me as a *barynya* and said to someone: "A Frenchwoman has come to the people of Slepnyovo." And Ivan Yakovlevich Derin, a bearded bumpkin in glasses who was the head of the Zemstvo, was almost dying of embarrassment to find himself seated next to me at the table. He could think of nothing better than to ask: "You probably find it very cold here after Egypt?" The fact is, he had heard that because of my incredible thinness and (as it seemed to them at the time) my mysteriousness, the local youth called me the famous London mummy who brought misfortune to everyone.

Nikolai Stepanovich [Gumilev] could not abide Slepnyovo. He yawned, grew bored, and left for obscure places. He wrote, "these boring, far from golden, old-world ways" and filled the album of the Kuzmin-Karavayevs with mediocre poems. But some things he did realize and learn.

I did not ride horseback and did not play tennis; I only picked mushrooms in both Slepnyovo gardens. Behind my shoulders Paris still glowed in a kind of final sunset (1911). . . .

Once I spent the winter in Slepnyovo. It was wonderful. Everything seemed to be a return to the nineteenth century, almost to the time of Pushkin. There were sleighs, felt boots, bear-skin lap-rugs, enormous fur coats, ringing silence, snowdrifts, diamond-brilliant snow. It was there I saw in the New Year of 1917. After oppressive, wartime Sevastopol, where I suffocated from asthma and shivered in a cold rented room, it seemed to me that I had arrived in the Promised Land. Meanwhile, in St. Petersburg, Rasputin had already been killed and people were waiting for the revolution, which had been scheduled for 20 January. (On that day I ate lunch at

---

* Protaganist in Pushkin's novel-in-verse, *Yevgeny Onegin.*—ed.
** A literary almanac of the early nineteenth century.—ed.

Natan Altman's. He gave me his drawing on which he had written: "On the day of the Russian Revolution." On another drawing (still preserved) he wrote: "To the soldier's wife Gumileva* from the draftsman Altman.")

• • •

I think of Slepnyovo as an architectural arch . . . small in the beginning, then larger and larger, and finally—total freedom (if you leave it).

• • •

No one really knows in what epoch one lives. Thus, we too did not know in the early 1910s that we were living on the eve of the first European war and the October Revolution.   1957

THE 1910S

The year 1910 was the year of crisis for symbolism and the deaths of Lev Tolstoy and Komissarzhevskaya. The year 1911 brought the Chinese Revolution, which changed the face of Asia. It was also the year of the publication of Blok's notebooks, which were filled with forebodings . . . and *The Cypress Casket.*** . . . I recently heard someone say: "The 1910s were the most vulgar time." Perhaps that is what one feels compelled to say today, but I replied that along with everything else, it was the time of Stravinsky and Blok, Anna Pavlova and Scriabin, Rostovtsev and Chaliapine, Meyerhold and Diaghilev. Mandelshtam, Pasternak, and Tsvetayeva began their careers, and I have not even mentioned Mayakovsky and Khlebnikov. This was their time. In the Uffizi Gallery in Florence, statues of Dante, Petrarch, Boccaccio, Michelangelo, and da Vinci are displayed. I thought they were the busts of famous men, but an Italian told me: "No, they're just native Florentines." It was the same in the 1910s.

In this decade, of course, like any other time, there were vulgar people with inflated reputations (for example, Igor Severyanin). Bryusov's "fame" also turned out to be dubious (it was already seriously flickering). Compared with the crude first decade, the second—the 1910s—represented a time of discipline and harmony. Fate cut off the second half and did so

---

* Nikolai Gumilev volunteered for the front and fought there from 1914 into 1917.—ed.

** A collection of verse by Innokenty Annensky, actually published (posthumously) in 1910.—ed.

with a lot of bloodshed. Someone told me: "Those you met in Paris in 1910 and 1911 were the last Frenchmen. They were all killed at Verdun and on the Marne." I read the same thing later in Sartre's *Le sursis*.

They were good fellows who in the summer of 1917 went to play tennis in the Crimean resorts. They have yet to return. Did the game wear on? It's horrible to think of those interrupted lives.

No other generation in history experienced such a fate, and perhaps there was no other generation like it. Though it is now an accepted thing to praise the twenties, they were not much—they reflected only the force of inertia. Blok, Gumilev, and Khlebnikov died almost at the same time;[*] Remizov, Tsvetayeva, and Khodasevich went abroad, joining Chaliapine, Mikhail Chekhov, Stravinsky, Prokofiev, and one-half of the ballet (Pavlova, Nijinsky, and Karsavina). Science lost Rostovtsev, Berdyaev, and Vernadsky; Boris Pasternak remained silent after completing his wonderful book[**] in the summer of 1917 (it was published in 1922)—he raised his son, read thick books, and wrote three poems.[†] According to Nadya [N. Ya. Mandelshtam], Mandelshtam was suffering from asthma and, moreover, had been declared an internal émigré by the Brik Salon,[††] and Akhmatova (1925) was immured in the first available wall.

In June 1941 when I read M. Ts. [Marina Tsvetayeva] a part of a poem (the first draft), she remarked rather caustically: "One must have a lot of courage to write about harlequins, Columbines, and Pierrots in 1941."[‡] She was obviously implying that my poem represented an artistic stylization of the world in the same manner as Benoit and Somov; i.e., what she as an émigré had opposed as out-dated drivel. Time showed that this was not the case; time worked for *Poem Without a Hero*. Something remarkable has happened in the past twenty years; i.e., before our eyes there has been an almost complete renaissance of the 1910s. And this strange process continues. The post-Stalin youth and foreign Slavonic scholars are equally filled with interest in the pre-revolutionary years. Mandelshtam, Pasternak,

---

[*] 1921, 1921, 1922, respectively.—ed.

[**] *My Sister, Life. Summer of 1917,* published in 1922.—ed.

[†] "1905," "Lieutenant Schmidt," and "Spektorsky."—ed.

[††] The salon of Osip Brik, a Soviet literary critic, which served to bring together writers and officials of the Main Political Department or "political police."—ed.

[‡] Marina Tsvetayeva strongly disliked the first sections of *Poem Without a Hero* that Akhmatova read to her in 1941.—ed.

and Tsvetayeva are being translated and published in Russian; Gumilev has been reprinted a number of times; dissertations on Bely are being defended in Cambridge and the Sorbonne; lengthy scholarly treatises are being written on Khlebnikov; the books of the formalists cost *les yeux de la tête;* second-hand booksellers are anxious to acquire Kuzmin; and practically "everyone" has a copy of Khodasevich.* Almost no one has been forgotten; almost everyone is remembered.

I mention this in connection with my poem because, while it remains a historical poem, it is very relevant to the contemporary reader who secretly wishes to roam the St. Petersburg of 1913 and wants to learn about everyone long admired (or disliked). Members of the Leningrad elite ask me what issue of *Russkaya Mysl* contains Nedobrovo's article about *Rosary*, and Antony Cross of Cambridge is writing a work to commemorate the fiftieth anniversary of this collection's first publication (30 March 1964).

B. P. [Boris Pasternak] thought he alone was of interest to people abroad. This was one of his mistakes. And there is something else: as interest in Blok decreases, it increases in Andrei Bely, about whom everyone is speaking now. But, Heavens! What will become of Sologub? Is it possible that he will remain so utterly forgotten? (Al. Remizov is well-loved and remembered abroad.)

There is a veritable cult of Vyacheslav Ivanov and his articles at Oxford. Bowra and Berlin went to pay their respects to him (between us: was this not a sight for the gods?!), he was allowed to do anything, even enter into a mixed marriage.

• • •

The twentieth century began with the war in the autumn of 1914, just as the nineteenth century began with the Vienna Congress. A calendar's dates are insignificant. Without any question, Symbolism is a phenomenon of the nineteenth century. Our rebellion against Symbolism was justified, because we felt ourselves to be children of the twentieth century and did not wish to remain in the preceding one.

★ Vladislav Khodasevich was not published in the USSR until 1986. Beginning in the 1950s, his poems, like the unpublished works of Akhmatova, Gumilev, and many other poets and writers, were typed on typewriters and distributed in the form of so-called *samizdat* (self-publication).—ed.

THE CITY

I have early recollections of St. Petersburg—in the 1890s. This was essentially the Petersburg of Dostoyevsky. A Petersburg before tramways, a city with horses, horse-drawn trolleys, the rumbling and screeching, the boats, the signs from top to bottom that mercilessly hid the architecture of the houses. It seemed especially fresh and pungent after quiet and fragrant Tsarskoye Selo. Inside Gostiny Dvor were swarms of pigeons; in the corners of the galleries were large gold-rimmed icons and burning icon-lamps. The Neva was filled with boats, the streets with the sounds of foreign languages.

The houses were painted mostly red (like the Winter Palace), crimson, and pink. There were none of these beige and gray colors which now merge so depressingly with the vapor of Leningrad dusk.

At that time there were still many wonderful wooden houses—manorial estates—on Kamennoostrovsky Prospekt and around Tsarskoye Selo Railway Station. They were taken apart for firewood in 1919. The two-story estates of the eighteenth century, some built by famous architects, were even better. "Fate dealt with them badly"—in the 1920s new stories were added to them. On the other hand, there was practically no greenery in the Petersburg of the 1890s. When my mother came to see me for the last time, in 1927, she involuntarily recalled, along with her memories of the People's Freedom organization,* St. Petersburg not just in the 1890s but in the 1870s (her youth). She marveled at the amount of greenery. And this was just the beginning! In the nineteenth century there was only granite and water.

Just now I was amazed to read in *Zvezda*** (an article by Lev Uspensky) that Maria Fyodorovna rode around in a gilded carriage. Nonsense! There were indeed gilded carriages, but they were supposed to be used only on very ceremonious occasions—coronations, marriages, christenings, the first reception of an ambassador. Maria Fyodorovna's equipage was distinguished only by the medals worn by her coachman. How strange that

---

* The most numerous and active of the underground antigovernment parties in Russia between 1870 and 1880. There is no concrete evidence that Akhmatova's mother, Inna Erazmovna Gorenko (1856–1930), was connected specifically with the People's Freedom.—ed.

** A literary magazine that began publication in Leningrad in 1924.—ed.

they can come up with such nonsense after only forty years. What will happen after one hundred?   1957

MORE ABOUT THE CITY

You can't believe your eyes when you read that the staircases of St. Petersburg always smelled of burned coffee. (There were often tall mirrors, sometimes rugs.) Not one staircase in one Petersburg home ever smelled of anything except the perfume of the passing ladies and the cigars of the passing gentlemen. No doubt the comrade had in mind the so-called "back staircase" (which has in most cases today become the only staircase). It is true that one could smell anything there, because the doors from all the kitchens opened to it. For example, there was the smell of *bliny** at Shrovetide, mushrooms and vegetable oil during Lent, and Neva fish in May. When something smelly was prepared, the cooks would open the door to the back staircase "to get rid of the fumes" (this was how it was put). But, unfortunately, the back staircases smelled most often of cats.

The sounds in the yards of St. Petersburg. First of all, the sound of firewood being thrown into the cellar; organ-grinders ("sing, my swallow, sing; soothe your heart . . ."); metal sharpeners ("I'll sharpen knives, scissors . . ."); ragmen ("housecoats, housecoats"), who were always Tatars; tinsmiths; "I have pretzels from Vyborg." . . . The sounds echoed through the yards like voices in a well.

Smoke above the rooftops. The Dutch ovens and fireplaces of St. Petersburg—futile fires in the freezing weather; the ringing bells drowning out the sounds of the city. The beating of drums that always brought to mind executions. Sleighs banging into posts on humpback bridges that today have all but lost their humps. The last green branch on the islands always reminded me of Japanese engravings. The horse's head frozen with icicles is almost on your shoulder; the smell of wet leather in the horse-drawn cab with its hood rolled up against the rain. I composed almost all of *Rosary* in such surroundings, only getting the last drafts down at home. . . .

• • •

---

* A kind of pancake.—ed.

In the 1920s Tsarskoye Selo was something indescribable. All the fences were burned; rusty hospital cots from the First World War stood over open manholes, the streets were overgrown with weeds, roosters of all colors and goats, for some reason called Tamara, roamed around crowing and bleating. On the gates of the once magnificent Stenbock-Fermor home a large sign read: "Mating Station." But on Shirokaya Street the autumn oaks—witnesses of my childhood—gave off the same astringent smell, the crows on the cathedral crosses screeched the same as when I walked along Soborny Park to the gymnasium, and the statues in the Tsarskoye Selo parks looked the same as in the years of my youth. I sometimes recognized the tattered and frightening figures as residents of Tsarskoye Selo. Gostiny Dvor was closed.

· · ·

. . . In 1936 I began to write again, but my penmanship had changed and my voice was different. By the bridle, life brings before me a Pegasus a little like the Pale or Black Horse of the Apocalypse from yet unwritten verse. [. . .] There can be no return to the former way. It is not for me to judge which is better or worse. Nineteen forty is the apogee. My verses are non-stop, one immediately following the other. They come quickly, breathlessly, and sometimes, probably, they are bad.

FROM A LETTER TO XXX
(IN LIEU OF A FOREWORD)

In the first half of March 1940, the margins of my notebooks began to be filled with irrelevant lines. This was the case especially with my draft of "Vision," which I wrote during the night of the attack against Vyborg and the announcement of a truce.

At that time the meaning of those lines seemed obscure, even frightening. For a rather long time they did not promise to become anything whole, seeming to be ordinary, stray lines until their hour came and they were forged into the shape you see them in now.

In autumn of the same year I wrote another three non-lyrical poems, wanting in the beginning to add them to *Kitezhanka* and write a book entitled *Small Poems*. But one of them, *Poem Without a Hero*, exploded, ceased to be small, and, most important, would not tolerate a companion. The other two, "Dostoyevsky's Russia" and "Arms of a Fifteen-year-old," suffered another fate: apparently they perished in the siege of Leningrad, and what I recalled from memory here in Tashkent was but a hopeless fragment. Thus, *Kitezhanka* remained in proud solitude, as our forefathers used to say.

In Tashkent, out of "evacuation loneliness," I wrote "The House Was One-Hundred-Years Old." There, in a typhus-induced delirium, I constantly heard the sound of my heels on Tsarskoye Selo's Gostiny Dvor— me walking to the gymnasium. The snow around the cathedral grew darker, crows screeched, bells rang; someone was being buried.

• • •

I started to write my autobiography several times but with, as they say, intermittent success. The last time was in 1946. . . . As far as I remember it was not very detailed, but it included my impressions of 1944— "Leningrad after the Blockade," "Three Lilacs," about Tsarskoye Selo, and a description of my trip in late July to Terioki, at the front, to recite poems to the soldiers. It is difficult for me to recall them now. The rest has become so indelible in my memory that it will disappear only with me.

1957

• • •

How long ago it all was. . . . The first day of the war, which seemed so recent; Victory Day, which, it seems, was just yesterday, and 14 August, 1946.* . . . It is already history. Not long ago there were translations, some I handed in, some I didn't; daily life in Zamoskvorechye; the little pines that now sway angrily against the background of a white night.

"We are way in the north here, and this year I chose autumn as my friend,"** I wrote last year. It was so long ago, and here I am trying to describe the nineties of the nineteenth century.   1957

---

* The day the Central Committee adopted the infamous resolution on the magazines *Zvezda* and *Leningrad.*—ed.
** From "Let someone enjoy southern skies fresh and clear. . . ."—ed.

About the book that I will never write, though it exists nonetheless, and people have deserved it: At first I wanted to write it in its entirety, but now I have decided to take some pieces from it and make a narrative about my life and the fate of my generation. The concept for this book is old, and my friends are acquainted with some of it.

•   •   •

Who would have thought that I would be destined to last so long, and why did I not know it? My memory has become incredibly sharp. The past surrounds me and demands something. What? The kind shadows of the distant past almost speak to me. Perhaps for them it is the last occasion when bliss, which people call oblivion, will pass over them. Flowing from somewhere are words spoken half a century ago and which I have not recalled once in these fifty years. It would be strange to try to offer as the only explanation for this my summer solitude and closeness with nature, which for a long time has only reminded me of death.

•   •   •

Most days I am busy with my autobiography. I see that it is very boring to write about oneself and very interesting to write about other people and things (St. Petersburg, the smell of Pavlovsk Station, sailboats in Gungerburg, the Odessa port at the end of the forty-day strike). One should write as little as possible about oneself.

•   •   •

Without doubt January 9* and Tsushima** were the shocks of a lifetime. And as they were the first, they were the more frightening.

•   •   •

I'm afraid that everything I write here belongs to the somber genre— "*La Fille de Faust*" (see Daudet's Jack), in other words, it simply does not exist. And the more there is the less I believe it. This is because I see and

---

* On this day in 1905 a peaceful demonstration in Petersburg was fired on.—ed.

** On May 14 and 15, 1905, near the island of Tsushima in the Korean Gulf, the Russian Pacific fleet was routed by Japan, forcing Russia to begin peace talks as the defeated side.—ed.

hear so much beyond these words that it completely wipes out the words themselves.   22 November 1957, Moscow

• • •

If I could manage to write one-hundredth of what I have in mind I would be happy. . . .

• • •

Nonetheless, the sister book to *Safe Conduct* and *The Noise of the Time*,* should come out. I'm afraid that compared to its rich sisters it will appear uncouth, a simpleton, Cinderella, etc.

Both of them (Boris Pasternak and Osip Mandelshtam) wrote their books barely having reached maturity, when everything they remembered was not so incredibly long ago. But it is virtually impossible to view the nineties of the nineteenth century from the height of the mid-twentieth century without feeling dizzy.

• • •

I have no intention of trying to resurrect the "physiological sketch" genre and filling the book with innumerable unimportant details.

• • •

Regarding memoirs in general, I warn the reader that 20 percent of all memoirs are false in one way or another. The arbitrary introduction of direct speech should be recognized as a criminal deed because it easily slips from memoirs into respected literary works and biographies. Continuity is also a delusion. The human memory is constructed in such a way that, like a projector, it illuminates separate moments, leaving the rest in impenetrable darkness. Even a wonderful memory can and should forget some things.

• • •

It makes no difference at all where one starts: in the middle, in the end, or in the beginning. For example, right now I want to start with the fact that these green houses with glass-enclosed terraces (I live in one of them)

---

* Autobiographies of Pasternak and Mandelshtam.—ed.

were always before my (closed) eyes in 1951 when I lay in Soviet Hospital No. 5 (Moscow) after a heart attack and, no doubt, was under the influence of pantopon. These houses did not yet exist; they were built in 1955. But when I saw them, I remembered where I had seen them before. This was why I wrote in "Epilogue":

> I live in a strange house I have dreamed,
> Where, perhaps, I have died.*

• • •

Pro domo mea [as for me], I can say that I never abandoned Poetry, though the frequent hard knocks of the oars against my numbed hands clinging to the side of the boat beckoned me to sink to the bottom. I admit that at times the air around me lost its moisture and ability to transmit sound. As it was lowered into the well, the bucket gave not a joyful splash but a hollow sound of striking a rock. In general, suffocating times began and lasted for years. Today it has become customary to "introduce words," to "bring them together." After forty years, that which used to be daring begins to sound trite. There is another way—the way of precision; and something even more important—having each word in its proper place in the line, as if it were there for a thousand years, yet the reader hears it for the first time. This is very difficult, but when one is successful people say: "That's about me: it's as if I wrote it." I have (rarely) experienced this feeling when reading or listening to the poems of others. It is something like envy, but more noble.

X asked me if it was easy or difficult to write poetry. I answered: either someone else dictates them, and then it is very easy; or one dictates them to one's self, and then it is impossible.   1959

• • •

The poet has a mysterious relationship to everything he has written, and it often contradicts what the reader thinks of a certain verse.

For example, of the poems in my first book *Evening* (1912), I now truly like only the lines:

---

* From "Let someone enjoy southern skies fresh and clear. . . ."—ed.

> Intoxicated by a voice
> That sounds exactly like yours*

I even believe now that a large number of my poems grew out of these lines.

On the other hand, I very much like several dark poems that are quite uncharacteristic of me and without continuation: "I have come to take your place, sister . . ." Here I like the lines:

> The tambourine's beat is no more to hear
> I know silence is what you fear

I am quite indifferent to those poems mentioned so often by the critics.

Poems (for the poet) are also divided into those which the poet can remember writing and those which seem to have written themselves. In some, the poet is destined to hear the voice of a violin, that once helped him to compose the poems; in others—the sound of a carriage, hindering him in his composition. Poems may be connected with the smell of perfume and flowers. The dog rose in "The Sweetbrier Blossoms" cycle did indeed have an intoxicating smell at a particular moment.

This is not just the case with my own poems, however. In Pushkin I hear the waterfalls of Tsarskoye Selo ("these living waters"**), which I managed to see before they disappeared.

DIARY ENTRIES

24 December 1959 (European Christmas Eve)

A light snow storm. A quiet, very calm evening. T left early. I was alone the entire time; the telephone did not ring. The poems keep coming, and I, as always, drive them away until I hear a genuine line. Despite the constant pain in my heart and frequent attacks, the whole month of December was fruitful for poetry. But "Melkhola" is still resisting; i.e., something inferior is there. But I will achieve it, nonetheless.

My efforts to write my memoirs stir up unexpectedly deep layers of the past: my memory is increasingly, unbelievably clean: voices, sounds, smells, people, the brass cross on the pine in Pavlovsk Park, and so on,

* From "White Night."—ed.
** From Pushkin's poem "It was the time of our young holiday. . . ."—ed.

without end. I remember, for example, what Vyacheslav Ivanov said when I first read my verse to him. That was in 1910, fifty years ago.

Poems must be kept safe from all this.

These last few days I always have the feeling that something is happening to me somewhere. It is unclear in what way. Either in Moscow or somewhere else something is drawing me in, like the hot air of a huge stove or the propellers of a steamboat.

On the twenty-ninth I'm going with Irina to the House of Creativity* in Komarovo. It's only for ten days. Perhaps I'll rest, but most probably not.

Everyone knows that some people begin to sense spring right after Christmas. Today I seemed to sense it, though winter has not yet come. So much wonder and joy is connected with this that I don't want to say anything to anyone for fear of spoiling it. Somehow I also seem to be connected with my Korean rose, with my demon hydrangea, and with all the silent, dark life of roots. Do they feel the cold now? Do they have enough snow? Do they know the moon looks down upon them? All this concerns me deeply: Even in my night dreams I don't forget about them.

BIRCH TREES

First of all, no one has ever seen such birch trees. It frightens me to recall them; it is an obsession—something threatening, tragic, like the "Pergam altar"—majestic and unique. Surely crows ought to be there. There is nothing better on earth than these birch trees—large, powerful, ancient as the druids, even more ancient. Three months have passed and I can't get over it, like it was yesterday. I don't want them to be a dream; I need them to be real.   1959–1961

• • •

It's common knowledge that everyone who left Russia took with him his last day. I was recently convinced of this after reading Di Sarra's article about me. He writes that my verse comes entirely from the poetry of M. Kuzmin. No one has thought this way for forty-five years. But Vyacheslav Ivanov, who left St. Petersburg for good in 1912, took with him an image

---

* A writers' retreat.—ed.

of me that was connected with Kuzmin, only because Kuzmin wrote the foreword to *Evening* (1912). This was the last thing Vyacheslav Ivanov could remember, and, of course, when asked about me abroad, he said I was a student of Kuzmin's. Thus, a double, an alter ego, grew around me and lived peacefully in some people's imagination all these decades. It had no relevance to me or to my fate.

Involuntarily the question arises: how many such doubles or alter egos roam the world and what role will they finally play?

• • •

. . . One (not very honest) critical approach deserves attention: the desire to distinguish my first book (*Rosary*) from all else I have written, to proclaim it my *livre de chevet** and immediately destroy everything else; i.e., to make of me something between a Sergei Gorodetsky (which is to say, a poet without a creative path) and Francoise Sagan—a "sweetly frank" young girl.

The fact is that *Rosary* came out in March 1914, but it was destined to live only two-and-a-half months. At that time the literary season ended in late May. When we returned from the village we were met by the war. A second edition of three thousand copies was needed about a year later.

Approximately the same thing happened with *A Flock of White Birds*. It came out in September 1917 and, due to lack of transportation, was not even sent to Moscow. But a second edition was needed a year later, just like *Rosary*. The third edition was printed by Alyansky in 1922, then came the Berlin edition (the fourth). This was the last, because after my trip to Moscow and Kharkov in 1924 [. . .], they ceased to publish me. This was true until 1939 [. . .].

The two-volume work already prepared for publication by Hessen's publishing house (*Petrograd*) was destroyed; condemnations were no longer sporadic but regular and planned (Lelevich in the magazine *Na Postu*, Pertsov in *Zhizn Iskusstva*,** etc.). A storm with a force of 12, i.e., life-threatening, was measured in some places. I was not given any translations (aside from the letters of Rubens in the 1930s). However, my first work on Pushkin ("Pushkin's Final Folk-tale") was published in *Zvezda* [No. 1,

---

* Favorite book (literally, "book at the bed's headboard").—ed.
** See *Na Postu* in appendix.—ed.

1933]. The ban affected only my poetry. This is the simple truth. And this is what I have found out about myself from the foreign press. It turns out that after the Revolution I stopped writing poetry altogether and did not write another poem until 1940. But why then were new editions of my books not published, and why was my name cursed in the most vulgar terms? Apparently, there was a strange desire and temptation I do not understand to inextricably immure me in the 1910s.

• • •

I listened to the dragonfly waltz from Shostakovich's ballet suite. It is marvelous. It seems that grace itself dances it. Is it possible to do with words what he does with sound?   November 1961

• • •

If Poetry is destined to flourish in my native land in the twentieth century, I am proud to say that I was always a happy and reliable witness. . . . And I'm certain that even now we don't know what a wonderful choir of poets we have, that the Russian language is young and malleable, that we have been writing poems for not such a long time, and that we love and believe them.

For Remembrance

I consider it not only appropriate but also extremely important to return to 1946 and the role Stalin played in the August 14 Resolution.* This has not yet been discussed in the press. I think the comparison of what was said about Zoshchenko and Akhmatova and what was said about Churchill is a felicitous one. It is impossible to supply Zhdanov's direct quotes, those that evoked in us the atmosphere of a scandal in a communal apartment. On the one hand, youth today (post-Stalin) does not remember it and can learn nothing from it; and as for the philistines who have not yet read my books and still call them Akhmatova's "alcove verse" (as Zhdanov did), there is no need to heat up their favorite dish. It is totally unsuitable to use an objective tone and citations; the author's indignation concerning the fact that someone who, considering himself to be a critic, writes obscenities, must

* On the magazines *Zvezda* and *Leningrad*.—ed.

be apparent (as with something like: "We refuse to believe our eyes"; "It is impossible to explain why [this is being said] about a woman poet who never wrote an erotic poem"). The abusive articles—numbering in the thousands and appearing over a number of years—were published not only in *Culture and Life* . . . but in all the major and local papers. And for many years they were used to edify the young; they provided entrance examination material for all the higher institutes in the country.*

Zoshchenko and Akhmatova were expelled from the Writers' Union; i.e., they were condemned to starvation.

(From Akhmatova's workbooks, 1962)

FIFTY YEARS AS A WRITER: LECTURES
Akhmatova on the Campaign against Her

In spring 1911 my poems were published [in *Apollon.*]** Burenin reacted immediately in *Novoye Vremya* [*New Times*], believing to have ruined me with his parodies without so much as mentioning my name.

In 1919 Bunin ruined me in Odessa (with his epigram to "the Poetess") and Bryusov ruined me in Moscow (in honor of Adeline Adalis).† Beginning in 1925 my work ceased to be printed at all, and the press initiated a planned and consistent campaign to ruin me (Lelevich in *Na Postu*, Pertsov in *Zhizn Iskusstva*, Stepanov in *Leningradskaya Pravda*, and many others). (The role played by Chukovsky's article "Two Russias.") One can imagine the life I lived at that time.†† This continued until 1939, when Stalin asked about me at a writers' awards ceremony.

---

* The "Resolution on the magazines *Zvezda* and *Leningrad*" was actually studied in Soviet institutes of the humanities.—ed.

** This was her first publication.—ed.

† Valery Bryusov was reported in an article by Marina Tsvetayera to have derided Akhmatova at a poetry reading on 11 December 1920.—ed.

†† Naturally, after the first Central Committee Resolution (1925?), which M. Shaginyan told me about on Nevsky Prospekt and which was never published, no one invited me to give readings. This is evident from the speech list. After a considerable amount of time I was invited to read my poems at a Mayakovsky commemoration (the tenth anniversary of his death) in the House of Culture in Vyborgsky district. Zhuravlev was invited as well. This (first) Resolution, it seems, was not as comprehensive as the famous Resolution of 1946, because I was allowed to translate *The Letters of Peter Paul Rubens* for the Academia Publishing House and two of my poems on Pushkin were published. But they stopped asking me for poems. At this time I left the Union out of sympathy for Pilnyak and Zamyatin. In 1934 I didn't fill out the application forms and thus did not join the Union of Soviet Writers that had then been created. [See *Pilnyak* in the appendix.—ed.]

A few of my poems were published in Leningrad magazines, and then Sovetsky Pisatel Publishing House received instructions to publish my poetry. Thus, the highly selective collection *From Six Books* appeared; it was destined to exist for approximately six weeks.★ *(Willow)*★★ was never published separately despite instructions from abroad.

Then, as is well known, I, who had already been totally ruined innumerable times, was once again devastated in 1946 by the concerted effort of certain people (Stalin, Zhdanov, Sergievsky, Fadeyev, Yegolin), the last of whom died yesterday. My poems are more or less alive, but my name is not mentioned in the press (perhaps in keeping with the old and honorable tradition). There has not been any mention of my book *Verses,* which came out in 1958.

• • •

"Over the icy Neva" and over Moscow River, this was the way it was. But we all know that this sort of thing is contagious.

"The campaign against her" was carried beyond the borders of our homeland, where my position was even more hopeless, because my only defense, my poetry, was absent. In its place were horrible word-for-word translations with confused meanings (see Einaudi's Italian and Laffite's French). Just as horrible were the rumors of my alleged unrequited passion for A. Blok, which for some reason people are still eager to believe.† Moreover, my failings were piling up. Someone accuses me of not being a symbolist; someone sets me in opposition to the "innovators" and insists on sending my works to the archives. Shatsky claims that Gumilev considered my poetry "the hobby of a poet's wife" (despite all the reviews by Nikolai Stepanovich). At the bidding of Odoevtseva, Georgy Ivanov spent his entire life trying to vex me, starting with the cheap literary work *Petersburg Winters*.

★ The following circumstance played a role in the fate of this book: Sholokhov proposed it for the Stalin Prize (1940). The proposal was seconded by A. N. Tolstoy and Nemirovich-Danchenko. N. Aseyev was supposed to receive the prize for his poem "Mayakovsky Begins." There were denunciations and everything else that usually occurs in such situations. My *From Six Books* was banned and removed from book shops and libraries. For some reason the Italian Di Sarra believes this collection is a complete collected works. Foreigners think I stopped writing poetry, though between 1935 and 1940 I wrote *Requiem,* among other works.

★★ The title of a section in the collection *From Six Books* (1940).—ed.

† Once again I repeat that this rumor with its provincial origin appeared in the 1920s, after Blok's death. In the 1910s everyone knew perfectly well who was having an affair with whom. It was said aloud that Delmas was "Carmen"; no one doubted it, etc.

I don't know at whose bidding and for what purpose, but Harkins wrote something so obscene in his *Dictionary of Russian Literature* that when I try to retell it to my acquaintances, no one can believe it. What were his sources?! Pierre Segers has put on the cover of a translation of my poems (1959) the titillating news that I was divorced twice (on the cover!). The fact is, I was forced into the first divorce, which occurred before the Revolution. My pitiful divorce! (In early August 1918.) Was there any hint that in another forty years it would be accorded the honor of a worldwide scandal? I didn't go anywhere or speak to anyone, and I have absolutely no idea how this happened. I simply received a note saying I had been divorced from a certain person. There was starvation and terror. Many left (some for good). There was no private life; everyone was being divorced. Everyone was accustomed to seeing us apart, and no one meddled in anyone else's affairs. As if there were time for that! And now forty years have passed, and I discover that I was forced to get a divorce before the Revolution. Why "before"? Why "forced"? Whom do I have to thank for this information? Clearly, the author of this rich gossip wanted to remain anonymous.*

(By chance I took a book off the shelf of some friends—the Rozhanskys—and discovered I was an *amie intime* of—guess who?—Pasternak. This was Payne's discovery and no doubt no one will argue with him.)

MISCELLANEOUS NOTES

The Poets' Guild was conceived in the autumn of 1911 as an alternative to the Academy of Poetry, which was under the leadership of Vyacheslav Ivanov. Nikolai Stepanovich Gumilev was not previously well acquainted with Gorodetsky, who was much older than all of us and had already tried out Chulkov's "mystic anarchism" and "*sobornost*." Seryozha Gorodetsky had quickly gone out of fashion and ceased to be a "wonder boy." Now he was searching for another life preserver (S.O.S.). The first Guild meeting (very impressive) with Blok and the Frenchmen took place at Gorodetsky's home, and the second, at Yelizaveta Yuryevna Kuzmina-Karavayeva's home on Manezhny Lane. That was the day I met Lozinsky.

Soon we were talking about the need to stay away from symbolism, which, by the way, had declared itself in a state of crisis a year earlier (in

---

* Out of mischief I looked into the matter: Harkins singled me out to write about my divorce, though almost everyone about whom he writes is divorced, most more than once (Tolstoy, Simonov, Olga Bergholtz, etc.).

1910). At this time Nikolai Stepanovich was writing poems that were to be included in his book the *Strange Sky*, which he then considered to be his first acmeist collection. *Pearls* appeared in the spring of 1910, a long time before the initial talk about a new trend. In an obituary written in 1921 (a review of *Bonfire Pillar*), Georgy Ivanov claims that *Strange Sky* marked the beginning of the real Gumilev; but even he does not note the unbroken path from the first book [*Pearls*] to *Bonfire Pillar*.

There is an interesting notation in the new edition of Blok: "We were right in fighting the pseudo-realists, but are we right now in fighting Gumilev who, perhaps, is our own?" Time will judge; to be more precise, it has already judged them. But how terrible it was when this literary enmity ended with the simultaneous ruin of both.

I learned of the arrest of Nikolai Stepanovich at Blok's funeral. The "fainting-sweet smell of decay" in my poem "Fear," written the night of 25 August 1921, refers to that funeral.

I learned of Nikolai Stepanovich's death (I read it in a paper at the train station) on 1 September in Tsarskoye Selo, where I was living (opposite Kitaeva's home) in a half-hospital, half-sanatorium. I was so weak I did not once walk to the park. On 15 September I wrote "Tearful autumn (like a widow). . . ." That summer a forest near Petersburg had burned, and the streets were filled with acrid yellow smoke (as in 1959). In autumn a huge vegetable garden had been destroyed in Marsovo Polye and there were clouds of crows. After arriving from Tsarskoye Selo, I walked (everyone walked then) to Mramorny (through Marsovo Polye) to see Shileiko. He cried. (I see that I am not writing what I should: there are almost ten topics on two pages and they are all muddled.)

ON THE HISTORY OF ACMEISM

It is impossible to understand the birth of acmeism without a knowledge of the facts and the following observations. The last time I spoke on this topic with M. A. Zenkevich, he drew my attention to the point that the acmeists had never had any patrons, something that could not be said of the symbolists. This is true, but it is not the most important thing.★ We bought up the issues of *Giperborei* ourselves, and Lozinsky ran the

★ In some fourth edition, Volkov, in an extremely mild manner, continues his oratory about the link between the acmeists and the bourgeoisie.

magazine almost unaided. Zhirmunsky admits that he made a mistake about Kuzmin and his "wonderful clarity" (see Kuzmin's article several weeks after the death of Nikolai Stepanovich).

To speak about acmeism one should have a clear understanding of when it appeared and not quote the Gumilev of 1910 as did Gleb Struve ("We cannot but be symbolists"). Gumilev hoped that Bryusov (*Russkaya Mysl*) would help him spite Vyacheslav Ivanov, who immediately revealed his open hostility (see the letter). But what would Bryusov have left if he renounced symbolism? So Bryusov attacked acmeism, and in his article, Nikolai Gumilev became Mr. Gumilev, which in the language of the time meant someone outside literature.

But while all this information is useful, it is secondary. It is more important to understand Gumilev's character and what was most important in his character: as a boy he believed in symbolism as people believe in God. It was an inviolable sacrament. But the closer he approached symbolism, specifically *The Tower* (V. Ivanov), the more his faith faltered. He began to believe there was something profane in him.

Andrei Bely says somewhere that he gave Gumilev an acmeist program he had carelessly sketched on a piece of paper. Gumilev took it, saying that this was something to his liking. I have never heard anything more far-fetched and absurd. I might add that when Gumilev invited Bely and his wife to visit us at Tsarskoye Selo, Bely was almost rude in his refusal. And he finds acmeism in 1910. And why should Bely, one of the pillars of symbolism and the author of a fundamental work on symbolism, depose himself?

In 1914 there was an inner split in the Guild. Gumilev and Gorodetsky quarreled. Gorodetsky's letters to Gumilev have survived. Recently someone acquired them from Rudakov's widow, to whom I had given them for safekeeping. But, as everyone knows, she bargains with everything entrusted to her. We will not, however, go into that here. There was an attempt at a reconciliation in 1915. We visited the Gorodetskys at their new apartment (near the mosque) and even spent the night there. But evidently the rift was too deep, and it was impossible to return to what had once been.

Other shops were formed later; some invited me, others did not. But none of them had any significance for the history of acmeism.

Mandelshtam's article "Morning of Acmeism" was in all probability written in 1913 and not when it was published in *Sirena* (1919). Neither we nor our friends (there were none, only enemies) carried the term acmeism to the next generation.

I remember how Osip and I, while still in the editorial office of *Severniye Zapiski,* urged the syndics to close the [first] Guild. We wrote an appeal of sorts in my notebook, and I forged all the signatures. (S. Gorodetsky passed a resolution: "Hang them all, but for Akhmatova—for her, life imprisonment at Malaya 63." It was all a joke, but still. . . .)

It was there I recall hearing, much to my displeasure, Gorodetsky vilify Blok's poem "Song of the reed . . ."

N. Klyuev publicly repudiated us at this meeting, and when the defeated N. S. asked him what this meant, he answered: "Fish search for where it's deeper; man—where it's better."

It was not easy being an acmeist at that time.

As was only to be expected, a general battle was being waged in the Academy of Poetry. I returned from my mother in Kiev and came down with a fever.

In the winter of acmeism's *Sturm und Drang* we sometimes gave recitals as a group. Gumilev and Gorodetsky read lectures. I remember how the elderly Radetsky, with his great beard, shook his fist and shouted: "Look at these Adams* and this skinny Eve," referring to me.

This group had plans to take me out of circulation, because they had a ready candidate to fill the vacancy. This was why Georgy Ivanov described these soirees in his cheap memoirs (*Petersburg Winters*) in the following way:

> Not even one-tenth of those who wanted to hear Akhmatova were able to get into the small auditorium of the Writers' House [*Dom Literatorov*]. Later there was a repeat performance at the university. But even the huge university premises proved to be inadequate. A triumph, one would think?
>
> No. Most of the listeners were disappointed.
>
> "Akhmatova is a has-been."
>
> Well, of course.
>
> For five years she had not been heard or read. They were expecting that for which she was loved—the left glove on the right hand gives a new pair of gloves. But they heard something completely different:
>
> All is lost and betrayed and sold out
> Why then is it all now full of light?

---

* The acmeists were initially called adamists.—ed.

There is something mysterious and wonderful
Coming close to our ruined, soiled homes
Unfamiliar to anyone, strange to all,
What we dreamed of for years—it comes . . . *

The audience was perplexed: "What Bolshevism!"** For old time's sake they clapped, but they had already decided: "A has-been."

The critics eagerly accepted "the voice of the people." Now every literature student knows that nothing can be expected of Akhmatova.

"Nothing" is right. The public at large, which at one time had given Akhmatova fame, unusual fame—resounding and swift as lightning—for a contemporary poet, had been deceived by Akhmatova. All the female students of Russia who had given her a mandate to be mistress of their souls were deceived.

But the paragraph is not completed in either translation. On the contrary, they show my "fall" as final and irrevocable. I myself allegedly admitted as much (in 1932) and ceased to write poetry until 1940, when, for some reason, a "complete" collection of my works came out. At the same time a book called *Willow* was also published. This was the name of the first section in the collection *From Six Books*. Containing a handful of the poems I wrote from 1922 to 1940, it had never been published separately. As to the completeness of that collection, the title itself refutes this claim. But for some reason foreigners want to immure me in the 1910s, and nothing, not even the circulation of my books, can change their minds. From 1940 to 1961 *ninety-five thousand* copies of my books were printed in the USSR, and now it is *impossible* to buy my collections of poetry. Concerning the early 1920s (the so-called NEP period), after K. Chukovsky set me in opposition to Mayakovsky ("Two Russias"), V. Vinogradov wrote a well-known article, "Akhmatova's Stylistics," B. M. Eikhenbaum wrote an entire book (1922), the formalists took up my poetry, lectures were given on them, and so on. All this (like everything in my life, by the way) ended rather sadly. In 1925 the Central Committee issued a resolution (not published in the press) for the withdrawal of my work from circulation. A two-volume collection (*Petrograd*) ready for publication by Gessen was banned, and my poems ceased to be printed.

* Tr. by Yana Glukhoded.
** To understand what kind of Bolshevism, see the afterword to the book by Al. Syrkov (1961).—ed.

The fact is that I believe poems (especially lyrics) should not flow like water from a faucet or be a poet's daily occupation. It is true that I wrote little from 1925 until 1935, but my contemporaries (Pasternak and Mandelshtam) took similar intermissions. Even the small amount of poetry that I wrote could not appear because of the pernicious personality cult. I did write the Tsarskoye Selo poem "Russian Trianon" at that time. It was not preserved because I heard some intonations of Onegin in it (a few stanzas were printed).

4 APRIL 1963

It is only today that I realized the nature of my guilt before humanity, the crime I committed for which they ceaselessly take their revenge: I wrote poems that people liked and continue to like. Apparently this is something not to be forgiven. See how tenderly and politely S. K. Makovsky speaks of my contemporaries. Vera Nevedomskaya—a beauty, a student of Kardovsky, and such. Tanya Adamovich is made mysterious and given the name Tatiana Alexandrovna A. She is also a beauty and she is brilliant. Gumilev was desperately in love with her, and all that. But as soon as I appear, the tone changes. I suppose it was out of jealousy that I brought Gumilev together with her and even gave her my bed in Tsarskoye Selo while I slept in an adjoining room(!).

[Makovsky] was unscrupulous and wrote with unprecedented audacity to accuse a Russian poet of engaging in filthy pandering without a shred of evidence. This is like the local Samarin, who assured G. A. Shengeli that he had proof of my having had an affair with Nicholas II.

Of course, Vera and Tanya are close by and someone could probably defend them. But this is not important. Neither of them wrote *Rosary*, *Triptych*, or *Requiem*. There is no reason to take revenge upon them; let them live in peace and flourish. Once again I hear the serpentine hiss of my epigraph: "How similar slander is to the truth."

12 JULY 1963

When Innokenty Annensky was told that the brother of his *belle-fille* Natasha [Stein] was to marry the elder Gorenko, he remarked: "I would have married the younger." This decidedly measured compliment was something Anna [the younger Gorenko] treasured very much.

By the way, when Anna's family moved away from Tsarskoye Selo (1905) she was rescued from the more or less open persecution of the brutal residents. Gumilev, however, had to endure it. In this terrible place, everything above a certain level was subject to destruction. N. N. Punin writes eloquently of this in his unpublished memoirs. Vsevolod Rozhdestvensky, who has been unmasked, writes little today. Apparently, neither Gollerbakh nor Otsup know what was going on.

About such a tremendous, complicated, and important phenomenon of the late nineteenth and early twentieth centuries as symbolism, the people of Tsarskoye Selo knew only this: "Oh, close your pale legs" and "We will be like the sun."*

Thus, Otsup (in his foreword to the selected works of Gumilev), repeating one of the innumerable tales about Gumilev, relates that Nikolai Stepanovich told some young lady while riding with her in a carriage: "We will be like the sun." Everyone who lived in Tsarskoye Selo at the time knew this was a lie, and to write such a thing was the same as writing that Gumilev said this to a young lady while they sat in a bath. But Otsup left Tsarskoye Selo when he was still almost a child and was not a part of the "society" at that time. Many years spent in Paris had erased the distant, half-childish memories, but malicious gossip and the desire to make the poet appear ludicrous remained. Yes, it did!

•   •   •

I lived in Tsarskoye Selo almost uninterruptedly from the age of two until I was sixteen. During this time my family spent one winter (when my sister Iya was born) in Kiev (on Institutskaya Street**) and another in Sevastopol (on Sobornaya Street in the Semyonov home). Our main residence in Tsarskoye Selo was the house of the businesswoman merchantess Yelizaveta Ivanovna Shukhardina (on Shirokaya Street, the

---

* The first is a line from Valery Bryusov; the second is the title of a collection of verse by the symbolist poet Konstantin Balmont.—ed.

** This was where the incident with the bear in Chateu de Felur occurred. My sister Rika and I had run down from the hills and into the fenced area [with the bear]. Everyone around was terrified. We promised our governess we would hide the event from Mama. But upon returning, little Rika shouted: "Mama! Bear—both—face—window." Up in the Tsarskoye Selo garden I found a pin shaped like a lyre. My governess told me: "It means you will be a poet." But the most important thing happened not in Kiev but in Gungenburg when we were living in the Krabau dacha: I found a Tsar-mushroom. Our "Kalugan" nanny said about me: "She will be spicy"; "Our affairs are up in smoke"; and "Looking backward, you'll never see enough."

second house from the train station, on the corner of Bezymyanny Lane). But the winter of the first year of the century my family lived in the Daudel house (on the corner of Srednaya and Leontyevskaya). There was measles and perhaps even smallpox there.

• • •

On 25 April 1910 I married N. S. Gumilev and returned to Tsarskoye Selo after a five-year absence (see the poem "First Return").

It is time I finally clarify Nikolai Stepanovich's attitude to my poetry, because I am still reading in [foreign] publications false and absurd information. For example, Strakhovsky writes that Gumilev considered my poetry "the hobby of a poet's wife," and . . .* that after he married me, Gumilev began to teach me to write poetry, but soon the student surpassed . . . etc. This is all nonsense! I began writing poems at the age of eleven completely independent of Nikolai Stepanovich. As long as they were bad, he told me so with characteristic integrity and frankness. Then this is what happened: in the Bryullov room of the Russian Museum I read the galleys of *Cypress Box* (when I traveled to Petersburg in early 1910) and understood something about poetry. In September Nikolai Stepanovich left to spend a half-year in Africa, and I spent the time writing what would later for the most part become the book *Evening*. Of course, I read these poems to many new writer-friends. Mayakovsky took several for *Apollon* (see *Apollon,* No. 4, April 1911).

When Nikolai Stepanovich returned on 25 March he asked me if I had written any poetry. I read him everything I had written, and he said those words which, evidently, he never retracted (see his critical review of the collection *Orion*). At the same time, parenthetically and once again in answer to D. D. Di Sarra and Sophie Lafitte, I reiterate that I married not the leader of acmeism but a young symbolist poet, the author of *Pearl* and critical reviews of books of poetry (*Letters on Russian Poetry*).

Acmeism emerged in late 1911. In 1910 Gumilev was still a faithful symbolist. The break with "the Tower"** evidently began with the publication of Gumilev's review on *Cors Ardens*† in *Apollon.* I have written many times in other places (for instance, in my article "The Fate of

---

* There is a gap in the text.—ed.
** The coterie surrounding Vyacheslav Ivanov (1866–1949), poet and theorist of symbolism.—ed.
† A collection of verse by Vyacheslav Ivanov.—ed.

Acmeism") about what happened next. There was something in this review
for which V. Ivanov never forgave [Gumilev]. When Nikolai Stepanovich
read his *Prodigal Son* in the Academy of Poetry, Vyacheslav Ivanov attacked
him with almost obscene language. I remember how we returned to
Tsarskoye completely crushed by what had happened, and afterward
Nikolai Stepanovich always considered Vyacheslav Ivanov his open enemy.

The situation with Bryusov was more complicated. As can be seen
from his letters to Bryusov, Nikolai Stepanovich had hoped that he would
support acmeism. But how could a man who considered himself to be a
pillar of Russian symbolism and one of its founders reject it for the sake of
anything? What followed was Bryusov's devastating attack against acmeism
in *Russkaya mysl*, where Gumilev and Gorodetsky were even referred to
as "mister;" i.e., as people outside literature.   1910

Everyone, especially those abroad, want me to have been "discovered"
by Vyacheslav Ivanov. I don't know who started this story. Perhaps it was
Pyast, who used to come to "the Tower."

But this is what really happened: after we returned from Paris (in the
summer of 1910), Nikolai Stepanovich brought me to see Vyacheslav
Ivanov. He did indeed ask me if I wrote poetry (we three were alone in
his apartment), and I read: "And when we wished each other dead and
worse . . ." (from the Kiev notebook, 1909) and something else (I think it
was "We came and said . . ."). Vyacheslav commented with indifference
and mockery: "What truly heavy romanticism!" At that time I didn't
understand his irony. It was that autumn, after earning the eternal disfavor
of Ivanov with his review of *Cors Ardens* (see: *Apollon* and Ivanov's letter
to Gumilev), that Gumilev left to spend the half-year in Africa, in Addis
Ababa. Vyacheslav met me at the Rayevsky Courses where he was giving
lectures and invited me to come on "Mondays" (no longer "Wednesdays").
I did read my poems several times there, and he did praise them. But at that
time everyone was praising them (Tolstoy, Makovsky, Chulkov, etc.). They
had been accepted and published by *Apollon*. But the hypocritical Ivanov
advised me to visit with Zinaida Gippius. Aleksandra Nikolayevna
Chebotarevskaya led me into an adjoining room and said: "Don't go. She's
mean and she'll insult you." I replied: "I have no intention of going to see
her." Moreover, Vyacheslav Ivanov tried hard to persuade me to leave

Gumilev. I remember his exact words: "You'll make him a man if you do."
As for how he would cry over poems tête-à-tête and then take them into
a "salon" and vehemently criticize them, I have so frequently and so long
ago discussed this that it's boring to write it down.

Vyacheslav was neither grand nor magnificent (he thought this up himself), but a "catcher of men." Berdyaev's *Autobiography* described him best.

N. V. Nedobrovo, who was in indisputable favor with "the Tower"
and Blok, whom Vyacheslav called "nightingale" to his face, knew [Ivanov]
very well and did not believe a word he said. The youth today—i.e., our
genuine heirs—are puzzled by reading *Cors Ardens* and call it "a bad
Balmont."

Anyone who takes the trouble to read about Vyacheslav Ivanov
in Einaudi's anthology—where, by the way, he has first place (Blok is
second)—will discover whom [Ivanov] "wished" to appear to be.

We (the youth of the time) were amused that this perfectly healthy
forty-four-year-old man who was destined to live until 1949 was doted on
by grey-haired ladies. M. M. Zamyatina ran down from "the Tower" to
wrap a blanket (in April) around the Teacher's legs when he was riding
with me to the Academy on Moika [Street]. He was "acting" at being
someone who never existed and who, in my opinion, should not have
existed. I especially disliked his acting at being a "one-woman man," as he
liked to call himself, because I loved and pitied poor Vera.

It is terrible to hear what X. has to say about [Ivanov's] "family pastime." I didn't read Kuzmin's *A Dead Woman in the House.*

CLEARING UP A MISUNDERSTANDING

Now it is Makovsky's turn. I have just read that for some reason the
Makovskys became my confidants and Sergei Konstantinovich printed my
poems in *Apollon* against Gumilev's will. I will not allow ludicrous and
foolish gossip to besmirch a poet's tragic memory, and those who printed
this nonsense should be ashamed.

In the beginning my poetry was indeed insipid, and Nikolai Stepanovich
did not hesitate to tell me so. And he did indeed advise me to take up
another form of art—dance, for example ("You are so limber"). When
Gumilev left for Addis Ababa I remained alone in the Gumilev home (on
Bulvarnaya Street; the Georgievsky house). As usual I read a good deal,

traveled frequently to Petersburg (mostly to see Valya Sreznevskaya, who was then still Tyulpanova), visited my mother in Kiev, and was crazy about *Cypress Box*. My poems flowed smoothly, like never before. I searched, found, and lost. I felt (somewhat dimly) that I was beginning to succeed. It was then that the praise began. And how they could praise at the Parnassus of the Silver Age! To all this wild and extravagant attention I rather flirtatiously replied: "But my husband doesn't like them." This was remembered and exaggerated; finally it was put into someone's memoirs, and half a century later this disgusting, malicious gossip emerged with the "noble goal" of depicting Gumilev as a base envier or as someone who knew nothing about poetry. "The Tower" rejoiced.

On 25 March 1911, old style—the Annunciation—Gumilev returned from his trip to Africa. During our first conversation he asked me: "Did you write any poems?" Masking my joy, I answered, "Yes." He asked me to read them, listened to a few, and then said: "You are a poet. You must do a book." Soon my poems were in *Apollon*. . . .

• • •

Rosary—15 March 1914. Lozinsky had the galleys. When we were discussing the size of the edition, Gumilev mused thoughtfully: "It might be sold in every bookshop." There was a first printing of 1,100 copies, which sold out in less than a year. The most important review was by N. B. Nedobrovo. There were two unfavorable ones by S. Bobrov and Talnikov. The others were favorable.

"We are all of us drunkards . . ." is a poem about a lonely, capricious young girl and not a description of debauchery, as is thought today. . . .

In a year *Rosary* will mark its half-century.

ROSARY (A CONTINUATION)

The book came out on 15 March 1914, old style, and was destined to have approximately six weeks of life. In early May the Petersburg season began to die down and gradually everyone began to leave. This time the parting with St. Petersburg turned out to be forever. We returned not to St. Petersburg but to Petrograd, passing immediately from the nineteenth century into the twentieth; everything was different, beginning with the face of the city. You would expect that a small book of love lyrics by a beginner would have drowned in the sea of events. This is not what happened with *Rosary*. . . .

Later, after being placed on the executioner's block, enhanced among lists of banned publication (*Index librorum prohibitorum*), and representing stolen goods (Efron's publication in Berlin and the Odessa counterfeit under the Whites in 1919), [*Rosary*] would emerge many times from the sea of blood and icy polar waters.

Habent sua fata libelli.＊　　　　　　　　　　　　　　　24 June 1963

• • •

Dmitry Yevgenevich Maksimov asserts that *Rosary* played a special role in the history of Russian poetry, that it was destined to be the tombstone on the grave of symbolism (see also Matezeus). To a certain extent he repeats what I was recently told by Viktor Maksimovich Zhirmunsky and M. Zenkevich, one as a researcher and the other as a witness.

• • •

Rosary, as I have said, was published on 15 March 1914; i.e., soon after the campaign to destroy acmeism was over. With unusual fervor and rare unity everyone eagerly sought to suffocate the new trend. From Suvorin's *Novoye Vremya* to the futurists, the symbolist salons (the Sologubs and Merezhkovskys), literary societies (the so-called Fiza), the former "Tower" (i.e., V. Ivanov's circle) and so on, and so on—all mercilessly clawed the *Apollo* manifestos. It was hopeless to fight the symbolists; they held total command. They had enormous experience in literary policy and struggles; we had no idea of these things. It got so bad that the editors had to announce that *Giperborei* was not an acmeist magazine. The titles alone of anti-acmeist articles give an idea of the tone the polemic took ("Freezing Parnassus," "At the Feet of an African Idol," "Bereft of God, of Inspiration," and so on). And then there was Bryusov's reference to Nikolai Stepanovich as "Mr. Gumilev. . . ."

I mention all this in connection with my recollections of *Rosary* because in the dozens of laudatory reviews the word acmeism is not mentioned once. It was almost a swear word. The first real [article] on it was Zhirmunsky's "Overcoming Symbolism."＊＊　　　　　　　　December 1916

＊ "Books have their own fates"—ed.
＊＊ Akhmatova miswrote the title as "Overcoming Acmeism."—ed.

Zhirmunsky's Reminiscences

A half-century has passed. Grandchildren have become grandfathers. First readers of *Rosary* are becoming more rare than aurochs outside Belovezhskaya Pushcha.* This, of course, was inevitable. The orthography changed as well as the calculation of time (new and old styles; not 15 March but . . .) and the name of the city where it was published (not St. Petersburg but Leningrad) and the country (not Russia but the USSR).

The reader, then, waits (with some perturbation) to see if the verses, at least, are the same. It would have been fine if they were! But I submit that the poems are different as well, that the predictions (Kuzmin in his foreword, Khodasevich) that have come true force us to understand certain parts differently, that after innumerable imitations, that which in 1914 was spectacularly new now seems ordinary. In this way the hundredth kiss surely erases the first.

• • •

When *Rosary* was published, Chatskina, the publisher of *Severnye Zapiski* and *Socialist Revolutionary*, invited us to her home. (I wore the same blue dress I had on in the portrait by Altman). There were a large number of guests. Around midnight people began to leave. The hostess allowed some to go and asked others to remain. Then we all went into the dining room where a magnificent table had been set. We found ourselves at a banquet in honor of the Narodnaya Volya [People's Freedom] members just freed from Shlisselburg. I sat by L. K. [Leonid Kanegisser] opposite Herman Lopatin. Later I often recalled with horror how L. K. said to me: "If I were given *Rosary* I would agree to be kept in prison until our vis-à-vis."

Someone introduced me to Stepun. He immediately said to me: "Walk around the table and raise your glass with Herman Lopatin. I want to be present at such a historical moment." I went up to the old man and said: "You don't know me, but I want to meet you." He said something half-polite, half-impudent, but this is not interesting.

26 June 1963, Leningrad

* Aurochs—a species of wild bison now almost extinct. The few remaining animals are protected on a game reserve in Byelorussia (Belovezhskaya Pushcha).—ed.

A FLOCK OF WHITE BIRDS

This collection appeared under even more dangerous circumstances than *Rosary*. It came out in September 1917. Whereas *Rosary* made a late debut, *A Flock of White Birds* did not appear until "after the ball was over." Transportation was paralyzed—the book could not even be sent to Moscow; all the copies were sold out in Petrograd. The paper was coarse, almost like cardboard.

Magazines and newspapers were shut down as well. So, unlike *Rosary*, *A Flock of White Birds* did not have a lot of publicity. Famine and dislocation grew with each passing day. Strangely enough, for some reason these circumstances are not taken into consideration today and it's assumed that *A Flock of White Birds* was less successful than *Rosary* [as a book].

A year later, Mikhailov [Prometei] bought from me the rights to the second edition. This was in 1918 when Petersburg was already starving and half-empty. In 1918 an abridged counterfeit came out in Tiflis. Later Blok and Alyansky published *A Flock of White Birds* (an additional edition in Berlin) at Petropolis Publishing House, and Alyansky alone published it at Alkonost [Publishing House] (1922). Like *Rosary*, *A Flock of White Birds* was included in single-volume books (*From Six Books,* 1940; Sovetsky Pisatel; Chekhov Publishing House in America, 1952; and in the green book* of 1961). The title was given to the Czech single-volume collection of my poems translated by Marie Marcanova with a sensible afterword by Matezeus. (Two editions came out, one before the war.) I was never aware that *A Flock of White Birds* was not successful.

From Six Books contains bits and pieces of *A Flock of White Birds* and, by the way, *Rosary*. For example, the poem "I have a smile . . ." was taken out because of the word "lectern"** (1913). The same is true of the 1961 collection. So modern readers do not know my poetry, new or old.

•   •   •

As for the third collection—*Anno Domini*—the situation is more complicated. It was published (second edition) in 1923 in Berlin (Petropolis and

---

* *Verses.*—ed.

** The word was objected to because of its religious connotation. From 1930 to 1950 such words were carefully extirpated from Soviet literature.—ed.

Alkonost) and was banned at home. All the copies, a significant number for the time, remained abroad.

My culpability prompting the first Resolution about me (1925) can be divided into thirds: one-third—the poems [in *Anno Domini*] that had not been published in the USSR; one-third—K. Chukovsky's article "Two Russias (Akhmatova and Mayakovsky)"; one-third—my reading "New Year's Ballad"* at the *Russky Sovremennik* soiree (April 1924) in the conservatory auditorium (Moscow). It was published (without its title) in the No. 1 issue of *Russky Sovremennik,* and Zamyatin, who was very friendly toward me, showed me a stack of clippings and said to me with unexpected irritation: "You have spoiled the entire issue for us." ("Lot's Wife" was also there.)

Pertsov (*Zhizn' iskusstva*) recalls this recital in the conservatory auditorium in his article "On Literary Watersheds" (1925). The article was taken away from me, but I remember one phrase: "We can have no sympathy for a woman who did not know when it was time to die. . . ." In addition, mild surprise was noted over the fact that just the year before Akhmatova was able to fill the Moscow Conservatory auditorium with young women.

                                    • • •

In 1924 I dreamed of X three times in a row. I spent six years collecting *Works and Days* and other material**: letters, drafts and recollections. I did everything I could for his memory. It is amazing that no one else cared. [His] so-called students acted shamefully. Georgy Ivanov's doings. They all repudiated him abroad.

                                    • • •

The feeling I had while reading the quotation from *Petersburg Winters* that referred to my recitation (House of Writers, 1921) can only be compared to the last chapter of Kafka's *The Trial,* when the protagonist is led to slaughter before everyone and they all consider it perfectly normal. There is not a word of truth in the quotation. The author claims that the poem

---

* This and "Lot's Wife" were seen as hostile to the social order.—ed.

** Akhmatova and the poet Pavel Luknitsky were collecting material for the biography of Nikolai Gumilev.—ed.

All's betrayed and sold out and plundered
Death has flashed over us her black wing
All's devoured by despair and hunger . . .

reveals the corruption of lyrics and shows me to be a has-been. The audience allegedly "clapped out of habit." But no one claps out of habit. Perhaps the doors slam as they leave. People still recall those evenings with emotion and write me about them.

But Georgy Ivanov and Otsup were already remarkably busy trying to discredit my poetry in whatever way they could. They knew certain details about my biography, and, thinking my place was vacant, they decided to give it to I. Odoevtseva.

I was not even invited to [write for] *Drakon* or the Poets' Guild almanacs.

. . . I would not have brought up the events of such by-gone days if this page from G. Ivanov's memoirs had not met with special success in the foreign press. For the whole world it became the outline for my post-revolutionary biography. Strakhovsky translated and printed it in his book (*Gumilev, Akhmatova, Mandelshtam,* 1949), and I recognize it in the writing of Harkins, Di Sarra, and Rippellino. But friends ask me: "Why do you care?" Perhaps I don't, but their advice is strange. If I didn't object to anything in the fifty years of my literary career, this would mean something. And my objection should be taken seriously.

Why foreigners have taken this bait is totally incomprehensible. It was too tempting to announce that the Revolution had destroyed a young talent, the more so since my poetry ceased to appear in the press after 1924 (i.e., was banned), mostly for religious reasons.

But foreigners are the least of it all. What I cannot understand is how a Russian writer, who knew the real situation, could so quickly be corrupted.

Georgy Ivanov had to know that during NEP my books were quickly sold out (15,000 through Alyansky's Alkonost [publishing house]). That B. M. Eikhenbaum's book on my poetry was published, as well as a long article—"Akhmatova's Stylistics" by Vinogradov—in the first issue of *Literaturnaya Mysl,* and there were chapters in the books of Chulkov (*Our Fellow-Travellers*), Aikhenvald, and others. Chukovsky gave his lecture on "Two Russias," and I have already mentioned the recitations. The formalists were involved with these, as V. Vinogradov and Zhirmunsky can testify.

This prosperity ended with my trip to Moscow (April 1924), where I read "New Year's Ballad" at [the] *Russky Sovremennik* soiree, after which I was taken out of circulation by the Central Committee decision until 1939.

During the time of the personality cult my name was banned. I was defamed right and left;* during searches my pictures were removed from walls (1927).** Pasternak had considerable difficulty in persuading the editors of *Novy mir* to permit printing my name over the poem he dedicated to me†—*I think I will choose (a word)* . . . (1930?).

And I think it is finally time to expose these stinking "memoirs" of G. Ivanov†† and no longer write sympathetically of them, as Signore Logatto does in his recently published book.

Apparently he did this because there was nothing else he could say. But, in my opinion, better nothing than deliberate slander.

Dixi [I have spoken].   13 August 1961, Komarovo

• • •

After my soirees in Moscow (spring 1924) a resolution was passed barring any literary activity on my part. Magazines and almanacs no longer printed my work, and I was no longer invited to attend literary soirees. (I met Marietta Shaginyan on Nevsky Prospekt and she told me: "See how really important you are. The Central Committee issued a resolution about you—don't arrest, but don't publish.")

In 1929, after *We* and *Mahogany*, I left the [writers'] union.‡

When the application forms for joining the new union were being passed around in 1934 I didn't fill them out. I have been a member of the union since 1940, as my card shows.

From 1925 to 1939 my work was not published at all (see the criticism beginning with Lelevich, 1922–33). That was the first time I witnessed my death as a citizen. I was thirty-five. . . .

* For example, by Pertsov, Malakhov, Lelevich, and others.
** They were also removed from exhibits (Della-Vos-kardovskaya).
† "To Anna Akhmatova," published in the magazine *Krasnaya Nov* in 1929.—ed.
†† Just recall what he writes there about Gumilev and Mandelshtam! Now, it seems, the entire group has repudiated Gumilev; i.e., Peter denies and Judas betrays.
‡ Persecution of Boris Pilnyak and Yevgeny Zamyatin (authors of *We* and *Mahogany*, respectively) began after the books appeared abroad.—ed.

Note No. 3 (to the article "Akhmatova on the Campaign against Her")

Normal criticism disappeared in the early twenties as well (the efforts of Osinsky and Kollontai were immediately sharply rebuffed). It was replaced by something perhaps unprecedented but at any rate unambiguous. It did not seem plausible that one could survive such publicity during those times. Gradually life became a constant waiting for destruction. It was hopeless to try to find work, because after the first articles by Pertsov, Lelevich, Stepanov,* and the others, the job would have immediately fallen through.

Another Note

Two poets created entire hordes of students—Gumilev and Mandelshtam. The former, immediately upon his death (Tikhonov, Shengeli, Bagritsky). In the 1920s all the writers of southern Russia were crazy about him. The latter—right now (1961). Almost all the young writers in Moscow and Leningrad.

• • •

After the resolution of 1946 I began to work on the topics "Pushkin and Dostoyevsky" and "The death of Pushkin." The first topic is vast, with inexhaustible sources of material. In the beginning I was lost and didn't feel confident in my ability. Irina Nikolaevna Tomashevskaya always tells me that this was the best thing I ever did. (I burned it with all my archives when Lev was arrested on 6 November 1949.)

• • •

All the places where I grew up and lived in my youth are gone: Tsarskoye Selo, Sevastopol, Kiev, Slepnyovo, Gungenburg (Ust-Narva). What remains: Khersones (because it is eternal), Paris, because it was overlooked somehow, and Petersburg-Leningrad, so that there would be a place to lay one's head. Moscow, providing shelter to what was left of me in 1950, was a kind abode for my almost posthumous existence.

---

* For some reason I recall one of the titles: "Lyrics and Counter-Revolution."

PSEUDO-MEMOIRS

Contemporary literary criticism is impossible without the criticism of sources. It is time we learn to distinguish between putrid (Mako) and malevolent (Nevedomskaya) ravings and the conscientious work of the memory. Due to the circumstances of the twentieth century, many people have been left without any kind of archives and have learned very well to do without them. It was Rousseau who said: "I lie only where I don't remember."

I am an anti-Browning. He always wrote in the second person or for the second person. I don't let anyone else speak for me (in my poems, of course). I speak for myself, saying everything that is permissible and much that is not. Sometimes when my memory falters I recall a phrase not my own and turn it into verse.

There is a hidden poison in these journeys. On the whole, I was "happiest" in Konnitsa, when I was suffering from an endless and rather debilitating viral infection. I missed Friday after Friday (the only day sixteen-year-old Anna was free and which was to be my *wegleiterin* [guide] to Moscow). This was probably in 1956. How certain I was at that time that not a line [of my verse] would be published; how comfortably I lived with this certainty, never feeling the least amount of distress. How easily and openly I said to the three young men from *Lizhy* who had come to ask me for some poems: "You won't print them anyway. . . ." This was the life for a decent person! And now . . . I gave them "Summer Sonnet,"[*] a new poem, and something else. So, it will soon be ten years that I am once again in print. Such chains . . .

FROM HER FINAL DIARY ENTRIES
6 FEBRUARY 1966 (HOSPITAL, MOSCOW)

I felt bad all yesterday. I breathed from two oxygen bags, swallowed something, and was given some kind of injection (morphine?). The most frightening thing is that they can't find the reason. But somehow they've stopped the attacks. Today everything seems to be normal. Irina called yesterday. All is well there. It is bitterly cold and looks like it will stay that

---

[*] "Summer Sonnet" and "Music" finally appeared in the USSR in the newspaper *Literature i Zhizn*, 5 April 1959.—ed.

way. It seems to me that I have written everything about Lozinsky. It will be included in a book of [character] portraits (Modigliani, Mandelshtam, and others). It would be good to divide it into two sections: verse and prose. Marusya came in the morning and brought a letter from Tolya.* His translations of Eliot (from *Four Quartets*) are interesting.

Verse
V.S.S. To Valya) 2.
1913 and 1964.
To Pasternak (three).
Ante (. . .).
To Bulgakov (1940).
To Marina (1940).
Teacher (to Annensky).

Prose
Gumilev (Amand's dissertation collect written parts and continue).
+ Modigliani (Paris).
+ Mandelshtam (acmeism, Poets' Guild, *Sturm und Drang*).
Lozinsky (almost finished).
Blok (almost finished).
Pasternak.
Bulgakov.

7 FEBRUARY. MONDAY

This morning I had an X-ray. They said they didn't find anything. But if they had, would they really tell me? Yulya will come.

Yulya was here.

Yesterday evening I listened to Prokofiev's *Obsession*. Richter was playing. It was fantastic; I still haven't come down to earth. No words (in any order) can ever convey what it was like. It was near impossible. A huge symphonic orchestra directed by a supernatural force (and the first violin was played by Satan himself) filled the air and floated to the blue, frosty window.

---

* From Anatoly Naiman.—ed.

8 FEBRUARY. TUESDAY

There is still a full moon. I feel ill after the X-ray. Didn't sleep last night. I am lying in bed. Ira will call tonight. My health is not getting any better. Was it the same in Gavan* that January in 1961. I think in horror about the sanatorium (any sanatorium). In Gavan I wrote *Native Land* and something else, but here there is suffocation and silence! The tenth is the day of Pushkin's (death) and Pasternak's (birth). I know I should write about Boris after Lozinsky. *C'est complique*, as that villain [Petr] Tolstoy said about the luring of the Tsar's son, Alexei, away from Italy.

They are reading Pushkin's poetry over the radio (*Village*).

10 FEBRUARY

It is three months today that I have been in the hospital. I can now write the following with conviction: there is a law by which a long-term stay in a hospital slowly but surely turns it into a prison. In another six days they will declare a quarantine and make the analogy complete. Our parcels will be wrapped in pillowcases, the front door will be locked like an asylum, the doctors, nurses, and aides will wear masks, it will be a terrible bore.

Remember the lines from Pushkin: "Or I die of Boredom somewhere in quarantine."

They will not allow the convalescents to stroll outside. The doves, that we are strictly forbidden to feed, will pace by the windows.

14 FEBRUARY (HOSPITAL)

Larisa Alexandrovna has fallen ill and there is no one to sign for my discharge. Tolya came at five yesterday. [He spoke] a good deal about Leningrad. He himself is in good shape, as the athletes say. Our conversation will continue today.

* The Leningrad district where Akhmatova was hospitalized in 1961.—ed.

CONTEMPORARIES ON AKHMATOVA

Valeria Sreznevskaya
RECOLLECTIONS

Valeria Sreznevskaya (nee Tyulpanova, 1888–1964) became a friend of Akhmatova back in their school days at the gymnasium. Sreznevskaya's recollections were written at the insistence of Akhmatova herself. The poet read and corrected the work while Sreznevskaya was in the process of writing. In the end, however, according to a variety of sources, Akhmatova was not happy with the result.

The time approaches when I will be unable to say or write anything. My writings are without plan or system, and I have never intended or wanted them to become a part of history.

I have seen and experienced much in my life; I have met many famous people. Some were close to me, others more distant, and still others were only passing acquaintances. But a cross–examination of views and opinions helps to reveal the truth. Each witness, then, is valuable in his own way, as long as he does not lie or fabricate facts.

I will try to adhere to this rule, and as precisely as possible to recall the still glimmering images of the dear people I knew so long ago.

I met Anna in Gungenburg, a rather fashionable resort at the time located near Narva. Our families had summer cottages there. We both had governesses, both spoke fluent French and German, and both strolled with our "Madames" in the square near the Kursaal resort. Here the children would play while the "Madames" sat gossiping on benches.

Anna was a slender young girl with cropped hair. She was altogether unremarkable, rather quiet, and reserved. I was very gay, mischievous, and outgoing. We didn't become close friends then, but we saw each other often and chatted amicably. It was here that the foundation of our future friendship was laid. Our close, lasting relationship emerged later, when we lived together in the same house in Tsarskoye Selo. The house was near a railroad station, on the corner of Shirokaya Street and Bezymyanny Lane. We lived in the apartment on the ground floor; the Gorenkos had the rooms above us. We moved there after a fire had destroyed everything we owned, and our families were very happy to find comfortable lodgings so close to the railroad station. (Our fathers frequently traveled to St. Petersburg on official business, and the older children would soon be continuing their education.)

The house had a wonderful, large garden where the children could play the entire day without supervision, and this was one less worry for our parents and governesses. It was at this time that Anna and I became close friends. She was writing poetry and reading many books, some of which were banned. And she had changed a great deal, inwardly and outwardly. She was now tall and slender with the lovely, delicate figure of a girl on the threshold of womanhood. Her long black hair was thick and straight as seaweed, her arms and legs white and shapely. She had large grey eyes that contrasted strikingly with her dark hair, eyebrows, and lashes.

Anna was a veritable nymph in the water and she loved to hike. She climbed like a cat and swam like a fish. For some reason she was thought to be strange and was not in good favor with the "virtuous" inhabitants of Tsarskoye Selo—like all suburbs, a stuffy and backwards locality with all the shortcomings of the nearby capital but with none of its advantages.

Our families kept to themselves: our fathers had all their contacts in St. Petersburg and our mothers were busy caring for their many children and households. Living expenses were high; there was no longer any hint of the leisure of the nobility. Servants were impudent and careless about their work; governesses, most of whom were Swiss or German, were pretentious and not at all well-educated. So it was difficult to raise a large family. This created a lack of harmony in the home and among family members. It was understandable, then, that we enjoyed getting away from watchful eyes and wandering around the gardens of Tsarskoye Selo, a beautiful, melancholic spot, once the site of much activity but now abandoned.

Unfortunately, Anna did not keep her early poetry, so no study of her works will ever include the first stirrings of her great talent. But I can share one important fact about her work: she foresaw her destiny. When she was still a young girl she wrote about the mysterious ring (later she described it as the "black" ring of her grandmother) bestowed upon her by the moon:

> It was fashioned for me by the crescent's blue ray;
> Putting it on my finger, he begged of me, "Pray,
> Pray take care of this gift! Do not give it away!"
> So my ring and proud dreams I will keep, come what may!*

Later, while living with me in 1915 and 1916, she did give the ring away. And under what circumstances! What dark depths my memory holds!

Many lives became entwined with Anna's, but we should take them in order. She met Nikolai Gumilev, a [. . .] pupil at the Imperial Gymnasium at the time, on Christmas Eve in 1902. We—Anna, my younger brother Seryozha, and I—were on our way to buy Christmas tree ornaments. Anna was fourteen, Nikolai was seventeen. It was a beautiful, sunny day. We met Nikolai and his older brother Dmitry, a cadet at the Naval Military School, by the Gostiny Dvor [a department store]. I already knew the two boys, for my brothers and I shared with them the same music teacher—Yelizaveta Bazhenova. She brought Dmitry, her pet pupil, to our home and, much later, introduced me to Nikolai.

The Gumilev boys accompanied us. I walked with Dmitry, Anna, with Nikolai. We made our purchases, and they walked us home. Anna displayed not the slightest interest in this encounter. As for me, I had always found Dmitry boring. I was already fifteen, and he did not impress me in any way. Apparently Nikolai did find the meeting interesting. When returning from the gymnasium, I often saw him walking in the distance,

---

* Tr. by Sergi Roy.

waiting for Anna to appear. He became acquainted with her older brother, Andrei, in an effort to gain entrance to their secluded home.

But Anna didn't care for him. I suppose girls our age were more interested in disillusioned young men over twenty who had already tasted forbidden fruit and sated themselves with its spicy flavor. But even then Nikolai was not one to give up easily. He was not a handsome young man, being somewhat stiff, outwardly arrogant, and inwardly unsure of himself. But he was well-read and loved the French symbolists. Though he wasn't very fluent in French, he could read it well enough without having to resort to translation. He was tall and thin with beautiful hands and a pale, rather elongated face. In my opinion, he didn't cut a striking figure, but he was not totally lacking in elegance. Like so many others in the north, he was blond.

Later, after becoming a man and making it through the rough military cavalry school, he turned out to be a fearless rider and brave officer (he was awarded two orders of St. George). His smart figure and broad shoulders made him quite dashing, and he looked especially nice in uniform. Many people were attracted by his smile and the bemused yet kind gaze of his large, slightly tilting eyes. He spoke in almost a sing-song manner, softly pronouncing his rs and ls, so that his speech had a special, not at all unpleasant character.

I liked to hear him read poetry, and we often asked him to do so. He was a frequent visitor in our home. After I married, he became a close friend of my husband and, for old times' sake, of mine as well. I had met him when he was ten years old, and our unsullied friendship lasted a lifetime, right up to Nikolai's tragic death.

But let us return to those early days. In 1905 family concerns caused the Gorenko family to move to Kiev. During this brief period Anna and I maintained contact only through correspondence. Unfortunately, these letters were lost due to the many upheavals in our difficult lives. Anna never wrote of loving Nikolai, but she often mentioned his persistent courting and his numerous marriage proposals. She described her flippant refusals and indifference to the whole idea. Her kind mother, feeling sorry for Gumilev, often mildly scolded her on this account.

Anna had family ties in Kiev: a cousin had married her older brother, Andrei. Evidently she found much to occupy her time and was not bored with her life there.

Then Nikolai moved to Kiev, and one fine morning I received news of their marriage. I was very surprised. Soon afterwards Anna returned to Tsarskoye Selo and came to see me. She briefly mentioned her marriage but didn't appear to have changed in any way. Unlike many newlyweds, she exhibited no desire to talk about it. It was as if the event had no significance either for her or for me. We talked for a long time on different topics. She read her poems, which were more feminine and profound than before. The image of her husband was absent. In her later work, there might be only a fleeting hint of him. In Nikolai's verse, on the contrary, the image of his wife loomed with authority, pervading his emotions and the diverse themes until the final days of his life. Sometimes she was a mermaid, sometimes a sorceress "concealing evil triumph in her eyes."

> The woman in the corner listened to him,
> concealing evil triumph in her eyes . . . *

This poem should really be quoted in full to show that my statements are based not on impressions but on admissions and facts.

Certainly they both were too free-spirited and important to turn into cooing love-birds. . . . Their relationship was more like a secret duel: she was fighting for self-affirmation as a liberated woman; he was striving to remain free of her spell, to maintain his independence and establish his authority over the complicated and indomitable woman who always seemed to be slipping away from him. Speaking of love (though I am not altogether sure what people mean by this word), if love is the haunting image of the person alternately loved and hated, then this image is found throughout Nikolai Gumilev's poetry. I will say with conviction that if Nikolai loved anyone it was Anna. Now I must make a reservation and add that there was perhaps someone else he loved in Paris, the "Blue Star"** referred to in pieces of his work. If Tenderness is Love, then Nikolai also loved and cared for the Blue Star. The rest of it, regardless of its name, evoked his ironic smile and jesting tone.

But, after all, can any man be said to be monogamous? I recall walking along the bank of the Neva with Nikolai and quietly discussing the feelings of men and women. He said to me: "I only know that a real man is a

---

* From Gumilev's poem "Iambic Pentameter."—ed.
** Yelene Dyubushe. See "Blue Star" in the appendix.—ed.

polygamist while a real woman is a monogamist." "Do you know such a woman?" I asked. He laughed and said. "I guess not. But I believe she exists." I thought about Anna but, not wishing to cause him pain, said nothing.

Anna's feelings were deep and complicated; I know this probably better than anyone else. But Nikolai, the father of her only child, played an insignificant role in her life. Perhaps this seems strange and incomprehensible, but it's the truth. Leo Tolstoy, that master at understanding affairs of the heart, described this trait in Anna Karenina. But analogies are pointless.

I can say this: Nikolai was a caring and devoted son, the pet of his intelligent and domineering mother. No doubt he was happy that his own son was raised under the same warm and comforting wing.

I won't take it upon myself to question Gumilev's whereabouts when his son was born. As a rule fathers were not present, and honorable gentlemen should have a better understanding of what happened than I. If Nikolai's friends managed to persuade him to accompany them to their usual spot for carousing, perhaps this merely indicated that he wished to try to shorten the time of anxiety by overcoming his inner turmoil. I think that if he had met up with different friends less dedicated to carousing, he might just as easily have gone to a monastery and there, with trembling heart, attended vespers.

Anna gave birth at the expensive and well-equipped clinic of Professor Otto. Nikolai called her there, and when it was all over, he went to pick up the mother of his son and bring them to Tsarskoye Selo, to the happy grandmother. My husband and I lunched with them, and we drank champagne to celebrate the happy occasion.

Anna and Nikolai were great poets, and their lives reflected the multi-faceted nature of their inner thoughts and outward actions, the variegated colors and shades of darkness that painted their world. I have thought a great deal about this: I believe it is a trait of male character to harbor extremes, some of which may be diametrically opposed. Yet despite these extremes, a man possesses deep feelings for that single individual he most cherishes and needs.

The birth of her son considerably restricted Anna's life. She nursed the baby herself and rarely left Tsarskoye Selo. At that time there were no wonder-fathers who strolled baby carriages. Experienced nannies fulfilled that role. Like other fathers, Nikolai no doubt visited his son whenever he had the chance. If he were no better than other model fathers, he certainly was no worse. And who is to say that such ties do not represent love? Fathers and mothers play different roles, especially during the first years of a child's life. Anna herself gradually became less tied down with caring for her child (after all, the baby had a nanny and grandmother) and returned to the bohemian life of literature. Neither she nor her husband had any reason to want a separation. But other than poetry (and even that they understood in different ways) neither did they share any strong bonds.

Anna's verse was always filled with concrete images and facts, though she did not always call them by name. Gumilev's poetry was always filled with dreams and fantasy, the emotions behind which only those close to him could fathom. Reality turned to whimsy; perceptions crossed over into hallucinations and impressions of infinity and death. Gumilev's poetry revealed his longing for the unknown, his dreams of mysterious places and encounters. Readers and listeners were spellbound by his tempestuous verse. He was a meditative and prescient poet. Perhaps, while not knowing his tragic fate, he somehow felt it.

Anna wrote poetry even as a young girl, and her father jokingly called her a poet. Headstrong and perhaps too independent, she was a favorite in the family, but she wasn't altogether trusted. She caused too much trouble: leaving home for long periods without telling anyone, swimming far out at sea, climbing on top of the roof to talk to the moon. In short, she grieved her lovely mother and kind governess. This was my first impression of the tall, extremely thin girl with cropped hair.

A fourteen-year-old adolescent. The next time I saw her, Anna Gorenko had changed considerably and was now a tall young woman with a high bosom and small waist. Everyone in my family thought her beautiful but did not altogether approve of our renewed and deeper friendship. As it was, I caused enough concern to my family, for I was stubborn and difficult. But in the end it was hard to control us: Tsarskoye Selo had none of the restraints of city life, our family was large, and freedom simply sprouted.

Of all the members of her family, Anna was closest to her brother Andrei, two years her senior. He was a gifted young man, seemingly older than his years. They always spoke French between themselves (Anna's

mother addressed her children exclusively in that language), and I was
surprised to hear them use "vous" with each other. We had foreign governesses in our home, but no one used the formal "vous." On the other
hand, the Gorenko family was much less authoritarian than my family, and
I enjoyed spending time there. True, Anna's handsome father often raised
his voice, but at the same time he could be very witty and unexpectedly
jovial. (It should be remembered that this was the period of the *anlechter
Vater:* fathers were bellowing tyrants.) It seemed to me that Anna was
allowed great freedom. She never complained of any kind of physical,
much less mental, abuse.

The friendship Anna and I shared could by no means be described as
schoolgirl adoration, the kind of relationship so often depicted in literature,
especially French literature. We had an intellectual relationship, and it
endured a lifetime. I can state without exaggeration that we had the kind
of pure, unselfish friendship that poets and writers are so reluctant to
ascribe to women.

Anna and I both loved Russia. My feelings were inculcated by my
nanny and from reading Pushkin and Blok. Anna's love developed through
reading Pushkin in Slepnyovo:

> Those pastel plains where mind is muffled
> And haze to mute all hues contrives,
> The damning gaze of those unruffled
> And weatherbeaten country wives.*

We took long walks together. Frequently, especially when we strolled
home from the gymnasium, Nikolai would be lurking around a corner
somewhere and suddenly join us. We didn't like his company and, I must
confess, naughty girls that we were, that we often set about to tease him.
We knew that he detested German so we would begin to recite aloud a
long German poem. The rythmic, florid verses, which we never forgot,
lasted until we reached our house. Poor Nikolai would patiently endure
our recitation the whole way. We were so naughty. Even now it causes me
amusement and pain to remember how we acted.

Only someone truly dedicated to a goal could tolerate such mockery.
I think Nikolai's determination to win Anna's favor was a trait of his

* Tr. by Peter Tempest.

masculine character, and this trait was evident in his approach to every-thing: to Lebanon, to the war, and to his military career. He was also very ambitious. In one poem he speaks of giving his name to a river and acting as a lawgiver to five foreign tribes. But he also writes of having grown weak and weary in spirit. Was it because of the duel he fought with Anna?

Only once did I believe that Anna had been conquered and broken. But this lasted only briefly.

> But unconcerned and calmly raising
> My open palms I blocked my ears,
> Not letting such unseemly phrases
> Profane my soul in grief and tears.*

Sitting on my large sofa, Anna told Nikolai she wanted to leave him, forever. Nikolai turned deathly pale and, after a prolonged silence, finally spoke: "I have always said you were perfectly free to do whatever you wanted!" He stood up and left.

It took considerable effort for a man like him—a man who wanted to command a woman according to his own desires and caprices—to speak those words. Less than a year later he married again. His second wife he sent to his mother in the provinces to live a lonely and totally joyless life. This was the Gumilev who had been defeated only once, but mortally so, in combat with a woman.

I don't know how poets or writers define the duels between men and women, but I think it is sex, though in the broad sense of the word. If it is love, it certainly differs from the descriptions rendered by such masters of the affairs of the heart as Tolstoy, Turgenev, Flaubert, and Shakespeare and the poets Pushkin and Blok.

Gumilev was perhaps the victim of his fervid imagination. He did not want to have a docile, kind, and modest wife who would bear him several children and manage his household. If he had, he might have met a different fate. But a person has only one fate, and it is not for us to make idle speculations.

At any rate, Nikolai married for love and of his own free will. As for whether or not it was a happy marriage, who is to say what happiness is to each individual? It was Pushkin who sadly observed that there was no

* Tr. by Peter Tempest.

happiness on earth, only serenity and will. Nikolai had little serenity but possessed a great deal of will. Anna? I believe that women as freedom loving and complex in character as she are only happy when they are totally independent. To a certain extent Anna was able to achieve this. She depended on neither her mother-in-law nor her husband; her work was published early in her life, and she had her own money. . . . But I never saw her happy. She was, however, serene, much more so than her husband. At times I would say she had a "bright serenity," and for the most part this came from within her.

> The swaying of branches that you
> Touch lightly, the jingle of your spurs,
> This dream that at last has come true,
> Is sweeter than all of my verse.*

Gumilev? No, she wasn't writing of Gumilev.

In one thing Anna was different from many modern poets and closer to Pushkin: the love and sincerity she felt toward others. Only rarely, and for well-grounded reasons, did she express disdain or indifference. I never saw her judge anyone around her or reveal any hatred, except for the "enemies of humankind" who considered themselves to be "supermen."

She had a great ability to mock, and at times offended people. But it was inner gaiety that prompted her. It rarely seemed to me that her mockery prevented her from loving even those whom she mocked. There were a few exceptions. One, for example, was the stupid, malevolent, and envious Shura Sverchkova. But this was a witch that no one loved, not even her hapless children. Unfortunately, Anna's son, Lev, was often in the company of this woman. And it was she who was most to blame for his withdrawn, discontented nature.

Anna had a pleasant disposition, and this made it easy for others to live around her. In my home, she stayed in a small but comfortable room with a window overlooking our clinic's shady, quiet garden. Her door was almost always opened, so we would talk without leaving our rooms. I had a very keen sense of hearing and sometimes would call out to her: "Why aren't you sleeping?" "How did you know I wasn't?" "From the sound of your breathing." Then she would come and sit on my bed and tell me why

* Tr. by Sergei Roy.

she was having trouble falling asleep. She would often whisper her poems at night, listening to how they sounded.

It was a wonderful time. But all around us shots were ringing out and the rumble of machine guns could be heard: we were living in Vyborgsky district, the first in Petrograd to revolt. But our clinic was secluded behind a large garden, and everything there seemed peaceful and calm. We were separated from the cruelties and turmoil of life by a high stone fence.

Yet we did experience some trouble: life could not be shut out forever. I remember one incident in particular. Anna and I were calmly sipping our tea in my dining room when suddenly we heard a loud noise, a ring at the door, and the sound of men's voices. Our military clerk, a man by the name of Semyonov, along with a detachment of Red Army soldiers and sailors, was asking for my husband, who at that time was the director of the Naval Academy's mental clinic.

I went out to meet them (no one could ever accuse me of being a coward) and someone shoved a piece of paper at me—the death sentence for five people at the clinic, or so they said. My husband and for some reason I myself were on the list. I sent Semyonov to my husband, asking him to inform him of why he was being sought. Then I crossed the hall leading from our apartment to that of Professor Osipov. (I had been there often as I was a friend of his wife, Vera.) I told him what had happened, and he called the Cheka and asked to speak to one of the authorities. We were soon informed that a detachment would be sent to investigate the incident. I remained in Professor Osipov's apartment to see how the situation developed. The doctor on duty was sent for. Unfortunately, he turned out to be Dr. Dobrotovsky, a rich and excitable young man who loved a clamor. He approached the detachment and the ensuing altercation soon became a brawl. Finding ourselves in the midst of the fighting, Professor Osipov, with his tone of quiet command, put a quick end to the abusive shouts from both sides.

A representative of the State Health Organization, Dr. Semashko reviewed the documents, and our execution was postponed for an indefinite time. Later we discovered what had happened. The instigator of the entire affair turned out to be a mentally ill commissar who had been placed in the disturbed ward located next to our apartment. He had seen me from a window and, though I don't know what he had against me, for some reason wished to see me dead. The rest was more understandable; my husband was the one who had given the order to have the commissar confined. More than likely the commissar had included me just to keep my husband company. More unbelievable incidents than this occurred during those times. Still, we came through them safely.

One person did suffer injury, though—the mild and totally innocent assistant doorman, Lachenkov, who became our clinic's romantic hero. He had his eye blackened and an ear cut, but this only made him more interesting to the women. My heroism went unnoticed by anyone save the military clerk Semyonov, who admitted I was a "brave woman." But I am not vain.

Anna, who was left alone with Ruslan, was frightened at how this ridiculous episode might end. I returned to my apartment, soothed Anna and Ruslan, then, though it was already morning, we went to sleep.

Georgy Adamovich

MEETINGS WITH ANNA AKHMATOVA

The reminiscences of the poet and critic Georgy Adamovich (1892–1972) were first published in the almanac (fifth edition, New York, 1967).

I can't remember exactly when I saw Anna Andreyevna the first time. Probably it was around two years before the First World War at a Romance-Germanic language seminar at Petersburg University. I was not enrolled as a student in that seminar, but I often attended it: it served as a kind of headquarters of the just-emerging acmeist movement and at the same time a meeting place for the first formalists, who were not yet sure of themselves and were developing their theories more because they rejected all of neo-Skabichevsky's ideas than because they were firmly convinced of their own. The students in the Romance-Germanic faculty looked condescendingly on the Russian sector of the history-philology department, and not without reason. Gumilev, for example, scoffingly related how, during his Russian exam (where he intended to dazzle everyone with his knowledge and astute arguments), Professor Shlyapkin had asked him:

"What do you think Onegin would have done if Tatyana had agreed to leave her husband?"

The conversations and discussions at the Romance-Germanic seminar were on a different level, and I personally found it wonderful, mysterious, and incredibly interesting. Poetry readings were organized several times a year, not for the public but for the seminar's "own." To be included as one of the seminar's "own"—even if there was an element of condescension involved—was a great honor. One day K. V. Mochulsky, who would later become one of my good friends in Paris (and who, because of his volatile, somewhat erratic nature and over-sensitivity, could not become a true formalist), said to me: "You must come today without fail. Akhmatova will be there. Have you read her?"

Had I read her?! I had read everything I could find, from her first lines addressed to the wind:

> You and I, we were both free
> But too eager I was to live
> Now, wind, my dead body you see
> With no one to grieve.[*]

I was fascinated by the sudden change in rhythm in the line "With no one to grieve." As people loved to say at the time, I was "pierced" by her poetry, almost as much as I had been "pierced" as a student a few years earlier by the first lines I read of Blok.

Akhmatova was already famous, or at any rate famous in the same way Mallarmé used the word when talking to his friends about Villiers del'Isla Adam: "You know him and I know him; what else is there?"

She was highly praised in the small circle of advocates of modern poetry. Gumilev, her husband, was at first sharply critical of her poems and allegedly even begged her not to write. It's possible that he unconsciously allowed his personal feelings to affect his critical judgment. It was not literary envy but an insurmountable, skeptical hostility evoked by a feeling of deeply rooted difference in Akhmatova's style of poetry and his own. It was not until several years after their marriage that he acknowledged Akhmatova, without reservation, to be a poet.

---

[*] From the poem "Bury, bury me, wind . . ." (1909). Tr. by Yana Glukhoded.

But it was Kuzmin who grasped the uniqueness and beauty of Akhmatova's early poems and who "set her up," if one may use that expression here. Akhmatova's originality was recognized as well by Georgy Chulkov, the "mystic anarchist" who at one time was scoffed at by half of Russia for writing in the introduction to an important article the words: "A real poet cannot help but be an anarchist; how could it be otherwise?" Of course, Kuzmin's authority was much greater than Chulkov's, and it was primarily he who helped Akhmatova to acquire her fame. I remember an inscription Akhmatova wrote already after the Revolution in a copy of *Plantain* or *Anno Domini* that she was sending to Kuzmin: "To my wonderful teacher, Mikhail Alekseyevich." However, by the end of Kuzmin's life, in the 1930s, Akhmatova had ceased to see him. I don't know why.

I was stunned by Anna Andreyevna's appearance. When people recall her today they sometimes say she was beautiful. She was not, but she was more than beautiful, better than beautiful. I have never seen a woman whose face and entire appearance, whose expressiveness, genuine unworldliness and inexplicable sudden appeal set her apart anywhere and among beautiful women everywhere. Later her appearance would acquire a hint of the tragic: Rachelle in Phaedra, as Osip Mandelshtam put it in his well-known octet. He made this comment after a reading at the Stray Dog Cafe when Akhmatova, standing on the stage with her "pseudo-classical" shawl falling off her shoulders, seemed to ennoble everything around her. But my first impression was different. Anna Andreyevna almost constantly smiled, laughed, and exchanged cheerful, sly half-whispers with Mikhail Leonidovich Lozinsky, who tried to persuade her to act in a more serious manner, as becomes a famous poet, and to listen to the poems more attentively. For a minute or two she would be silent, and then once again begin to joke and whisper. When she was finally asked to read something, she immediately changed and almost seemed to go pale: the future Phaedra was lurking behind the scoffer, the "Tsarskoye Selo happy sinner," as she would refer to herself in her later years, in "Requiem." But it didn't last long. As we were leaving the seminar, I was introduced to her. Anna Andreyevna said: "Forgive me. It seems that I prevented all of you from listening to the readings today. Soon they won't let me come anymore. . . ." and having turned to Lozinsky, she burst out laughing again.

I then began to meet Anna Andreyevna rather frequently—most often in the Stray Dog Cafe, which she frequented. Numerous stories and recollections have made a legend of this small cellar with a wall-painting by Sudeikin, located on Mikhailovskaya Square. Akhmatova dedicated two poems to it: "we are all of us drunkards and harlots" and "Yes, I adored those noisy crowded nights." It really was a night crowd: people would come after the theater, after an evening get-together or a discussion, and stay until almost dawn. Boris Pronin, the owner, would show the door to anyone he sensed was an "outsider," someone who did not belong to literature and art. But it all depended on his mood: there were times when an evident outsider would be given a hearty welcome; it was impossible to predict. It was very crowded, very stuffy, and not exactly merry. I would have great difficulty in coming up with the precise word to describe the atmosphere in the Stray Dog. But no one who once frequented the place has forgotten it to this day.

Famous foreigners used to come. There was Marinetti—vivacious and flushed, amusingly like "the man from the restaurant"; the only thing missing was a folded, snow-white napkin in his hand. And there was Paul Fort, the "king" of French poetry for many years. Verhaeren, Richard Strauss, and others. At the insistence of Pronin, Artur Lurye (considered in our circle to be a rising music star) played his modern arrangement of Gluck's gavotte for Strauss. Afterwards Strauss stood up, walked over to the piano, and kindly complimented Lurye. But he flatly refused to play by himself. All the Petersburg poets frequented this cafe—symbolists, acmeists, and futurists. The latter were divided into cubofuturists, led by Mayakovsky in his yellow blouse, and by Khlebnikov, and egofuturists, the followers of Igor Severyanin, whom we were supposed to shun and slightly despise. Khlebnikov was already a mystery even then. He sat silently with his head down, oblivious to everything, immersed in his own secret thoughts or dreams. His presence emanated something important, as inexplicable as it was certain. I remember how Mandelshtam, who was by nature cheerful and sociable, was talking animatedly about something. He talked and talked, then suddenly looked around, as if looking for someone, and stopped short: "No, I can't go on talking when Khlebnikov is silent." Yet Khlebnikov wasn't even close by. The cellar was divided into two sections, and Khlebnikov was sitting in the second, a darker and more "intimate" room, without a stage or tables.

Despite claims among the émigré community abroad, Blok never visited the Stray Dog. As a matter of fact, another allegation still strongly believed among that community needs to be dispelled: that there was a kind of love affair between Blok and Akhmatova. Nothing of the sort ever existed; no one then ever heard or spoke of their attraction to each other in Petersburg. I don't know the basis for the rumors. They probably arose simply because the temptation to imagine such a pair—Blok and Akhmatova—was too great, even if it was contrary to reality.

Anna Andreyevna was always surrounded by people in the Stray Dog. But she never seemed as gay as the first time I saw her. Perhaps she was showing restraint, aware that strangers were looking at her with curiosity and, perhaps, little by little, something in her character, in her general outlook, began to change. All kinds of people—those she knew and those she didn't—would approach her and "half-tenderly, half-lazily" touch her hand. Mayakovsky was one. One day he held her delicate, thin hand in his huge paw and with derisive admiration exclaimed for all to hear: "My God! What little fingers!" Akhmatova frowned and turned away.

There were occasions when someone who was just introduced to her would proclaim his love. I remember Akhmatova saying about one such daring fellow: "Strange, he didn't mention the pyramids. Usually in these circumstances they would say: we met before in the time of Ramses II, don't you remember?"

She had two close friends who also frequently visited the Stray Dog— Princess Salomeya Andronikova and Olga Afanasyevna Glebova-Sudeikina, "Olechka," a dancer and actress, one of the rare Russian actresses who could recite poetry.

I was accepted into the first Poets' Guild not long before it closed and thus attended only five or six meetings. But poetry readings were often conducted outside the workshop as well, sometimes in Tsarskoye Selo, at the Gumilevs, or in my own home. My mother had no great love for these strange people and would go to the theater or to visit friends, leaving my younger sister to play hostess. Gumilev fervidly courted my sister and dedicated his collection *Quiver* to her. Akhmatova, however, treated her in a friendly manner.

A discussion would follow the reading of each poem. Gumilev insisted that remarks be in the form of "subordinate clauses," as he liked to say; i.e., not exlamations or ungrounded comments about one poem being good and another being bad but motivated explanations as to why it was good or bad. He usually spoke first and for a long time. His criticism was detailed and, as a rule, unerringly correct. He had an exceptional ear for poetry, an exceptional feel for words. But I confess that even then I felt that he was incomparably more perceptive to the poems of others than to his own. He seemed not to notice or sense some vapidness and decorativeness in his own work. Anna Andreyevna spoke little and became animated only when Mandelshtam read his poetry. She frequently observed that, in her judgment, there was no one to compare with Mandelshtam, and once, after a workshop meeting at Gorodetsky's home, she said something that positively amazed me:

"Mandelshtam, of course, is our number one poet . . ."

What did she mean by "our"? Was Mandelshtam greater, more important to her than Blok? I don't think so. Without exception, without question, and without reservation, though we might question his poetic method, we all recognized Blok's regal superiority. And Akhmatova agreed with us. But immediately after hearing a Mandelshtam poem, whose lines flowed like thick, molten gold, she could forget Blok.

Mandelshtam admired her: not just her poetry but her personality, her appearance. An early indication of his admiration, which lasted throughout his life, was the octet about Rachelle-Phaedra. I recall an amusing detail probably unknown to anyone at this time: the original of the next to last line of this poem was not "like the indignant Phaedra" but "like the poisoner Phaedra." Someone—if I'm not mistaken, Valerian Chudovsky—asked Mandelshtam:

"Osip Emilyevich, why do you say, 'the poisoner Phaedra'? I assure you, Phaedra never poisoned anyone, not in Euripides or in Racine."

Mandelshtam was nonplussed and remained silent: indeed, Phaedra had *not* poisoned anyone. He had [. . .] probably confused something, because of his absent-mindedness. In any case, he was perfectly familiar with Racine. The next day "the poisoner Phaedra" had become "thc indignant Phaedra." In a two-volume edition of Mandelshtam poetry published abroad in 1964 I was surprised to read the following lines in the same poem:

The sinister voice—a bitter hop
The soul unfetters entrails.

This may have been based on one of the earlier editions. But I heard the author read this poem many times, and I distinctly remember the words "resounding voice" not "sinister." There was nothing sinister in Akhmatova's voice, and Mandelshtam could not have said this about her. Moreover, it wasn't "The soul unfetters entrails" but "Unfetters the entrails of the soul."

After the Revolution everything changed in our daily life, but not immediately. At first it seemed that the political coup would not affect personal life, but this illusion did not last long. Anyway, this is all well known and there is no reason to discuss it here.

Akhmatova and Gumilev divorced, the first Poets' Guild was closed, and the Stray Dog shut its doors, to be replaced (but not really) by the Comedian's Stop-over (located in the Dobychina house on Mars Field and frequented by the capital's military governor, Savinkov, and later by Lunacharsky, another high-ranking personage). Blok died, Gumilev was arrested and shot. Times were difficult, dark, hungry. Because we had our wonderful Lithuanian passports, my family was able to leave the country. I lived two years in Novorzhev, occasionally returning to Petersburg. I saw Anna Andreyevna less frequently and not one of these meetings I remember distinctly, except the last.

It was during the time of NEP. There was some kind of crowded affair—either a musical performance or a poetry recitation by one of the Serapionov brothers—taking place at the House of Arts on Moika. When the performance was over, everyone broke up into groups and sat at small tables. There was vodka, hors d'oeuvres, pastries, and cakes—compared with the first years after the Revolution, a veritable feast. Anna Andreyevna was sitting with friends at the other end of the room. Knowing that I loved ballet, Akim Volynsky was showing me with his hands how to do a fouetté properly and how carelessly a ballerina from Moscow had executed it in a performance of Swan Lake yesterday or the day before. It was late. The bottle of vodka on our table was almost empty.

I saw that Akhmatova had stood up and appeared to be about to leave. She was wearing the same shawl around her thin shoulders; she had the same unique appearance. . . . Not waiting to hear the end of the choreographic monologue interspersed with quotes from Plato and Schopenhauer, I somehow made my way through the crowded room and approached Anna Andreyevna. Quickly, perhaps even a little feverishly, I began to talk about her, not about her poetry but about her appearance. I might have been mistaken, but it seemed to me that she was probably pleased. She smiled sweetly, gave me her hand, leaning forward, as if trying to keep others from hearing what she said, and whispered: "I'm becoming an old dog. . . ."

Recalling the words spoken by others decades ago, one involuntarily generalizes. But I clearly remember the word "dog." Why did she say this about herself? Perhaps she was remembering Chekhov's letter to his wife? Something else? I don't know. But these were the last words I heard Akhmatova speak in Russia. Soon after that evening I left to join my relatives in Nice, thinking to return in half a year.

But almost thirty years went by. I had long ago stopped thinking about returning. The name Akhmatova was mentioned less and less in the press, there was little news about her. After the war came the crude and stupid Zhdanov resolution concerning her and Zoshchenko. Now even her life was in jeopardy. No one knew anything about her. I was certain I would never see her again.

With the advent of the "thaw," things changed somewhat. The papers reported that Akhmatova would be traveling to Italy. The next year she journeyed to Oxford, where university officials bestowed upon her an honorary doctorate. England is not so far from Paris. Was there a chance she might come to Paris? Would I be able to see her? I didn't know her mood, how she felt about the Russian emigrants and those involved with the émigré press. Nor did I know how free she was to act on her own. I told myself that I would not take the first step toward meeting her until I was sure it would not be against her wishes.

Late one night I received a telephone call from London. There were a few words in English and then: "This is Akhmatova. I will be in Paris tomorrow. Shall we meet?"

I must admit that I was both nervous and happy. Then, looking at the clock, I thought: My God! Russia has not changed. A telephone call at two in the morning! In the West, this was something we no longer did. Then I wondered how Akhmatova had obtained my phone number. It turned out she got it in Oxford from the daughter of the late Samuel Osipovich Dobrin, a professor of Russian literature at the University of Manchester where I had once lectured.

The next day I went to see Akhmatova in her room at the Napoleon Hotel on Freedland Avenue.

Among the comments made by [Lev] Tolstoy that one reads and thinks upon, how true is one that states that all the changes in a person's appearance are noticed in the first moment after a long separation. But a minute later amazement abates, and it sometimes seems that the person has always been this way. This is how I felt when I saw Akhmatova.

Sitting in the chair was a stout, heavy, old woman—attractive, regal, and smiling pleasantly. It was only by her smile that I recognized Anna Andreyevna. But a minute later, as Tolstoy predicted, my surprise vanished. I was looking at Akhmatova, only she was perhaps more loquacious than before, as if she were more certain of herself and of her judgments. At times she even imbued her words and gestures with a hint of the imperial. I recalled what I had heard not long before from a Soviet writer who had come to Paris: "No matter where Akhmatova goes she is a queen." There was indeed something majestic in her carriage that brought to mind Serov's portrait of Yermolova.

Little by little Akhmatova became animated. She began to recall the distant past, to tell stories, to ask questions, to laugh and argue, and generally seemed more at ease. She switched to the breezy, rapid Petersburg style of conversation where everything is considered to be understood and grasped in half a sentence, without wordy explanations.

What did we talk about? Mostly about poetry, of course. And I regretted, once I returned home, that I had not recorded the conversation. But it was not so long ago, so I remember almost everything Anna Andreyevna said. . . . In reconstructing our conversation, I am hindered only by the necessity of having to relate what I said as well. . . . I will try to call as little attention as possible to myself.

Anna Andreyevna spent three days in Paris, and I visited her three times. At our first meeting I offered to drive her around Paris, a city she had visited twice in her youth, more than fifty years before. She eagerly accepted my offer and began immediately to talk about Modigliani, her young Paris friend who would later gain world fame but was at that time unknown to anyone.

It was a remarkable summer day, one of those early, fresh, crystal summer days when Paris is especially beautiful. Some Parisian friends of mine who owned a car went with me to pick up Akhmatova. They were happy to have the opportunity to meet her. First of all, Anna Andreyevna wanted to see the Rue Bonaparte, where she had once lived. It was an old house, like many in this quarter of Paris, probably from the eighteenth century. We stood in front of it for several minutes. "There's my window, on the second floor . . . how many times he had been here." Once again Anna Andreyevna was remembering Modigliani and trying with great effort to conceal her agitation. Then we went to the Bois de Boulogne, where we sat for a long time on a cafe terrace bathed in sunlight. Finally, we went to Montparnasse and ate at Couple, a noisy, overcrowded restaurant that, before the war, was the night meeting place of the Parisian literary and artistic bohemians, including the Russian emigrants.

Akhmatova sat down, carefully looked around the square room, sighed, and said:

"If you only knew what it means . . . to sit here . . . and all these people, these young people . . . they come and go, they are happy and carefree. . . ."

She stopped and did not explain what she meant by "if you only knew." But there was no need for explanations. And it would have been unforgivable to press her. It was clear enough. Soon the conversation turned to literature: Akhmatova seemed to evade other topics, touching upon them only accidentally and unwillingly. Before breakfast, for example, she had used the word "Leningrad" several times. I asked her:

"You say Leningrad, not Petersburg?"

I asked because I had heard that the Soviet intelligentsia—at any rate, most of them—preferred to say Petersburg or simply Peter rather than Leningrad.

Akhmatova answered in a cool voice:

"I say Leningrad because the city is called Leningrad."

I understood that it was difficult and painful for her to speak about many things and immediately regretted having opened up such a subject.

I thought I heard a hint of reproach, even a challenge, in her voice: why ask me such questions?

As I mentioned before, I met with Akhmatova three times in Paris. We had a number of conversations. I will share excerpts from them without trying, after two years, to follow any kind of artificial pattern of consistency or continuity. I remember the general content of the conversations, but not the order.

I was interested in what Akhmatova thought of Marina Tsvetayeva. Long ago in Petersburg she had spoken of her coldly, once even evoking the following response from Artur Lurye:

"You treat Tsvetayeva as Chopin treated Schumann."

Schumann praised Chopin, who made only polite, evasive comments about Schumann in return. Compared to "the golden-tongued Anna of all Rus," Tsvetayeva was much like Schumann. Once, before they met personally, Akhmatova showed me with amazement Tsvetayeva's letter from Moscow. Tsvetayeva had just read Akhmatova's "Lullaby" and praised it, saying that she would give everything she had written and would write in the future for a single line from that poem: "I am a bad mother." I thought Tsvetayeva's early poetry, for example the "Moscow" or "Blok" cycles, were wonderful and showed unusual talent. But Akhmatova did not like them.

Judging from two lines of a 1961 poem:

That is an elder, its boughs dark and lush
As was Marina's verse[*]

I assumed that Anna Andreyevna had changed her opinion of Tsvetayeva. Akhmatova remarked in a restrained voice: "She is very popular among us now. People love her, perhaps even more than Pasternak," but she added no personal comment. In a later conversation I mentioned the device which Tsvetayeva increasingly abused with each passing year—the running over of the logical content of a line to the beginning of the following line. "Yes," Akhmatova agreed, "you can do it once or twice. But she did it all the time, and so the device was losing its power."

(In checking and re-examining my many years' impression about

[*] Tr. by Sergei Roy.

Akhmatova, I have decided that her coolness to Tsvetayeva's poetry was not just because she didn't appreciate her verbal and formal approach. I think there was something else she didn't like: the demonstrative, defiant, almost intrusive "poeticism" of Tsvetayeva's verse; the inherent similarity and at the same time the extraneous sharp differences to Balmont; the ubiquitous posturing and at the same time the unquestionable sincerity; constant eccentricity. If this is so, Akhmatova was not the only one to be repelled by it. Nor was she the only one to find the poetry of Tsvetayeva—a woman of exceptional talent who suffered exceptional misfortune—abstruse.)

About Dostoyevsky:
"I find him very hard to read. When I was young I never finished any of his novels. I couldn't. I'd begin to read and wouldn't be able to sleep. I'd spend the entire night with the book. I felt like I had to quit reading or I would fall ill. In fact, once I almost did become ill while I was reading *The Possessed*. I can't cope with all that torment, grief, and suffering. There's nothing to be done about it; I just have weak nerves."

"At last you've admitted that you don't like Gumilev! I always knew it. But you must admit he wrote some beautiful poetry, 'The crazy streetcar', for example. Don't you think so?"
"It's 'Literature'"; literature in quotes. "True, it is good."
"Literature, literature! But a long time ago someone said, and rightly . . . I don't remember who it was . . . that Russia had only one poet who could sometimes be outside or above literature—Lermontov."

[Akhmatova:]
"No, I know practically nothing about émigré literature. Very little manages to reach us. I know the name Aldanov, for example, but I haven't read a single line he wrote. Bunin? I don't like his poetry and never did. But he wrote one story that I read even before the Revolution, a long time ago, and I'll never forget it. It's a wonderful story about an old vagabond, a drunkard and cheater who, ashamed of who he is, secretly comes to Moscow to see his daughter marry."
"'Kasimir Stanislavovich?'"

"Yes, that's it. . . . Do you remember it?"

(I was surprised at her mentioning this story. I've always thought this was one of Bunin's best, although it was one of his early works. It's much more important and profound than "The Man from San Francisco," which is actually nothing more than a skillful variation on the theme in "The Death of Ivan Ilyich.")

[Akhmatova:]

"There are so many stories without a word of truth; everything has been made up! How many times I've read or heard that at some large meeting of poets Vyacheslav Ivanov praised my "glove" poem . . . you know the one . . . "the left-hand glove?" Supposedly he came up and congratulated me, saying something about a new page in Russian poetry. . . . Nothing of the kind happened! I remember that he told me he thought the poem was good, but that was all. There were no congratulations, no ebullience.

[Akhmatova:]

"Not long ago we had the Silver Age of Russian poetry; soon we will have another Golden Age. I am not exaggerating. We have many young people who live for poetry. They write wonderful verse but don't want to publish. Entire days and nights they argue over poetry, discuss poetry, read poetry, just like before, even more than before! Have you read Brodsky? I think he's a remarkable poet, and he's almost reached his maturity."

I mentioned Yevtushenko. Anna Andreyevna spoke somewhat disparagingly of his stage popularity. I thought her scorn unjustified: stage popularity was stage popularity but you couldn't reduce everything to that alone. Akhmatova shrugged her shoulders, began to protest, then, evidently wanting to end the argument, said:

"You don't have to try to convince me that Yevtushenko is very talented. I know this."

About *Requiem.*

Anna Andreyevna wanted to know how her book was received, what people thought of it.

I recalled what Tsvetayeva had written long ago about "Lullaby"—

that she would give everything she had written for that one line—and said that the last lines of *Requiem:*

> The distant prison-dove will coo alone
> While the silent boats of the Neva sail on

no doubt evoked the same feeling in many poets. Akhmatova had forgotten about Tsvetayeva's letter and, it seemed to me, she was pleased to be reminded of it.

"It's hard to judge one's own poetry. You have to remove yourself from it, get away from it, like a separation. Then you will have a clearer idea about what is good and what is bad. I'm still too close to *Requiem.* But I think there are some good things in it. For example, this inserted word 'unfortunately' in the introductory quatrain."

What about the other quatrain about Golgotha!

> Magdalene wailed loud and tore her hair
> The loved disciple's face was stone.

"Yes, this is probably good, too."

"Are you happy that you came to Paris? Are you happy with the Oxford ceremony and everything else?"

"Yes, it was all fine, thank God. It would be a sin to complain. But there's always a fly in the ointment. . . . Just look what they write about me in your newspapers! I just read this yesterday."

She handed me a recent copy of *Novoye Russkoye Slovo* (*New Russian Word*) that carried a long article about her. I skimmed the article and asked in some surprise:

"What don't you like here? It's a well-meaning article without a word of criticism. . . ."

"Yes, that's just it—praise, compliments, not one word of criticism. . . . But between the lines you read what a martyr I am, how much I've suffered, how I'm alien to everything and everyone in modern Russia, that everywhere I am lonely. . . . You have no idea how this has hurt me and how it can still hurt me! If they want to write about me over here, let them write about me the way they write about other poets: this line is better than that one, this is an original use of imagery, this image does not work at all. Let them forget about my suffering."

"Anna Andreyevna, may I pass on your words to the editors of the émigré newspapers and magazines?"

"You not only may, you would be doing me a great service if you would. I beg you to. You don't have to make me your banner or mouth-piece. Can't the émigré critics understand this?"

The day of her departure from Paris Anna Andreyevna was not the same as the day before. She seemed to be worried or sad, even upset. For my own reasons, I did not want to go to the train station, so I went to the hotel to wish her goodbye. She said to me:

"There is no reason to go to the train station. I'm afraid of them, too."

It was not a fear based on superstition but on her health: two or three times before she left on a trip she had suffered heart attacks.

We no longer spoke of literature or poetry. I asked Anna Andreyevna what her financial situation was. "Believe me, I do not ask out of idle curiosity."

"They pay well for translation. I am translating Leopardi at the moment. . . . So I'll be able to make ends meet."

"But if you're sick, if you can't work?"

"Then it will be harder. I'll get a pension, but a small one."

And for the first time in three days she began to speak about herself, about her personal life, about what she had had to endure in the past decades.

"Fate spared me nothing. My lot was to suffer everything it's possible to suffer."

Someone knocked on the door. Some people walked in carrying flowers and candy. It was time for her to get ready, to pack the final odds and ends. In another hour she would have to leave.

Anna Andreyevna stood looking somewhat helpless in the middle of the room. She tried to smile:

"Well, goodbye. Don't forget me. God willing, I'll be in Paris again next year. Thank you."

It was more with gestures and the perplexed look on my face than with words that I asked: thanks for what?

"Well, for everything. . . . If not for the past, for the future. We are all tied to one another in some way. Especially now."

As I was leaving, I turned at the door. Anna Andreyevna waved and said: "God bless you. Goodbye."

There was not another meeting, nor will there ever be.

Boris Anrep
THE BLACK RING

Boris Anrep (1883–1969), a poet in his youth and later a mosaic artist, left Russia in 1917 and made his home in England. Anna Akhmatova addressed a number of her love lyrics to him.

Anna's grandmother bequeathed to her granddaughter her black ring: "It suits her, that fiery one, it will make her have more fun." At one time such rings were called mourning rings in England. It was a gold band of even width covered with black enamel; only the rims remained gold. In the center was a small diamond. Anna Andreyevna wore the ring always and attributed mysterious power to it.

Nikolai Nedobrovo introduced me to Anna in 1914 upon my return from Paris and before I left for the front. Nedobrovo had already written me about her; on our first meeting I was captivated by her charm. She was an intriguing woman capable of subtle and astute observations. More than that, she wrote beautiful, poignant poetry. Nedobrovo thought her to be the best poet of the time.

In 1915 I met Anna Andreyevna whenever I was away from the front on leave. Once I asked her to safeguard a copy of my poem "Fiza." She sewed it into a silk purse, promising to protect it like a sacred relic.

> Unlike my friends, unlike my foes
> He did not praise me or revile,
> He only told me—take my soul
> And keep it safe for me awhile.

> Now, one thing really worries me:
> Supposing he should die one day?
> The Lord's Archangel certainly
> Will come to take his soul away.

How can I hide it, how insist
And keep it from the Lord's own eyes?
A soul that sings and weeps like his
Must surely dwell in paradise.

JULY 1915

We went sleighriding together and met in restaurants. I was constantly asking her to recite her poetry. She would smile and chant the words softly. Often we sat silent, listening to the sounds around us. During one of our meetings that year, I spoke of my lack of faith and of the futility of religious hope. Anna strongly reproached me, saying that the key to happiness lay in faith: "One cannot live without faith."

Later she wrote a poem alluding to our conversation:

I'll strike it from your memory, this hour,
That your vague look might ask in helpless doubt:
"Where did I see these lilacs in full flower,
These swallows, and the tiny wooden hut?"

How often you'll remember indiscreet,
Unnamed desires' sudden secret pang,
And look in pensive cities for the street
That never was there on the city plan?

Strange letters coming suddenly your way,
A sound of voice behind a half-closed door
Will make you think, "She's come again today
To cure my lack of faith, as long before."*

4 APRIL, 1915

It was so. But I never received a letter from her, nor did I write her. She never came to help me with my lack of faith, nor did I call upon her to do so.

In early 1916 I was to be sent to England. I returned to Petrograd for a lengthy stay in order to prepare for my trip to London. At that time Nikolai Nedobrovo and his wife were living in Tsarskoye Selo, as was Anna Andreyevna. Nedobrovo invited me to his home on 13 February to

* Tr. by Sergei Roy.

listen to his tragedy, *Judith,* that he had just completed. "Anna Andreyevna will also be present," he added. Here I had just returned from the front and was now being invited to enjoy the elegant atmosphere of Nedobrovo's home in Tsarskoye Selo. It was a tempting proposition: I would listen to a recitation of *Judith,* a work Nedobrovo had spent years in writing, and once again see Anna Andreyevna.

Nikolai Vladimirovich Nedobrovo greeted me affectionately, as always. But when I embraced and kissed him I immediately felt his displeasure: he did not approve of demonstrative affection. His elegant body recoiled and I was lost in confusion. His wife, Lyubov Alexandrovna, came to my rescue. Kissing me on the cheek, she said she was going to prepare the tea while we listened to *Judith.* Sitting with her elbow propped on the sofa, Anna Andreyevna was watching us with a smile. As I approached her I became strangely agitated and felt an implausible sensation of pain. This is how I always felt when I met her or even thought about her. Even now, after her death, these memories cause me pain. I sat down beside her.

Nedobrovo sat behind a beautiful Italian Renaissance desk and opened his manuscript. Some spiteful people liked to claim he had married Lyubov Alexandrovna on account of her furniture. In all truth, Nikolai Vladimirovich did have a passionate love for all things elegant, beautiful, and stylish, as well as for articles representing the latest in technology.

Nedobrovo began to read his verse. He never chanted his poetry like the majority of his contemporaries; rather he read them, stressing the rhythm, effectively modulating his cadence: speeding up or slowing down the measure, underscoring the concept and dramatic significance of each passage. The tragedy unfolded slowly. Despite the irreproachable poetry and the marvelous reading, I listened but did not hear. Sometimes I looked at the profile of Anna Andreyevna and saw her gazing somewhere into the distance. I tried to concentrate. The measured verse filled my ears like the sound of train wheels. I closed my eyes and placed my hand on the seat of the sofa. Suddenly I felt something in my hand: the black ring. "Take it," Anna whispered. I wanted to say something. My heart began to pound and I looked questioningly at her face. Silently, she gazed again into the distance. I squeezed my hand into a fist as Nedobrovo continued to read. Finally, he finished. What could I say? "It was wonderful." Anna said nothing at first and said slowly: "Yes, it was very good." Nedobrovo

wanted to hear more. "My first impression is that it's remarkable," she said.
"I have to read it carefully; it's a wonderful composition." I praised the
poem, fearing he would discover that I hadn't heard half of it. Tea was
served, and Anna conversed with Lyubov Alexandrovna. I quickly departed;
Anna remained.

I was scheduled to leave for England a few days later. The day before
my departure I received an autographed copy of *Evening,* Anna's book of
verse. She had written:

> To Boris Anrep:
> One hope fewer now beguiles me,
> But one more song I have for singing.
> > Anna Akhmatova.
> > > Tsarskoye Selo. 13 Feburary 1916.

A short time before this date I gave Anna a wooden cross I had found
in a half-ruined, abandoned church in Galicia. I also sent her a quatrain I
had composed:

> I lost my words, I didn't say my pledge
> I stretched my hands to a defenseless girl
> To save her from a crucifix,
> A token of soul I'd given her.

This quatrain appeared among other poems dedicated to Anna Andreyevna in the third volume of *Ethereal Roads* (New York, 1963), with some
modifications*

I have no doubt that Anna Andreyevna herself made these changes,
but I'm not exactly sure why. Was she merely trying to improve the style?
Was this the only reason? The most significant changes are personal and
poignant: the replacement of "soul" with "meeting." Anna wrote of our
"meeting" in other poems:

> Like an angel, quiet waters scoring,
> You bent down into my face to see,
> And, my strength and liberty restoring,
> Took a ring to mark the prodigy.

---

* Anrep's poem was found in Akhmatova's album.—ed.

My hot flushes, feverish and morbid—
God-beseeching woe has cooled them off.
In my mind this month will live, the turbid
Arctic February, blizzard-rough.

FEBRUARY 1916
TSARSKOYE SELO

I left for London meaning to return in six weeks. But this was not to be.

On the lilacs' luscious sprays
Falls fine drizzle from the skies.
White Whit Monday spreads its rays
And on fast wings past me flies.

It's the last term for my friend
To return from distant lands.
In my dreams, the world's far end,
Rocks, high towers and white sands.

I could mount a tower like this
At a gloomy daybreak hour . . .
But 'mid marsh and field, there is
Not a single blessed tower.

I will just sit on the porch
Where an inky shade still lies.
Do not leave me in the lurch,
White Whit Monday—help me, please![*]

SPRING 1916
SLEPNYOVO

I never wrote to her, nor did she ever write to me.

Meeting you left no trace in my verse;
Unsung, sadness subsided, and pain.
Then cool summer drew near, at last,
Like life starting all over again.

[*] Tr. by Sergei Roy.

Now the sky seems a vault of dull lead
Licked by bright yellow flame at the rim.
Now I need more than my daily bread
To hear one single word about him.

Thou dear God sprinkling grasses with dew,
Save my soul by a sign from above—
Not for passion or pleasure: anew
I will live for a great earthy love.

17 MAY, 1916
SLEPNYOVO

The cross that I had given Anna was mentioned in one verse:

In the gloomy capital,
My hand still firm, if deadly tired,
I abdicated, putting all
I felt in honest black and white,

And through the window poured the wind—
A heavy, moisture-laden flow;
And heaven seemed to have been burnt
Down by a golden afterglow;

I looked not at the endless stream
In glowing granite neatly set.
I thought I'd see, not just in dream,
You whom I never could forget.

But unexpected came the night
To hide the city from the fall.
To help me in my headlong flight,
The ashy shadows spread their pall.

I only took the cross you brought
Me on the day of your betrayal—
To make the wormwood steppe break out
In bloom, the winds like sirens wail.

And now it hangs there on the wall
And keeps my bitterness at bay:
I do not fear my thoughts at all,
Not even thoughts of my last day.

AUGUST 1916
PESOCHNAYA BUKHTA

I remained in England, returning to Russia only for a brief period in late 1916. I spent January 1917 in Petrograd and left for London on the first train after the Kerensky Revolution. I said that I didn't know when I would return to Russia and that I loved the sedate English civilization of reason (this was my feeling at that time), not religious and political insanity. Anna Andreyevna answered me by writing this:

> By arrogance your spirit's dulled and swayed.
> You'll never know the light because of this.
> Our faith is nothing but a dream, you say,
> And but a mirage, this metropolis.
>
> You said to me, "Your country's steeped in sin."
> "But yours in godlessness," meekly I replied.
> Our guilt lies heavy with us, I concede—
> Still, all can be redeemed, and all set right.
>
> You live amid bright colours and warm seas,
> Then why do you knock on this poor sinner's door?
> I know what your relentless illness is.
> You seek out death—of which you stand in awe.*

1 JANUARY, 1917
SLEPNYOVO

Later that same year she wrote:

> You're a renegade—you have betrayed
> For a green island our native land.
> Icons, songs, and the old pines that swayed
> On a cliff high above a still pond.
>
> What's the matter with you, Volgan hotspur?
> Did you really go clean out of your mind
> That you hoped in their castles to prosper,
> That for their red-haired women you pined?

---

* Tr. by Sergei Roy.

Go on, blaspheme and brag, conceited,
And your Orthodox soul sell out,
Try to live in that grand royal city,
Fall in love with freedom newfound.

Why come moaning and pestering me,
By my high window at dead of night?
You know well you won't drown in the sea
Nor get hurt in the deadliest fight.

Who've fallen from grace, they indeed
Need not fear either battles or seas.
This is why you so piteously plead
"In the orisons remember my sins."*

SUMMER 1917
SLEPNYOVO

With the Kerensky Revolution in progress the streets of Petrograd were filled with people. Here and there one could hear shots ring out. Railway communication was disrupted. But I gave the revolution little thought. My one and only desire was to see Anna. At this time she was living in an apartment with the Sreznevskys. Professor Sreznevsky was a distinguished psychiatrist whose wife was Anna's close friend. Their apartment was behind the Neva, either in the Vyborgskaya or Peterburgskaya district, I don't remember which. I walked across the frozen Neva River in order to avoid the barricades around the bridges. I recall seeing a boy of about eighteen in the middle of the river. He was fleeing from prison and in a panic-stricken voice asked me the way to Varshavsky Station.

I reached the Sreznevsky house and rang the bell. Anna Andreyevna opened the door.

"Is it really you? On a day like this? They are seizing officers on the streets you know."

"I took off my epaulets."

She was obviously moved that I had come to see her. We went into her room and she reclined on her sofa. For a while we spoke of the significance of the revolution. She was worried, saying that enormous changes were in store:

* Tr. by Sergei Roy.

"It will be the same as it was in France during the Great Revolution, perhaps even worse."

"Let's not talk about it any more," I said, and we were silent. She looked at the floor.

"We will never see each other again. You are going away."

"I will come back. Look, I have your ring." I opened my jacket and showed her the black ring I wore on a chain around my neck. Anna touched the ring. "Good, it will save you." I pressed her hand to my chest. "Wear it always," she said. "Always," I whispered and then added, "It is sacred." Her eyes clouded with emotion, and she stretched out her hands to me. I burned with spiritual ecstasy, kissed her hands, and stood up to leave. Anna smiled gently: "It's better this way."

> The Legend of the Black Ring
> (1917–1936)
>
> Suddenly the house is quiet,
> Bare stand poppies by the wall,
> I sit drowsy, stock-still, tired,
> Watching early darkness fall.
>
> Dark's the night, the wind is wan,
> And the gate is firmly closed.
> Where's the worry and the fun?
> Where are you, my sweet betrothed?
>
> Lost for good, my secret ring,
> Though I waited to the last.
> The sweet song I used to sing.
> Died a captive in my breast.[*]

JULY 1917

I took the first train to England. For years I wore the ring on the same chain around my neck.

The war was over. The Bolsheviks were in power; there was famine in Russia. I sent Anna two food parcels. The only news I received from her was a formal card with the words: "Dear Boris Vasilyevich. Thank you for feeding me. Anna Akhmatova."

[*] Tr. by Sergei Roy.

I wanted to write her but I had been warned that this might endanger her so I gave up the idea. I remained in London and gradually became involved once again in working with mosaics. Once when I was getting undressed I broke the chain around my neck and the ring rolled across the floor. I placed it in a small mahogany box lined with velvet in which I kept the articles most dear to me: my military medals, a gold cigar case given to me by Locker-Lampson, commander of the British armored unit in Russia, the cufflinks of a man I buried after he committed suicide, and other objects. I intended to have the chain fixed, but I never did. Gumilev was in London then, and we saw each other practically every day. He was anxious to get back to Russia. I tried to persuade him not to go, but it was useless. He was homesick. I had never felt that way. I left Russia in 1908 and settled abroad. Before Gumilev left I asked him to give Anna a large and well-preserved coin of Alexander the Great and some silk to make a dress. He unwillingly took the objects, saying: "What is this, Boris Vasilyevich? She's my wife, after all," I gasped at him in surprise. "Don't be a fool, Nikolai Stepanovich," I said coldly. But I don't know whether or not she received the gifts. Poor Gumilev! A great poet perished.

Another poet and a close friend, Nikolai Nedobrovo, was stricken with tuberculosis of the kidneys. They moved him to the south, where he soon died. He was a great friend of Anna's. I remember how deeply the news of his death affected me. Before he died I had written him a letter. I still recall one stupid but sincere line: "Please do not die, my dear Nikolai Vladimirovich. You and Anna Andreyevna are all of Russia to me!"

• • •

The years passed. The wound I carried in my soul had begun to heal. I often opened my little box of treasures and touched the black ring. To wear it would have seemed either sacrilege or farce. I concentrated on my art, on my work with mosaics. But the past continued to glimmer in my heart. And in my mind the ring was with me always.

Another war. I was in Paris at the time, but I fled from the Nazis the day they entered the city and two weeks later, by following a circuitous route, arrived in London. German bombs landed close to my studio and destroyed it. I lost consciousness, but managed to get out once I came to. It all happened at night, and the next morning I returned to salvage what remained. At first I couldn't find my small box of treasures. When I did, I saw that it was broken and empty. I was angry at the thieves and ashamed of myself. I had not safeguarded the sacred object. Tears of despair filled my eyes. Why had I not kept the ring in a safe-deposit box? Because I needed it with me, like a captive, so I could look at it whenever I wanted. But I had gone to Paris and not worried about it. Clearly the blame was mine. What would I say if Anna asked about it?

When the war ended in 1945 I sent Anna a color photograph of my mosaic of Christ titled "Cor sacrum." It depicted the Christ figure with a flaming Heart. I didn't know her address, so I sent the envelope to the Writers' Union in Leningrad with the request that it be passed on to Anna Andreyevna. On the photograph I wrote: "For memory's sake." There was no answer, and I didn't know if she received it.

Life went on. I worked in London, in Paris, and in Ireland. Creating the mosaics was strenuous and difficult work. Thanks to Gleb Struve, I managed to read almost everything Anna Andreyevna published. Her poetry affected me as strongly, perhaps even more strongly, than before. The acute suffering I experienced when I first lost her ring gradually subsided into quiet sorrow. But my feelings of guilt continued to cause me anguish.

In 1965 Anna Andreyevna was honored at Oxford. People were coming even from America. I was in London, but I didn't want to be lost among her swarm of admirers. I asked Struve to give her my warm greetings and best wishes and then left for Paris. For health reasons, I was giving up my work with mosaics, and I needed to put my affairs in order before closing my studio in Paris.

I envisaged Anna as she was in 1917: charming, young, and slender. I asked myself if I had done the right thing in leaving London. I was a coward and I had run away for fear she would ask about the ring. She was "my Russia," but was it not better to preserve my memories of her as she was? Now she was an international name, the muse of poetry! But all this seemed unreal to me.

That Saturday morning as I sat drinking coffee in my Paris studio, my thoughts were confused, my mind filled with self-reproach. . . . Suddenly the telephone rang and I jumped up to answer it. A deep masculine voice in a somewhat peremptory manner asked:

"Are you Boris Vasilyevich Anrep?"

"Yes."

"Anna Andreyevna Akhmatova has just arrived from London and would like to speak with you. Wait a moment."

"Of course."

Once again the imperious voice:

"Anna Andreyevna is coming to the phone."

"Hello?"

"Boris Vasilyevich? Is it you?"

"Yes. It's good to hear your voice, Anna Andreyevna."

"I've just arrived. I'd like to see you. Can you come right away?"

"Unfortunately I can't just at the moment. I'm waiting for the movers to come and move my mosaics."

"Yes, I know. [How?!] And I'm busy at five."

"Would you like to have breakfast with me or meet somewhere for lunch?"

"Oh no! That's impossible. [Why?!] Come to me at eight this evening."

"I'll be there."

The movers never came. I was in a state of agitation all day. To see Anna Andreyevna after forty-eight years of separation and silence! What would we talk about? So much had happened: so much personal grief, so much general suffering! Recollections emerged haphazardly, and they were all distorted by the lapses in my memory. What would I say about the black ring? What was there to say? I had not safeguarded the treasure, I had not the courage to admit it. Sending flowers was a banal gesture, but I went to a flower shop nonetheless and ordered a bouquet of roses to be sent directly to the Hotel Napoleon.

The hotel was filled with Soviets. A young, very attractive young woman walked up to me:

"Are you Mr. Anrep?"

"Yes."

"Anna Andreyevna is waiting. I'll take you to her."

We walked to the elevator.

"I saw your mosaics in London. I especially liked the ones in Westminster Abbey."

The young girl turned out to be Anya Kaminskaya, the granddaughter of Nikolai Punin, Anna Andreyevna's husband. She accompanied Anna on trips.

We went up to the second floor. Anya opened the door to Anna's room and then disappeared. Sitting in an armchair was an imperious, heavy-set woman. If I had run into her by chance I would not have known her, so greatly had she changed.

Catherine the Great, I thought to myself.

"Come in, Boris Vasilyevich."

I kissed her hand and sat in the chair next to hers. I found I couldn't smile. Her face, too, remained expressionless.

"Congratulations on your triumph in England."

"The English are very kind. As for my triumph. . . . You know, when I walked into my room and saw all the flowers I thought to myself, 'This is my funeral. Should poets really be exalted like this?'"

"Your admirers feel the need for it. It's how they express their admiration."

We spoke about contemporary poets. More than anything else I wanted to avoid personal subjects.

"Whom do you like?" I asked her.

Anna frowned and said nothing.

"Mandelshtam? Brodsky?"

"Oh yes, Brodsky! He was my student, you know."

She began to speak about Nedobrovo:

"You gave Struve his letters to you. Tell me, when were they written?"

"All the letters were written before 1914. And there's absolutely nothing in them. Do you have any of his letters, Anna Andreyevna?"

"I burned all of them."

"What a pity."

I was afraid to continue talking about Nedobrovo, but Anna Andreyevna did not want to drop the subject.

"Nikolai Vladimirovich was a wonderful critic. He wrote an excellent review of my poetry. Not only did he understand me better than anyone else, he even predicted how my poetry would develop in the future. Lozinsky also wrote about my work, but he didn't have the same understanding."

I listened and occasionally made comments, but my mind was blank. My heart was pounding and my throat was dry. Any moment now I was sure she was going to bring up the ring. I had to keep up the conversation about literature.

"Where is Lyubov Alexandrovna buried?"

"In a cemetery in San Remo."

We fell silent for several moments. "You know," said Anna Andreyevna, "I never read Nedobrovo's *Judith*."

I froze. She wanted to recall 13 February 1916, when we both listened to the recitation of *Judith* and she gave me the black ring. It was a direct challenge! Very well, then, I would accept it. I felt an evil impulse. Could she possibly be blind to the state I was in? I spoke with cool indifference.

"*Judith* is a purely academic piece. The composition of the verse is artistic, but on the whole it's rather boring. Still, it deserves to be read, and no doubt it will be included in the collection of verse that Struve, I hope, will publish."

"Struve," said Anna Andreyevna, changing the subject, "works hard and is a literary critic. But he supports the cold war and I'm adamantly against it."

"I think Struve is most interested in modern Russian literature."

"Have you read *Requiem*?"

"Yes. It is a magnificent tragedy, written with your blood. It's painful to read."

"If you'd like I'll read you my latest poem.* You might compare it with *Judith* since it's also on a biblical theme: Saul, David, and his unfaithful wife."

Anna Andreyevna opened a small notebook and began to read in a chanting voice. The chanting sounded like howling to me, it had been so long since I had heard anything like that. After *Requiem,* the whole business seemed to me to be an exercise in poetry writing. I couldn't get the gist of the words.

"What do you think?"

"Like everything else, wonderful."

"It isn't wonderful at all," she answered with irritation. I felt the need to say something clever, but I couldn't utter a single word.

"Very objective."

---

* Apparently the poem "Melkhola."—ed.

"Yes, very."

I didn't know what else to add to this stupid observation so I said nothing for a while. Then I recovered and asked: "How are you getting by?"

"By translating," she replied, understanding my question only in the material sense. "I translate the ancient poets."

"You yourself translate?" I asked in surprise.

"No, of course not. A few skilled translators prepare word-for-word translations and I make Russian verse out of them."

"Do you stay in Leningrad? Where do you vacation?"

"I vacation at my dacha in Finland. Do you remember sending me a colored photograph of your mosaic of Christ? I kept it on my desk a long time. Then it disappeared."

Here I might have simply noted that the same fate had befallen her ring. But the photograph was one thing, the ring something else entirely. I said nothing. I felt uncomfortable and wanted to leave.

"I'm afraid I'll tire you, Anna Andreyevna. I'd better leave."

"No, please. It's such a pleasure to see you; you haven't changed at all."

I flushed with embarrassment.

"As a personal favor. Stay another twenty minutes."

"Of course. Just tell me when I should go."

The conversation never clicked. Anna Andreyevna was waiting for something.

"How did you survive the siege of Leningrad?"*

"Stalin saved me [everyone knew this]. He was fond of me and he sent a plane to take me away from Leningrad. Later his kindness turned to indifference or perhaps hate."

Another silence.

"Well, go now. Thank you for coming. You might send me a card for New Year's at least."

Anna Andreyevna rose majestically from her chair and walked with me to the small foyer. She leaned against the wall.

"Good-bye," she said and held out her hand. I suddenly lost my head and kissed her unresponsive lips. Half-dazed, I walked into the corridor.

* Akhmatova was evacuated from the besieged city of Leningrad on 27 September 1941 at the decision of the City Party Committee [see: *Throughout the Entire Blockade,* P. Luknitsky, Leningrad, 1964, p. 99].—ed.

I made a wrong turn, but somehow I found the exit. I walked along the
Champs d'Elysees for a long time and then sat in a cafe until late at night.

I have asked myself a thousand times: why? why? Because I was a
coward and a cad. It was my duty to tell her about the loss of her ring.
Was it that I was afraid to hurt her? Absurd. I hurt her even more by
off-handedly treating her as a literary phenomenon. When I was trying to
think of something else to say or ask about contemporary poets, she had
blurted out: "Boris Nikolayevich, don't ask me the same stupid questions
as everyone else!" She longed in her soul to be simply a human being, a
friend, a woman. She had wanted to cut through the woods that had
grown up between us. But a heavy, sepulchral stone weighed upon me;
upon me and the entire past, and I was unable to move from under it.

During our conversation the door to the next room remained half-
opened and every now and then there was a rustling sound. Who was it?
A political watchdog? A friend? I don't know. The sense of unseen presence was unpleasant. It was clear that someone was listening to our conversation. Could it be this that prevented our final meeting from turning
into a warm, heart-to-heart talk? I'm seeking self-justification, am I not?

On 5 March 1966 Anna Andreyevna died in Moscow. I am incon-
solably bereaved and ashamed.

Kornei Chukovsky
FROM MY DIARY

*Kornei Chukovsky (1882–1969) was a literary critic, translator, chil-
dren's writer, and the author of several articles on Akhmatova's work.
Yelena Chukovskaya published excerpts from Chukovsky's diary in the
magazine* Novy Mir *(1987, No. 3).*

1920

19 January. Yesterday I saw Anna Akhmatova. She and Shileiko are
together in one room, with the bed behind a screen. The room is dank and
cold. Books are on the floor. Akhmatova has a strident voice. It's as if she's
talking to me over the phone. Sometimes her eyes seem to be blind. She

is tender with Shileiko, sometimes brushing away the hair from his fore-head. He calls her Anichka; she calls him Volodya. She told me what a wonderful translator of poetry he was and that he dictated an entire ballad to her in finished form. "Then he succumbs to lunacy."

25 January. It is terribly cold; the house is uncomfortable. Yesterday I put on two vests and two jackets and went to see Anna Akhmatova. She was very nice. Shileiko was ill with pleurisy. Akhmatova seems to know Pushkin by heart. She gave me details about where he had lived, and quoted from his letters and from variations of his work. But today she was something of the social lady, talking about fashion: and how do they wear skirts in Europe now, long or flounced? Fashion stopped for us in 1916.

30 March. A few days ago Grzhebin phoned Blok: "I bought Akhma-tova," meaning that he had managed to get hold of her poetry. What had happened was that they had brought Akhmatova a dress that she instantly liked, a dress she had always dreamed about, and she had gone immedi-ately to Grzhebin and sold him her books for seventy-five thousand rubles.

Blok, Zamyatin, and I ran into her as we were leaving World Litera-ture Publishers. It was the first time I had seen Blok and Akhmatova together. It was very interesting: Blok's face was impenetrable, except that something almost imperceptible and "responding" was in constant motion around his mouth. The same with Akhmatova. Nothing about their eyes or their smiles expressed anything, but much was said nonetheless.

1921

3 February. Yesterday, in the vestibule of the House of Scholars, I met Anna Akhmatova. She looked young, cheerful, and she had put on some weight. "Come see me today and I'll give you a bottle of milk for your little girl." I went that evening , and she gave it to me! Just imagine—in February of 1921, to offer a bottle of milk!

24 December. I've just come from Anna Akhmatova. She is living on No. 18 Fontanka in the apartment of Olga Afanasyevna Sudeikina. "Olechka is not in Petersburg. I am staying here for the time being but when she returns I will have to leave." The room was small; the large bed unmade. An icon of the Holy Mother in a silver frame was nailed to the left door of the cupboard. Next to the bed was a little table on which there was butter and rye bread. An old woman servant opened the door. Akhmatova had a blanket around her legs: "I have a cold and a cough." We talked for a long time. "They want me to go to Moscow, but Shchegolev is trying to talk me out of it. He says that they hate me there, that the imaginists will kick up a scandal. And I don't know how to act in a scandal. Blok was also berated in Moscow." Later, the old woman lit the small stove in the room and said that there was no firewood for the next day. "Never mind," said Akhmatova, "I'll bring a saw tomorrow and the two of us will cut some." (I sent Kolya [Nikolai Chukovsky] to her today.) She was lying on her bed in her coat. She put her hand under the blanket and pulled out some large sheets of paper rolled up into a scroll. "This is the ballet 'Snow Mask,' based on Blok. Listen to it and tell me what you think of the style. I can't write prose." And she began to read the libretto she had written, which I thought was a wonderful and accurate commentary on "Snow Mask." I don't know if it's a good ballet, but as a critique it's wonderful. "I've not come up with the death scene in the third act. I'm writing this for Artur Sergeyevich Lurye. He asked me to. Perhaps Diaghilev will stage it in Paris."

Then she began to recite her poetry. But when she had finished reading about Blok, I let out a sob and ran out.

1922

14 February. I saw Akhmatova yesterday. It was dark on the staircase. I went to the door and knocked. Akhmatova opened it right away. She was sitting in the kitchen talking to "granny"—Olga Sudeikina's cook. "Sit down! This is the only warm room. . . ." I began telling her that the poem "Slander" was too cold and classical. "Volodya (Shileiko) says the same thing. He says that if Pushkin had lived another ten years, he would have written such a poem. Isn't that mean?" She gave me some sardines and bread. We spoke a great deal about Anna Nikolayevna, Gumilev's widow. "The Nappelbaums suggested that I become the 'Syndic' of the 'Singing Shell,' but I refused."

I said to her: "You have a difficult job now—you are Gorky, and Tolstoy, and Leonid Andreyev, and Igor Severyanin—all in one. It's frightening."

And it's the truth: she's at the height of her fame. Yesterday The Free Philosophical Association organized a recital of her poetry, and the editors of different magazines are calling her from morning till night: "Give us something, anything."

26 March. Today I foolishly made an appointment to see Akhmatova exactly at four o'clock. On the way I bought a roll (with my last coins!) and headed for Fontanka. Akhmatova was waiting for me. The kitchen was clean, and there at the stove sat Olga Sudeikina's cook darning one of Akhmatova's black stockings with white thread. "Light the fire, Granny!" Akhmatova said. We went into her narrow room, three-fourths of which was taken up by a double bed covered by a large blanket. It was terribly cold. We sat at the window. With the gesture of a hostess entertaining an important guest, she gave me the just-published issue of the magazine *Novaya Rossiya*. "Read the criticism. It's about me. They really berate me!"

At the back of the magazine I saw the very respectful but not too enthusiastic article by [Erich] Gollerbakh. "This Gollerbakh," she told me, "sent me some panegyric in verse. But just look what he writes about me in the book about Tsarskoye Selo.* Look! It turns out that Akhmatova's maiden name is Gorenko!! How dare he? Who gave him permission? I have already asked Lerner to tell him that this is unacceptable. . . ."

I developed a great pity for this suffering woman. She showed me her large square notebook of new poems. There is enough there for a new book. But the critics will say once again: "Akhmatova is repeating herself. . . ."

"So, you have a lot of money now?" I asked her. "Yes, a lot, I received 150 million right away for *A Flock of White Birds*.** I could afford to have a dress made. I sent some money to Levushka and I want to send some to Mama in the Crimea. I've had some terrible news: there were four of us sisters, and now the third is dying from tuberculosis. Mama writes that she is dying in a hospital. I know that they're in great need, but it's impossible for me to send anything. Mama says, 'Don't send anything by mail!'"

We began to talk about the people who were starving. I told her my idea for her to write a children's book for Europe and America. She heartily consented.

The room grew hot. She made me coffee in a pot and quickly pulled out the table herself. She expertly took care of the damper, and it was only

---

* *Tsarskoye Selo in Russian Poetry,* compiled by Gollerbakh, appeared in 1922.—ed.

** The third edition, published in 1922.—ed.

then that I noticed how becoming her new dress was. "The material is from the House of Scholars!"

I took the roll from my pocket and hungrily began to eat. This was my dinner.

Later she asked me: "Would you like to listen to poetry?" She read "Judith,"* which resembled "Three Palms" in its meter. "I wrote this on the train when I was going to Levushka. I had begun it in Petersburg. I opened the Bible—at random—and found this episode. It was just what I was thinking about."

15 December. Yesterday I stopped by to see Anna Akhmatova. Should I describe the visit? The staircase was dark and dusty—a typical back entrance. I knocked on the door and heard a voice say: "It's open!" In the small kitchen a watery soup was on the stove. Anna Andreyevna was not there. Then she walked in with Nikolai Nikolayevich Punin. We went into the living room with icons hanging on the walls, formerly belonging to the Sudeikins, and began to talk—about personal, not worldly, matters. I saw her once as a hungry and ascetic nun (when she was living on Liteiny in 1919); I saw her later as a woman of the world (three months ago); and now she was . . . just a young woman from a very ordinary family. The crowded rooms, kitchen entrance, the mother, cook . . . who would have thought that this was the same Anna Akhmatova who today has surpassed in fame Gorky and Lev Tolstoy and Leonid Andreyev, who is the subject of dozens of articles and books, whose poetry is known by heart by the entire province?

I left with a good feeling. Behind all the nonsense, one still perceives the genuine Anna Akhmatova, the woman who finds it awkward, as it were, to be genuine in public and who, involuntarily, out of shyness, puts on the most trivial guises. But all this is only a shield in order to preserve untouched what is dear to her. This was the case with, for example, Tyutchev.

1923

19 March. Saw Akhmatova. She was very kind to me. She complained about [Boris] Eikhenbaum: "Since he wrote his book about me, we no

---

* Apparently the reference is to Akhmatova's poem "Rachel."

longer know each other." We looked over Nekrasov, which we will be editing together. She had crossed out the very same poems that I had discarded in Grzhebin's edition. There was complete agreement. In reading "Masha," she recalled how she had quarreled with Gumilev when sometimes she had stayed in bed too long, and he was working at the table.

14 May. Saw Akhmatova. She showed me some pictures of Blok and a letter from him. The letter was very crumpled and had been torn by a pin. It had to do with the poem "By the Sea." He praises and criticizes, but he's always truthful. I showed her my corrections of her comments on Nekrasov. I don't think the comments are appropriate. Apparently, Anna Akhmatova, like Gumilev, cannot write prose. Gumilev couldn't even translate prose. When he had to write a foreword to a book put out by World Literature, he said: "It would be better if I wrote it in verse." It was the same with Akhmatova. . . .

November 14 Wednesday. Saw Akhmatova yesterday. She has moved to a new apartment—No. 3 Kazanskaya, apt. 4. She is renting two rooms from some friends. She wants to go with me to Kharkov. She doesn't have a warm coat and wears only a jersey underneath with a light sweater over it. I went to see her to check the proofs of Blok's letter with the original. She spent a long time looking for the letter in the chest of drawers where she kept in great disorder pictures of Gumilev, books, papers, etc. "This is a rarity," she said and showed me an agreement in French between Gumilev and some French officer concerning the purchase of horses in Africa. In the chest of drawers there were many photographs of the ballerina Spesivtseva—evidently they were for Olga Sudeikina, who made an incredibly pretty and graceful clay statuette of the dancer for a porcelain factory. The statuette has already been cast in porcelain, and it's wonderful. "Olenka is going to paint it," she said.

Irina Karnaukhova was with me. Since Anna Andreyevna had to hurry to a meeting of the Writers' Union, we took tram No. 5. I had bought some apples and offered one to Akhmatova. She told me: "I won't eat it on the street: after all, there are *gaiduki** around. But give it to me and I'll

---

* *Gaiduki* (guerilla warriors) are mentioned in her poems about the czar. Unaware of the subject of the poems, critics today have written that Akhmatova herself rode with *gaiduki*. Also see appendix. —ed.

eat it at the meeting." She didn't have enough money for a tram ticket (which now costs 50 million; she had only 15 million). "I thought I had 100 million, but it turned out to be only 10 million." I said: "I have a generous nature on a tram: I'll buy you a ticket." "You remind me of an American I met in Paris. It was raining and I was standing under an arch waiting for it to stop. The American whispered to me: 'Mademoiselle, come with me to a cafe and I'll treat you to a glass of beer.' I gave him a disdainful look, and he said: 'I'll treat you to a glass of beer, and you won't be obliged in any way at all. . . .'"

26 November. I stopped by to see Akhmatova. She was lying down, a copy of Stendhal's *De l'amour* beside her. For the first time she greeted me with real warmth. "I was afraid of you," she said. "When Annenkov told me you were writing a book about me, I began to shake and I thought: *Lord, let this pass from me.*" She spoke a great deal about Blok: "Many people in Moscow believe that I dedicated my poems to Blok. It's not true. I could not love him as a man. Moreover, he did not like my early poetry. I knew this; he didn't hide it. Once we recited our poems at the Bestuzhev Institute. It was Blok, I, and, I think, Nikolai Morozov. Or was it Igor Severyanin? I don't remember because Blok and I were twice at the Bestuzhev, once with Morozov and once with Igor. Morozov had just been released from prison. . . . Anyway, there in the dressing room Blok suddenly wanted to talk to me about my work. He said: 'I recently corresponded with a girl about your poetry.' I was insolent: 'I know your opinion; tell me the opinion of that girl.' Then a car came for us. Blok still wanted to talk about poetry, but some young student was with us and Blok wanted to get rid of him: 'You might catch cold,' he told him (in a car!). But the student said, 'No, I won't. I splash myself with cold water every day. And even if I were to catch a cold I couldn't refuse to accompany such guests!' Of course, he didn't know who I was. 'Have you been in the theater long?' he asked me, when we were on our way."

1924

6 May. Akhmatova has moved to a new apartment on Fontanka. I went to see her three weeks ago. It's a huge house, the former premises of the court laundry. She was sitting in front of the fire; it was daylight, but a candle was burning in the kitchen. "Why?" I asked. "No matches.

I wouldn't be able to light the stove." I extinguished the candle, ran to the painter working in the next apartment, and bought some matches for her.

7 June. Akhmatova said to me: "You are sly. But I am certain that when you write you cannot lie."

1954

8 March. We had *bliny*★ at Vsevolod Ivanov's. I saw Akhmatova there for the first time since her tragedy.★★ She is grey-haired and quiet, very fat, and very plain. She does not in any way resemble the modern, timid, and at the same time arrogant, slender poet with combed bangs to whom Gumilev introduced me in 1912—forty-two years ago. She speaks about her tragedy with composure and humor: "I have been very famous and very notorious, and I know now that essentially it's just the same thing.

"I have told Yevgeny Shvarts that I have not been in the theater for years. He told me, 'Yes, of those from your organization only Zoshchenko comes.'" (There are only two people in the organization.) She said, "They recently suggested that Zoshchenko go abroad. 'Where to?' I asked him, and he said: 'I was so frightened I didn't even ask.'"

Once again I felt the excitement in her presence that I had felt in my youth. One feels the greatness, the nobleness, the magnitude of her gift, of her fate.

1955

30 June. Akhmatova came to see me on the very same day that Nehru arrived in the USSR. Mozhaiskoye Highway was filled with people who had come out to meet him, and all traffic in the direction of Peredelkino was halted. We were faced with a wall of militia men repeating the same thing: "Go back." And there in my car sat Akhmatova, tired and exhausted. I so much wanted to take her to the countryside away from the oppressive heat.

As always, she was plain and kind, but at the same time, regal. I soon realized that she had not come for the fresh air but solely for her poem, as if in her tragic and painful life a poem offered the only ray of light, the only illusion of happiness. She came in order to talk about her poem, to hear it

---

★ Thin pancakes, generally reserved for periods of fasting (blĕeny).—ed.

★★ The 1946 Central Committee resolution against her, banning the publication of her poems.—ed.

praised, for a time, to live for it. She was dismayed to think that the meaning of the poem was beyond the comprehension of many readers. She maintained that it was entirely clear, but for most people it was gibberish. Akhmatova divides the world into two uneven parts: those who understand her poems and those who do not.

Nadezhda Mandelshtam

AKHMATOVA

Nadezhda Mandelshtam (1899–1980), wife of Osip Mandelshtam. The excerpt from her reminiscences on Akhmatova is taken from an earlier edition of her memoirs, The Second Book.

I

The book is inscribed: "For my friend Nadia, so that she will remember once again what happened to us." Out of everything that did happen to us, what was most significant and powerful was the fear and what it produced—a loathsome feeling of disgrace and impotence. There is no need to try to remember this; "this" is with us always. We admitted to each other that "this" turned out to be stronger than love and jealousy, stronger than all the human emotions that we shared. From the very early days, when we were still brave, up until the late 1950s, fear stifled everything human within us. And for every minute of hope we paid with nights of delirium, awake and asleep. Our fear had a physiological basis: well-scrubbed hands with short, fat fingers would rummage through our pockets; our nighttime "guests" had good-natured faces with eyes dim and reddened from lack of sleep. Calls would come in the middle of the night, the stomping of boots outside, the "black crows."* Some idiot would stand on guard duty in the street—not to find out additional information about us but to scare and intimidate us.** At night, during the hours of love, I would catch myself thinking: what if they come right now and

---

* Black paddy wagons.—ed.

** At that time the NKVD made a practice of overt surveillance, sometimes with no subsequent arrest.—ed.

interrupt? This is what happened, leaving behind a strange memory—the combination of two memories.

In addition to the physiological, there was another, something like a moral, aspect to the fear. In 1938 we learned that the "psychological methods of interrogation" had been replaced, and that "they" were now using the method of "simplified interrogation"; i.e., they were merely resorting to torture and beatings.* For some reason we decided that if there is no more psychology involved, there is nothing more to fear—let them break our ribs. . . . But she quickly changed her mind: how could one not be afraid? We had to be afraid. We didn't know what they might do. Perhaps they would break us and we would begin to say all kinds of things, now this one and now that one. And from our lists they would make one arrest after another. How can people know how they might act under inhumane circumstances? I learned much from her, and this as well: God help me, for I know I cannot help myself. . . .

More than anything else Anna feared the "fearless." In our circumstances these were the most dangerous people of all. A "fearless" person falling into their hands could, out of stupidity, bring down all relatives, acquaintances, and strangers. Trying to protect their children, parents raised them in ignorance. But the parents could be interned, leaving a "fearless" one to the whim of fate; or a "fearless" one—a kind person with an honest soul—could be interned; or no one might be interned (people were lucky!), and the "fearless" one might walk the streets and visit homes, speaking his thoughts, sometimes even writing letters or keeping a diary, and then others would have to pay for his idiocy. For us, a "fearless" person was worse than a provocateur: you are sly with a provocateur, and he understands what is going on; but the "fearless" person looks with innocent eyes and won't shut up. In our day, fear alone made people human, but only if it did not evoke cowardice. Fear was the organizing principle and cowardice the pitiful surrender of position. We could not permit this to happen to us, and to tell the truth, we were not tempted to do so.

During the most terrifying years Anna would always be the first to enter the house where the "dear guests"** had been at work. "All night

* Virtually every prisoner was subjected to a beating at the initial interrogation, an offically sanctioned practice in 1938.—ed.

** Members of the NKVD. From Mandelshtam's poem, "Leningrad."—ed.

long while waiting for my dear guests," she said, "I check the fetters of the door chain." Not long ago I asked Tata—a remarkably beautiful woman who was fortunate enough to get only five years—"Did she come?" "Of course." Tata replied. "At once . . . the first one to arrive . . . we hadn't even cleaned up yet. . . ." "And who was it, you or she, who said that all that was needed now was an ashtray and a spittoon?" "She, of course," Tata answered in surprise.

This charming woman, the widow of L., symbolizes for me the senselessness and horror of the terror. A sweet, delicate, and sensitive woman— what did she do to deserve what happened to her? This was a woman who was like a flower. How dared they destroy her life, kill her husband, spit in her face during interrogations? They separated her from her small son, whom she never saw again, because he also died while she rotted in prison. Why? This was her sacrifice to the idea that the world must be remade, that all people must be made happy.

On the other hand, my Tata, who retained her charm even in old age, is a symbol of feminine strength, of unprecedented resistance against those who turned strong men into submissive, trembling creatures with well-organized collective reasoning. Who was it who said that collective reasoning always characterizes low creatures? When the prosecutor told Tata she could always marry again—sometimes they were so kind as to say this when informing us that our husbands had been shot or otherwise killed— she replied: "I do not divorce the dead."

The women were not so broken by the suffering as the men. They had fewer psychoses and were not so quick to submit, though they, too, were beaten and deprived of food and sleep. And the women endured penal servitude better than the men. Shalamov told me that women sometimes came to see their husbands in Kolyma to try to cheer them up. It was a journey entailing unbelievable hardship; they were mocked and raped. . . . But they came nonetheless, and they stayed. But Shalamov said he never once heard of a man coming to see a wife or sweetheart.

What did we learn from this accursed time of bestial fear, that might justify it? Perhaps I could find enough if I took the time to think, but for now I can say that we learned this: there were certain people who remained people, an isolated few, a drop in the ocean, but not everyone became inhuman beings. Another thing: under such conditions a human being is recognized faster and easier than in situations where inhuman beings, hiding behind conventional forms of polite address and correct behavior, masquerade as people. Finally, acute illnesses, if they do not result in death, lead to a more complete recovery than chronic and slow-progressing illnesses that leave behind permanent after-effects. These three lessons I have come up with on the spur of the moment. They are probably more negative than positive.

Anna and I were much interested in the question of what constitutes courage. We immediately realized that courage, daring, and fortitude were not synonymous. We knew that miserable cowards in everyday life—lickspittles and spineless yes-men without the courage to think their own opinions, much less speak them—sometimes turned out to be brave officers and invincible warriors during war. What was it that strengthened their spirits? Wasn't it because they were simply carrying out orders, freeing themselves from responsibility for what was happening? What happened to us can be described as a spiritual crisis. And the so-called real, courageous males, the "he-men," as the British say, were the first to cast off responsibility for everything that was occurring and to line up meekly with those voting "aye." Yet those who were weaker, those about whom it was said: "What a poor excuse for a man," demonstrated the greatest resistance. Unexpectedly, a spark of spirit showed up in the weak body. It might not have been much, but by our standards it was at least something. Together with the women, they somehow struggled through, keeping up faith in humanity, in its ability to be resurrected, to repent, and to begin a new life. The strong climbed upward on the social ladder, the weak were stranded on the lower rungs. With the new times came a large category of young people who conscientiously renounced well-being and careers. This was the first sign of healing, and Anna and I noted it as a good symptom. Nonetheless, one shouldn't take it for granted that young people, who have everything ahead of them, will not revert to the old ways. Who knows? It is the same with them as with the "fearless"—it depends wholly on circumstance.

Village women tell each other their dreams the next morning. I will tell about Anna's dream. In it, time is condensed—three decades merge into one episode—and her terrible pain, no doubt mixed with guilt, concerning two people in her life, takes a symbolic form. In the corridor of the Punin apartment* stands the dinner table. Lev [Gumilev] sleeps behind the curtain at the other end (when they let him into the house—the older generation of Punins was more kind to Lev and did not always drive him away). "They" [Soviet Political Police] stand in the corridor and hand her a warrant for Gumilev. She knows that Nikolai Stepanovich is hiding in her room—the last door in the corridor to the left. She leads the sleepy Lev out from behind the curtain and pushes him toward the Chekhists: "Here's Gumilev." It is unclear which of the two Gumilevs they want; the elder, after all, has already been killed. "It torments me that I gave them Lev," she told me when she first related her dream to me. But what could she have done? They could have taken both of them. Even in her dream there was no way out.

Different epochs—different dreams. Many years, several decades are flattened into the first epoch where the dreams were of one type—being taken away and perishing. The next epoch was one of gradually overcoming fear, and it is typified by the dream I had in Pskov. Here as well someone who is already gone takes part. There is a desperate knock at the door. Osip [Mandelshtam] shakes me: "Get dressed! They've come. . . ." "No," I answer. "They won't come for *you*; you are no longer here. And if they've come for me, who cares? Let them break down the door. I'm tired of it all. . . . Enough is enough. . . ." Then I turn over on my side and go back to sleep.

A humorous consequence of that dream is that I cannot now be wakened by a knock or the ringing of a bell: I don't want to wake up. Once, when I was staying in Tarusa, the owner of the cottage asked some drivers to pick something up. They knocked at all the windows and doors until they practically brought the house down, but I wouldn't allow myself to wake up. To wake up and open the door would mean a kind of collaboration, and I had no intention of collaborating in this matter. If they wanted to crush me it would be without my consent.

Thus I overcame my fear. It did not occur early or late but at the proper time; i.e., when hand-copies of Osip's poetry had been distributed

* The apartment of Akhmatova's husband Nikolai Punin, where she took up residence in 1926.—ed.

and I ceased to be afraid: now it was impossible for them to be destroyed and, like a human being, wiped from the face of the earth. My deed was done. Things were more complicated for Anna: first, there was Lev*; second, the poems she had not yet written. Sometimes I would say to her: "What are you afraid of? We have nothing left to lose." And she would answer: "No, I do have something left to lose." In the new epoch Anna's fear was replaced by something for which Surkov praised her: "extreme tact." I called it "extraordinary caution." At one time people tried to convince her to send *Requiem* to the editors of some magazines—for example, *Novy Mir*. It did upset her that hand-copies of her poems were not widely circulated, but she rejected the idea of sending them to magazine editors. "Do you want me to be struck down again?" she asked me. But she tirelessly handed out Osip's poems, doing everything she could to see that they were distributed: "Nadia, dear, everything is fine with Osip," she said to me when I despaired because his books were not being published, "he doesn't need a printing press." This was so. Once you buy a book, you can lose it or choose not to read it. But who will forget the poems they take such trouble to acquire and then secretly retype? It is not so easy to turn away from this poetry. This was the advantage of our pre-Gutenberg epoch.**

In the second period of the new epoch Anna felt the ground steady under her feet and grew happy. By this time *Requiem* had slipped from her guardianship and was being met with critical acclaim. Her customary severity disappeared, and she even told me once: "That's enough of that. There's more to life than politics. . . ." Was there any way of knowing that we would live to see this day? We thought "he" was "immortal." That's the way it was. The new epoch began the day we were walking down the street toward the church park we used to visit and we saw a number of plainclothes detectives. They were everywhere, peering out of every gateway. "They are for us, not against us," Anna said. "Don't be afraid; something good is happening." It was the preliminary meeting held before the famous congress† took place. But we became calm only in the sixties, and the calm lasted one brief second. Anna's advice "to think about something

---

* After his third arrest, in 1949, Lev Gumilev was not released until 1956.—ed.

** Mandelshtam's poetry was not formally published in the USSR until 1974.—ed.

† The reference is evidently to the Twentieth Communist Party Congress in 1956, which marked the beginning of the disclosure of the crimes of the Stalinist period.—ed.

else" meant only that she had fallen under the illusion common to the elderly. Old people have periods of complacency when they see everything through rose-colored glasses. The very young suffer from this failing as well, and I had a bout of it myself. Anna reminded me that at the beginning of our friendship I was "pro-Soviet"; i.e., I calmly listened to her tales of arrests, believing that this could not continue and that sooner or later everything would be put right. This was one of the innumerable mistakes of my youth which cannot be corrected. Both of us were forced to remove our tinted glasses. Before the end, she once again felt fear.

Anna spent the last months of her life in a hospital. Before that she lived with the Ardovs.* She had very much wanted to see my new apartment and was preparing to come when she fell ill. We put it off for a couple of days, but when she regained consciousness she was not at my place but in Botkin hospital. Frightened, I hurried to her. Shalamov came with me. He stayed behind in the cloakroom while I went upstairs. I never saw her look so terrible. She was semiconscious, remote from the world, but she recognized me. Now and then, opening her eyes, she made a great effort to speak to me. I was touched by the careful way she chose the topics—the nicest things, what bound us together, the past: "Nadia, I was so sick in Tashkent, and you were with me. . . . I so much wanted to come to you. . . . Keep my papers.** . . . I will write again. . . ."

I went down to Shalamov feeling depressed. It was the end; how could I live without her? (Even now I don't understand how it is possible: she was always there.) But, as always, she did the unexpected; she got better. She was ready to go home. (What home!? She had no home, and I was afraid to take her with me. I had no telephone. What if something happened and we needed to call an ambulance?) Sitting in the corridor, she told me that the doctors least of all had expected her recovery. A doctor examined her later that day and expressed surprise that she had pulled through. "There must be something left for you to do," I said. "Oh, God!" she replied. "How much there is left to do."

Where did we get the notion that one leaves the world only after accomplishing one's purpose? The state taught us better than this. Osip died at the height of his ability, full of strength and ideas. When he left he

---

* The family of Nina Ardova-Olshevskaya.—ed.

** The reference is to Akhmatova's recollections of Mandelshtam—"Pages from a Diary."—ed.

was a strong and self-possessed man. What did they turn him into in a few months? He was one of those people who could not endure violence. Imprisoned, he ceased to be himself. He always had a premonition of a violent death. Break is the word. They knew how to do this and they never failed. Now things seem to be somewhat easier: one well-known writer recently commented on the case of D. and S.*: "What's all the ruckus about? In the twenties we shot people for less and nobody said a word. . . ."

No mere mortals lay in the privileged ward where Anna stayed. These were the mothers and mothers-in-law of high officials, and those activists of the 1920s who somehow managed to survive the cataclysm and clearly remembered how and why people were shot in order to preserve the achievements of the Revolution. Reading about the D. and S. case in the newspapers, they would comment loudly: "Serves the scum right! . . . In this day and age!" Anna complained about having to listen to them and whispered: "Let D. and S. make room for me. I belong with them." I began to quote [from Akhmatova's poem, "Others take away the loved ones . . ."]: "The sixth prosecutor had a heart attack . . ." She raised her hand: "Hush, they'll hear you. . . ." At once I saw that her old fear had returned. "Anna, what is it? They won't harm you. . . ." "What about *Requiem*?** It's the same kind of work. . . ." I couldn't look her in the eye and tell her that things had really changed for the better and that the dying were no longer being dragged from their hospital beds to be interrogated. That epoch was over and had been replaced by a new one: open trial by invitation, prosecutors nominated by the masses; a prosecutor, defense attorney, and a small handful of prison camp dust for the criminal printing of inappropriate literary works. To ensure that such literary works did not wind up in the [Western] world, writers were asked to take them from the editorial offices that had refused to print them and hide them at home or even destroy them. The latter suggestion is the more patriotic: why write and keep works that will never be published here? "But they won't harm you, Anna. Really, they won't. . . . They will forgive you for *Requiem*. . . . If need be, you will ask for forgiveness." This, just before she died, was her last bout with fear.

---

* See appendix for *D. and S.*—ed.
** Published in 1963 in Munich.—ed.

She left the hospital and no one tried to harm her. She died the day after arriving at a sanatorium. Her body was kept in the morgue three days: it was the March 8 holiday—International Women's Day. People called the Union [of Writers] for information, but they were told she was already in Leningrad. They were afraid of a big crowd at the funeral. On 9 March her body had been placed in a small room in the morgue, and a few people paid their last respects. Then her body was taken to the airport. A few people, including me, accompanied her on the plane.

Essentially, what they did was steal her body from Moscow—that's the Russian tradition. A few women created a row about this at the Union's Party meeting, asking why they had not been allowed to pay their final respects to Akhmatova. They say that one of the leading officials answered: "Comrades, there is no need to fear the dead." Is that so? The remarkable thing is that they fear both the living and the dead as much as we do. They have something to lose, and they are more afraid than we, who have nothing to lose. We were constantly oppressed by fear. Few have liberated themselves from this fear, but I am among those few. They cannot frighten me any longer, because my work is done.

· · ·

"We never suspected that poetry was so viable." This is what Anna said to me, having managed to live long enough to see people once again returning to poetry. But in the 1920s Tynyanov predicted the demise of poetry and a transition to prose. Several times throughout our long lives readers of poetry would appear, only to disappear again. The first wave of interest in poetry occurred in the 1910s, with the symbolists, who taught the new readers. For all the subsequent disparagement against the symbolists, they sparked an interest in poetry among a group of people, small though it was. The 1930s marked a sharp decline in interest. "No one knows Mandelshtam anymore," Katayev commented once. "Only Yevgeni Petrovich or I mention him now and then." "What impudence!" I thought. "An intermediary, no less!" But Osip was conciliatory: "That's the way it is now." It was true, though his name was banned for no more than ten years, and even in 1931 and 1932 his poetry and prose slipped through into publication. The most surprising thing was that Osip was so calm about the personal oblivion. It didn't bother him. What infuriated him was the ban on the publishing of his works. That readers had forgotten him he no doubt attributed to being out of print or, more than likely, he didn't even think about it. In fact, however, matters were much more serious.

A new wave of reader interest began with the war. The same Katayev (unlike other writers, he always recognized me; even in the center of Moscow or Tashkent* he would leave his girlfriend standing in the middle of the street and run up to greet me) came to Tashkent and told me: "Akhmatova is famous again. I must go to her and see." I'm afraid that what Anna considered a new awakening affected only the older readers, like Katayev. In Central Asia University my colleague Usova persuaded me to listen to a young poet from among the evacuees. This was an extremely popular youth from Odessa, and the only poets he recognized as authoritative were those published in thick magazines. But he was surrounded by admirers who believed in him as the Konstantin Simonov of the future. I inadvertently mentioned Akhmatova's name and the poet, along with his admirers, was aghast: what old rubbish!

It was also in Tashkent that I witnessed another incredible scene— Misha Volpin's gushing words, typical of the ungrateful reader of the twenties. Erdman and Volpin, youthful and smart in their military uniforms, arrived in the house on Zhukovsky Street where some of the evacuee writers were lodged. They went to visit my brother, E. Khazin. Erdman said little, as was his custom, while Volpin kept up the conversation. Volpin argued that he thought Yesenin and Mayakovsky were interesting poets.

Akhmatova was boring . . . what good was she to him? All this talk about loving or not loving. . . . In the free-wheeling atmosphere of the twenties the free-wheeling reader appeared, asking to be coddled, hungering for "innovation," and recognizing nothing else. The word signified a break with form and all ideas in the spirit of the present: Love? Give me a girl and I'll tire of her in three days.

Attempting to explain the rise and fall of reader interest, Akhmatova once said: "Poetry is such that if you accept a surrogate even once you'll never go back to it." This is partially true, but it isn't the entire truth by any means. There are plenty of surrogates today as well, but the reader knows very well what he wants, what he should copy, and whose books

---

* See appendix.—ed.

he should search for. But during the time of the cult of violence and the rejection of values, the reader looked to poetry for strengthening his own position and even for a justification of his cynical belief in the ability to adapt. This new reader was unaware of the pathos of Akhmatova's repudiation, seeing only what was easy prey for the cynics and totally ignoring her best qualities: severe restraint and the accuracy and strength of her aim. The spoiled reader never searched for authentic poetic truth: he never bothered himself with searching for that small bit of spiritual transformation, wanting only to be stunned and amazed, "before taking one step away from the cash register," as Anna put it. The reader never even noticed that Akhmatova was a poet not of love but of the repudiation of love for the sake of humanity.

The situation was even worse with Mandelshtam. An effort had to be made to understand him, and then an even greater effort was required so that, having understood him, one could extricate oneself from his power, from what he termed the "sense of the poet's being right." In the struggle with the power of the poet, no holds are barred, including slander, anecdotes, and allegations of a compromising though non-political nature, to resolutions passed by the highest bodies of authority and arrest warrants.

During those years our society possessed a very accurate measuring device for human substance: there were two poles, between which lay an entire spectrum of positions. At one pole stood promulgators of "innovation," voluntarists who rejected all values, theoreticians of force, and advocates of dictatorship; at the other, those who countered force with their own truth. These polar groups could not and would never understand one another. The spiritual pole appeared ludicrous to the force pole. One of my young acquaintances, a secret admirer of poetry, was married to a woman belonging to the other side. In the late 1950s he grew brave enough to hang a portrait of Akhmatova in the room he was renting. His wife, however, was often visited by the sons of powerful fathers forced into retirement after the congresses. These young men were being called upon to study the trades of their fathers in secret academies so that they could replace them as quickly as possible. Upon arriving at the home of their childhood friend, they gazed in disbelief at the portrait of Akhmatova and began to ridicule it. The woman pictured there was physiologically alien to them. Her beauty seemed monstrous. I have heard that these men are

now called "amoebas" and sometimes sycophants, though the latter func-
tioned under much more difficult circumstances—on the streets, not
behind closed doors. The "amoebas" do not understand the complex
nature of human nature. And at a time when precisely these individuals
represented the "re-evaluation of values" and most people support them,
readers of poetry were disappearing from the face of the earth.

In the late 1950s, the spiritual victory over the amoebas was marked
by a growth of interest in poetry. For Russian culture, it's evident that
poetry contains a liberating principle.

• • •

Leningrad. The church. Funeral services. A crowd of thousands
encircled the Church of Nikola Morskoi. Inside, people were crushed
together. Movie cameras whirred, but the films were later confiscated:
church funerals were dangerous propaganda, and the woman herself was
questionable—after all, no one had yet revoked the resolution about her.*
The films were hidden away in some archive, and the camera operators
(though they had obtained all possible forms of permission) had some
unpleasant experiences.

After the service I walked out of the church and went to sit in the bus
that had been prepared for the coffin. An unbroken line of people filed out
of the church as an identical unbroken line filed in. Saying good-bye was
a lengthy process. Among the crowd were some old women, her contemporaries, but most were young, unknown faces. Those who usually
attended the church, weary old women wearing tattered, old-fashioned
clothes, made desperate attempts to enter, chastising those who had come
for a special event like a funeral and were crowding them, the regular
church-goers, out. The organizers of the funeral were becoming concerned: it was taking too long for people to pay their last respects; they were
falling behind schedule. Who would have thought so many would come?

The second farewell and civil funeral rites were held at the Union of
Writers. A long crowd had been waiting here also and no more people
were being allowed inside. A doorman blocked the entrance. Lev and I

* The All-Union Communist Party resolution was revoked on 20 October 1988 at a meeting of the
Politburo.—ed.

were among those kept out. We tried to squeeze behind a corner where, hidden from view, we could wait out the official ceremony. Then someone from the administration recognized Lev and put us where we belonged. A stout academician spoke utter drivel about a golden cockerel,* something Akhmatova had repudiated long ago; female poets with hair of various hues hysterically claimed allegiance to Akhmatova: some poet or another droned on, and then the ceremony was over. Both at the church and in the Writers' Union I noticed Kushner's immobile, preoccupied face and Brodsky's sad eyes. The small number of Muscovites were easily distinguishable from the Leningraders: they behaved as if Akhmatova, whom they had accompanied on the plane, belonged to them. In Leningrad Anna had lived a much more secluded life. In Moscow, she was always visited by a crowd of friends, and gatherings called "Akhmatovka" were held in the apartment where she spent her customary two weeks. It wasn't until the very end that she became close to a group of young poets in Leningrad. "They are oddballs," Anna told me, and pointed out the most important "oddball"—the one with the beard, the very young Brodsky. I'm glad that these young men of Leningrad helped to brighten Anna's solitary life there.

The buses began to move. In our bus, the one with the coffin, were Koma [Vyacheslav Ivanov], Volodya, and Tomashevskaya. Anya [Anna Kaminskaya] stepped in for a minute, and Lev called her "niece." After a brief stop in front of Fontanka House, the vehicles moved toward Komarovo. We were preceded by a militia car. From what were the militia protecting the dead woman?

More than a little effort was expended to acquire a cemetery plot. There is a shortage of these also, and ideology creeps in. While the body was in the church, there were continuous negotiations with Moscow, where Surkov had managed to secure a plot. The head of the Komarovo cemetery finally gave in on the condition that a church service not be held at the grave. Life is hard, almost impossible, here. It is no easy matter to die, either. Even this final journey is complicated by a thousand instructions and directives, not to mention the fact that coffins are in short supply as well. Still, it is fortunate that Anna Akhmatova lay in her native soil without a name tag tied around her toe. It could have been otherwise.

---

* See appendix.—ed.

My final impressions: a small group of people at the cemetery, some of whom lived in Komarovo. Practically all the faces were known to me. Suddenly Sergei Mikhalkov, sent here by the Moscow Union of Writers after the scandal, appeared, made a speech, and left. The people began to disperse. A small service was held later at her cottage. Those present were unable to cross themselves—they had forgotten how. The priest conducted a wonderful ceremony, but it was hard for him—all around were people who didn't understand. The funeral feast was laid, and there was the same quartet that played for her at Komarovo. Tarkovsky was pale. Someone drove the two of us into the city. It was over. I would never see her again on this earth. She cherished every day of her life and struggled against death with all her might. Near the end, the darkness lifted somewhat, things became much easier, and it seemed that she could peer into the future. Though her last book [*The Race of Time*] was not picked over to the same extent as the others, even there she was made out to be a poet of love, not of rejection. But this woman with a zest for life had rejected all earthly things since her early youth.

II

How did it happen that three self-willed individuals, three nitwits with heads of straw, three incredibly frivolous people—Anna, Osip, and I—maintained and preserved throughout our entire lives our Triple Alliance, our indissoluble friendship? We were tempted to fan our tail-feathers, to play the pied piper, "to dance in front of the ark of the covenant." We teased each other and tried to get our own way, but our friendship and alliance were unshakable. We stood by one another. Determination and will were needed to preserve that friendship. Where did these traits come from? How did we overcome the inevitable crises of friendship and love? . . .

It would seem that love played a very important role in Anna's life, but at the first crisis each of these affairs crumbled around her like a house of cards. Yet her intensely personal and ardent relationship with Osip withstood every test. The first of these came a short time before I appeared. At some point in 1918 she decided to keep Osip from falling in love with her and asked him to visit her less frequently. In all probability she did this in her usual clumsy manner. At any rate, Osip was terribly offended. He was not in love with her, at least this is what he told me. He differentiated

between the nuances of a relationship, and he was constitutionally incapable of lying or concealing anything. Besides, he felt that Anna was his
equal or even above him; a woman, in other words, made for comrade-
ship not for love, which for him was either a lengthy affair or a momentary spark, a game, a madness—but always with someone weaker. His
Travels to Armenia contains a hidden sign of his lust: "An almond-shaped
eye of the Persian miniature is casting a delicate frightened glance at you.
. . . The invaders enjoyed them so much. . . . " The words "delicate" and
"almond-shaped" are added for form's sake. The real meaning is in the
frightened eyes. This could win him over in a second. He often complained to me that I no longer had that look of frightened surprise. His
youthful attraction to Salomeya Andronikova and Zelmanova was a trib-
ute to beauty from a great distance as could not have been the case
between him and Anna. Moreover, these Petersburg beauties were generally considered to be created for admiration, but Anna was a fellow-poet
with whom he would travel a difficult path. His love for Marina
[Tsvetayeva] contained something quite different and characteristic only of
that relationship: the splendid impulsiveness of the lofty feminine soul:
"In you I worship a divine boy of ten."* I met Marina but I do not know
her. Judging, though, from what she said about herself, I would think she
was the most generous and selfless of people. She was one of those Russian
women who yearned for excitement and would have probably washed the
wounds of Don Quixote if she were not otherwise occupied. Anna was
not a Great Russian; she was from southern Russia and of Petersburg stock,
more or less. She was more self-absorbed and incomparably more selfish
than Marina. Take her attitude toward mirrors, for example. When she
looked in a mirror she held her lips a certain way. It was she who said, "I
have sung over so many abysms and lived in so many mirrors."** She did
not look into mirrors, she lived in them. So Rozanov's observation that
writers can be separated into two groups—those who look in mirrors and
those who do not—does not apply here. What Rozanov has in mind is
watching the reader and toying with him, the acting trait in writers which
is invariably absent in real poets.

* From Tsvetayeva's poem "You throw back your head. . . ."—ed.
** From her poem, "What is it to us after all . . . ?"—ed.

This trait was totally lacking in Osip. Once in the Crimea the intelligent and strange Rozh told Osip that he had spent the morning with someone who by profession was the antithesis of Osip and all poets in general. Did Osip know what he meant by this oppositional profession? Osip nodded. I began to pester both of them, wanting to know what they were talking about and why they were laughing. It wasn't until decades later that I finally understood their explanation, that they had been speaking about an actor. It was only Pasternak who had something of an actor in him, and this did not appear until he grew old: actors do have the desire to be liked. Poets have not the slightest bit of actor in them. This was true even of Mayakovsky, though he spent half his life on the stage, and of Klyuev, even though he tried to conceal his brilliance and education under the guise of a peasant.

An actor looks into a mirror to discover how he should smile, move, and speak in front of spectators. Akhmatova entered into deep relationships with an unheard of number of people (after they ceased to be threatened with prison for being her friends) and looked at them as she might look into a mirror, as if seeking her reflection in their pupils. This was not egocentrism by any means: it demonstrated her spirituality, for she generously gave herself to each of her friends, living in them as in a mirror, searching in them for a reflection of her thoughts and feelings. This is why it is essentially unimportant to whom she wrote her poems. The only thing of importance is Anna herself, at once forever immutable and still developing in accordance with her own inner laws. For example, at one time I was certain that the poem about "an eternal stiff round dance of your mourning cypresses"★ was written in memory of Nedobrovo, especially since in the first edition the narcissuses were described as being "of Tsarskoye Selo," not "snow-white." This poem was written in 1928, the same year that Osip, upon returning from Yalta, told her he had found Nedobrovo's grave there. But Anna told me the poem was not in memory of Nedobrovo but of another person. (I know of a ballet-master from the Mariinsky Theater who also died of tuberculosis in Yalta.)

With a few people, especially Osip, myself, Khardzhiev, and, no doubt, Emma Gershtein, Anna formed a different kind of relationship—without mirrors.

★ From Akhmatova's "Moonlit horror's still splashing about. . . ."—ed.

Let me say a few more words about mirrors. Osip would look into a mirror during the difficult moments when we quarreled. Our quarrels always took the same form: he would accuse and revile me, sparing no effort or eloquence, while I, cornered, would attack. During the torrent of accusatory words I would sometimes take the initiative and mention Rozanov. But this was the usual female foul play. Putting his whole heart into the argument, Osip would look into the mirror, no doubt checking to see if his look was sufficiently convincing. He was usually right, but I would take advantage of his weaknesses, like the mirror, in order to confuse him and change the subject. Women, we all know, do not like to admit being wrong. And though I am not a "real woman," I knew some of the tricks of my sex. No matter how much I love women, it is still alarming that they consider themselves to be as impeccable as the Catholic Pope. And I understand Osip, who always realized how important it was for a human being to recognize his errors, mistakes, and stupidities. A human being is not a model, a doll, or a robot. Who has not made a terrible mess of life? But perhaps these mistakes are what give our lives warmth and humanity. Our masters canonized each other while they were still living. But we are people, not portraits. Osip once told me that if I chose a husband according to my taste he would be a hypocrite the likes of which the world had never seen. But it was Osip I chose and not a cunning hypocrite. And not for one second of my life was I ever miserable, depressed, or bored. Let Akhmatova look at people as if they were mirrors; let Pasternak charm his visitors; let Mandelshtam irritate people and get his face slapped ("It is senseless to approach a stranger with tenderness"); let Klyuev swagger about in his peasant attire; let Klychkov stagger "from dawn to dawn" down the bawdy streets of Moscow. Not one of them ever shed blood; all of them were people, not the faceless masses. They were complex, multicellular structures with eyes that looked in wonderment at God's world. They did not kill; it was they who were killed.

Writing, in and of itself, arouses in people a need for others and strengthens ties between them. Poetry flows from one person to another, from the living and the dead to other people. Each individual is a select vessel—if he does not renounce his humanity, if he does not claim to possess a higher mind with the right to control the fates of little people, if he does not violate the will of the living and the dead, and if he does not destroy the sacred values acquired by people throughout history.

Reminiscing about Anna Akhmatova, I for some reason recall my own life. This did not happen when I wrote about Osip Mandelshtam. His fate was such that it swept away the personal and intimate details I now recollect in thinking about our friend—Anna Andreyevna, Anush, sweet Anyuta.

Osip brought me to see her on Kazanskaya or to her apartment on the Neva. She lived in both places with Olya Sudeikina, and I can't recall now where our first meeting took place. Olya was dusting—she tried to keep the apartment as neat and attractive as possible—and said that she couldn't let Anna out of her sight for a minute or she would come up with some mischief. Osip immediately relaxed and smiled.

On our way to see Akhmatova Osip was rather perturbed. He had recently criticized Anna twice in the press and was now apprehensive about seeing his former ally and friend. He was also worried about how she would treat me: he remembered Marina [Tsvetayeva]. Both these indomitable women were capable of anything. Marina did in fact "rub my face in dirt" when she met me. Extending a friendly hand to Osip, she said she was taking him to see Alya.* Hardly bothering to look at me, she left me with the words: "Wait here. Alya cannot abide strangers." Osip turned green with anger but still he went to see Alya, leaving me behind in a kind of anteroom that was totally dark and filled with junk. Osip later told me it had once been a dining room with an overhanging light. But it had not been cleaned since the beginning of the Revolution, and the lamp was covered with such a thick layer of dust that not a ray of light escaped. The visit with Alya lasted a few minutes, and as soon as Osip returned he took me away and never went back to see Marina. I was not angry in the least, and Marina was wrong to think I was the jealous type. My major defect as a woman has always been my lack of jealousy. Essentially, this indicates an arrogant and superficial attitude toward people, and Osip as well as other friends, especially Anna, always reproached me for this. The only time I justifiably broke a dish and uttered the sacramental words: "Her or me,"

---

* Ariadna Efron, daughter of Marina Tsvetayeva.—ed.

Osip was elated: "You've become a real woman at last!" But this happened much later.

As for the relationship with Marina that never came to be, I now have these thoughts: why are people incapable of saying a kind word to others at the right time? Why do we make relationships between people so complicated? Why are they encumbered with foolish obstacles—vanity, pretense, popular rules of conduct, an era's rules of propriety concerning romance, love, friendship, and God knows what all else—that prevent people from approaching one another with open hearts and keep them separated by an eternal barrier? Anna made this apt observation: "A sacred line is present in all human intimacy . . ."* This line, this barrier, exists not only in relations of love and passion but in all human relations—everywhere and always. Why, for instance, did I not tell Marina that I was not the stranger she took me for, that there were too few of us left to reject each other out of capriciousness? Why did I prefer to laugh maliciously—what a fool I was!—and wait in a dark anteroom? How much easier it is to offend or ridicule someone than to cross this barrier. Despite our real closeness, Osip and I did not always manage to step over this "sacred line," and I, not he, was to blame. He was capable of being much more open and honest than I. He could recognize his faults and mistakes while I mostly needed to demonstrate my impeccability and "incomparable rightness." My secretiveness, which I once considered to be my trump card, caused me considerable harm: I never managed to tell Osip what was most important or to ask him many of the questions to which I will now never know the answers (even should there occur that meeting I secretly still believe in).

Something similar happened between me and Anna. She tried persistently for years to get me to answer questions about the crux of things, but I, just as persistently, evaded her questions, made jokes, and acted in a silly manner. If I had answered them, perhaps in some way I would have made her life easier, helped her to understand herself and certain aspects of her relationship with Gumilev. But even in my relationship with such a friend as her, I still never crossed that invisible line, that barrier, that wall, against which human relationships are broken. I have observed that the stronger the individual, the more open he is and the deeper his relations with

* The first line from one of her poems.—ed.

others—to the point that the barrier sometimes becomes transparent. I saw this in Anna and in Osip. But most people want always to put forth their best side and to this end conceal their real selves. It took me thirty years, which included many nights of endless thinking, bitter solitude, and the ultimate loss of Anna—the most jealous and prejudiced friend I ever had—finally to admit this.

Osip had no need to worry about my first meeting with Anna. There was no unpleasantness. As a matter of fact, Anna was marvelous toward me, showing the consideration she reserved for new friends. The most important issue was soon decided: when the time came to read poetry, Anna said: "You read first, because I like your poetry better than you like mine." Such remarks—off-handed comments that put everything in its proper place—were called "Akhmatova's barbs." Subsequently we visited her several times, and once she came uninvited to see us at Morskaya. She found me alone (Osip had gone to Moscow to collect some belongings) and sick, wearing my pajamas. Later, in my presence, she told Nina Pushkarskaya how I sent her off immediately for cigarettes and how she humbly obeyed me: "You know how docile I am." Perhaps my lack of formality in some way broke the ice: she did not much like or appreciate admiration and respect toward herself. But it was those who didn't know her who were inclined to this; among her own circle a little rudeness was in order. This is how her friends from the Poets' Guild, Narbut and Osip, treated her, and she loved it.

She was left with fewer and fewer close friends and equals, Khardzhiev being the last to join the group. She was delighted to learn that Khardzhiev, after listening to Chukovsky drip honey in her praise, finally became fed up and said: "She's a great old girl, good to have a few drinks with." When she heard this story, it made her look some ten years younger.

Anna and I did not become real friends until March 1925, in Tsarskoye Selo. This was the difficult time when Osip and I were experiencing the only crisis we ever had in our relationship. In January 1925 Osip accidently met Olga Vaksel on the street. He had known her since she was a young girl studying at an institute, and he brought her home. Two poems reveal how their relationship developed further. Out of a false pride I kept silent and secretly prepared my attack. In mid-March I packed my suitcase and waited for T. [see appendix] to pick me up and take me with him. Osip walked in by chance at that precise moment and showed T. to the door. Then he phoned Olga and broke with her in a rude manner (I was horrified and grabbed the phone from him, but he put down the receiver; I only managed to hear her crying). He took me in his arms and brought me to Tsarskoye Selo. To this day I'm astonished by the determination and will he showed in that affair. . . .

Poetry and sex share a mysterious connection so strong that it's almost impossible to describe. Anna was aware of this, and she tried to force me to admit it as well. Shalamov knew it, and he was angry at Osip for writing poems to other women. He also tried to convince me that everything was petty compared to poetry.

I know that the connection between poetry and sex is manifested in various forms, the most common being rapture about a woman. But if the passion is quenched, the poems immediately lose their intensity. The Lauras and Beatrices, those beautiful and unattainable women, do not merely represent the fashion of the day but something deeper and inherent in the physiology and the nature of poetry. Apparently one cannot live with these beautiful women. Blok's unhappy family drama lay in his marriage to one.

Anna never wrote poems to the men in her life until a crisis occurred. Osip cautiously discussed this subject with me several times, and from his words and my own observations I know of another, more complicated connection between poetry and sex, something that Anna was especially interested in—when the ecstasy of asceticism is replaced by the ecstasy of something quite different. I did not discover this until the 1930s. I lived an ordinary, humdrum married life only during that time when Osip was not writing poetry. Anna knew a great deal from her own experience and encountered traces of the same traits in her research into the lives of the poets of the past. I don't think either painters or musicians have such a direct connection between art and sex. The special intensity of poetry, its sensual and prophetic nature, has a much greater influence on man than do other arts or sciences.

Osip and Anna's renewed friendship (she often told me I was the one who brought it about) helped to restore the intimacy between Osip and me after he broke with Olga Vaksel.

• • •

Anna used to say that she would have written prose if her life had turned out differently. I find that hard to believe: in her Pushkin research her voice is strident and analytical; in some of her autobiographical passages she is too cautious, trying to soften and mitigate the truth. Letters are a good indication of a writer's ability to write prose, but she never wrote any, not wanting to give herself away by a careless word. She had a good pretext for not writing: how disgusting to know that your letters would be opened and read by people other than those to whom they were addressed. But she was the same when she was younger. Somehow she came to believe at an early age that all her indiscretions would be divulged by her biographers. She lived always aware of her own biography, but her volatile character would permit neither the secrecy nor the idealization she longed for.

"It is all in our hands," she would say, and: "As a literary critic I know. . . ." One part of her longed for a canonized portrait without the follies and foibles inevitable in any life, especially that of a poet. A beautiful, poised, intelligent woman, and a wonderful poet on top of all that—this was the image Anna had of herself. She once admitted to me that when she and Gumilev arrived in St. Petersburg she was astonished at her success, not as the author of first books of poems but as a woman. She was indifferent to her literary success in the beginning, believing Gumilev that they would share the same fate as the Brownings—in life the wife was famous; after death she was forgotten and the husband was celebrated. But her success as a woman went to her head, and herein lies the secret as to why she wanted to be perceived as a perfect lady.

It was Nedobrovo who gave her her first lessons in how a woman should behave. Like his extremely dignified wife, Nedobrovo was of "the best society," and he greatly influenced certain aspects of Anna's life. But while he exerted a calming influence on her frenetic behavior, Nedobrovo could also appreciate her spontaneity and untamed nature. "Anna is wonderful in every way," he would say, "Except for this gesture." Anna demonstrated it for me: she slapped her hand on her knee, turned her wrist, and shot her palm up almost to my nose. It was the gesture of a young, mischievous girl from the seaside. Behind the flimsy disguise of a lady (who was sometimes truly polite but more often a little funny) lived this feisty girl who made the earth tremble under her feet.

Anna was indifferent to performances and to the public, and cared nothing about applause, standing ovations, and other useless honors. But she adored sitting around a table drinking tea with friends of all ages; she loved the noise and lively table conversation. Here she excelled: people would fall off their chairs laughing when she gave in to her mischievous nature. She could not keep up the role of a lady for long, but whenever she was invited to a proper home she prepared for the evening. As for invitations, she accepted them all: she loved to visit people. Khardzhiev and I would be terrified: where can she be off to next?

She always took someone along when she went visiting; she was afraid to go out alone. I would go with her only when we were in Tashkent, and even there not very often. In Moscow we never went anywhere together. There were many reasons for this, but the most important was that in my presence she couldn't pretend to be a lady; she was afraid to meet my sardonic gaze. Also, she wanted to be the center of attention, and in later years she feared having to share some of that attention with me. We had virtually no common friends. Of her entire circle of friends throughout the years I developed a close relationship only with a few. Two she herself presented to me: Yulya and Nika, no one else. But my friends often became her acquaintances and even close friends. One morning, without calling in advance, I brought Rozhansky to see her (she stubbornly persisted in referring to him as an academician, refusing to believe me when I told her he only worked in the Academy). She was excited about being invited to attend one of his dinner parties. The Rozhanskys were very polite, and they always invited me as well. But I told them frankly that my presence would spoil Anna's fun. The dinner went very well.

The episode with Vilenkin, a theater critic, was more complicated. Anna informed me that Vilenkin had invited her to dinner and was horrified to learn that I had been invited as well. She didn't bother to conceal her mortification; what were we to do? To pacify her, I called Vilenkin and said I was sick. The dinner was a great success, and the next day Vilenkin came to the Shklovskys, where I was living at the time, to visit the sick woman. I was dressed in my robe and slippers and sweeping the corridor. Vilenkin looked at me in surprise: what did this mean? I had to tell this dear gentleman about my jealous friend and how she felt uncomfortable pretending to be a lady in my presence.

But what about her biography? How would she be depicted there? She wrote practically no prose, and in the poetry of her maturity she revealed too much of herself to pretend to be a lady. I love her strident voice:

I do not play the lover's lyre
To win hearts in this battle
The weapon that sings in my hand
Is the outcast leper's rattle.*

I think that for these lines even Nedobrovo would have forgiven Anna her habit of striking her knee during an argument.

She presented me with Yulya and Nika, but I took Nikolai Ivanovich Khardzhiev without her permission. It first happened during those days when she came to see me in Moscow and we arranged "beggars' feasts." Osip would call in the middle of the night from Voronezh, Nikolai Ivanovich joined our feasts, and Anna observed with alarm that we were getting along wonderfully. "Nadia dear," she told me, "be careful; Nikolai Ivanovich cannot abide forward women." "What about you?" I asked naively. "I'm different," she replied. This, of course, was pure slander against Nikolai Ivanovich, and we remained friends throughout life. When Osip returned he spoke with Nikolai Ivanovich as well. He told me that Nikolai had a perfect ear for poetry, and he wanted such a man to publish his poems. It was already clear that his work would only be published posthumously. According to Osip, a poet was truly fortunate to have such an editor. He even asked me to give Nikolai *The Unknown Soldier*, saying that he could do anything he wanted with the composition because he, Osip, was tired and couldn't do anything more with it. But after this bout with fatigue, the poem—a kind of oration as Osip described it—took its final form.

Osip disappeared and later came the news of his death. By this time I was already an outcast: everyone turned away from me. The only place I could take refuge was in a small room in a wooden house in Marina Roshcha. It was here that I came after a parcel I had sent [to Osip] was returned marked: "addressee deceased." I lay flat on my back on Nikolai

* Tr. by Andrew Bromfield.

Ivanovich's mattress. He boiled wieners and forced me to eat. From time to time he would offer me a piece of candy, saying: "Eat it Nadia; it's expensive." He was trying to make me smile. It was during this period that Anna would come from Leningrad to send parcels to Lev* or to try to petition his case; i.e., to stand in line at the offices of prosecutors who never answered a single question and only further frightened already terrified people. In our whole, vast country we had but one friend, only one who never turned away from us. This always served to distinguish Nikolai Ivanovich from the acquaintances that appeared later—after the terror was over and it became clear that friendship with us would not cost people their lives. "He was there when we were all alone," Anna would say, and, "He was the only one who never turned his back on us."

Nikolai Ivanovich was evacuated to Alma Ata. We heard that he made an unhappy marriage and then divorced. Anna was angry with both S. N. [Serafima Suok] and Shklovsky: "What riffraff. How could she have betrayed Nikolai Ivanovich!" After all, Nikolai had supported S. N. during those terrible years as well, and he virtually saved her life at the beginning of the war when he took her to be evacuated.** It was then that we discussed what constituted courage. The only one who did not succumb to cowardice was our "Black Man"—this was what we called him behind his back (we wouldn't have dared such familiarity to his face). "The master is strict but fair," Anna said, and both of us showed Nikolai Ivanovich the utmost respect, though he was the youngest among us. Anna used to frown and ask me: "Why do you call him Nikolasha? I always call him Nikolai Ivanovich."

At one time she got it into her mind to marry me off to Nikolai Ivanovich. In this way she would get two birds with one stone: I would be settled and Nikolai would not marry again someone else who would do as all wives do: take our "Black Man" away from us. To her dismay I rejected her plan: it was not something either he or I wanted. She told me that had she been rich (if she had a dacha or at least an apartment—this is what we meant by rich), she would have moved in with Nikolai Ivanovich and let people say whatever they liked. And people would have said a great deal, especially about the difference in their ages . . . meanwhile our charming

* Lev Gumilev had been arrested in 1938.—ed.
** I.e., after the arrest of Vladimir Narbut in 1937.—ed.

"Black Man" had no reason to suspect what we were plotting. Then Anna found a solution: "Let him be a husband to both of us!" I immediately agreed. We informed him of our decision by telegram, which in those days were delivered practically on foot. We didn't receive an answer for a while and Anna began to worry: what if our "Black Man" was offended? The answer came in my absence. Waving a telegram in her hand, Anna met me at the door (we were living together on Zhukovskaya Street in Tashkent). He was not offended; he had signed it "mutually yours."

Khardzhiev played an important role in Anna's life. During the most difficult periods she never took a step without asking his advice: "I will do what 'Black Man' or 'mutually ours' says" . . . (despite the situation with his real wife, she continued to call him "mutually ours"). Many of her poems have a connection with their conversations. This was how the leper theme came up. She was complaining to him that everyone thought of her as a love lyricist and did not notice anything else in her work. Nikolai Ivanovich replied: "There is no love or lyricism there at all; it's more like the leper's clanging bell."

When Nikolai Ivanovich was thousands of miles away, Anna consented to share "Black Man's" friendship with me, but she was by no means so generous in Moscow. With him so near, she tried to push us apart. But it was still a holiday for us all when we managed to get together and recall our "beggars' feasts." Only now no one called long-distance from Voronezh. Together we three relived our youth; we laughed and enjoyed the stolen moments of joy.

No matter how much Anna liked Khardzhiev, she could never forgive him one thing: how could he admire Khlebnikov as much as Mandelshtam?! Anna even suspected that he admired Khlebnikov more, and this infuriated her. No one could tell her that he preferred another poet to Mandelshtam. "He's a Pasternak fan," she would warn me; i.e., we should not waste our time with such a dilettante. Despite Punin's avant-garde sympathies, Anna could forgive him much: he had once printed a favorable article about Mandelshtam. It's funny, but it was not important to her that her own poems be admired. At any rate, she never avoided anyone because he was indifferent to her poetry. But she tried to get me as well to show Khardzhiev that I would not tolerate his inexcusable admiration for Khlebnikov.

Jealousy and intolerance are twins. These are emotions of the strong, not the weak. Nikolai Ivanovich also claimed that his judgments were ruled by predilections, and I found a passage in Hertzen in praise of predilections. Indifference is the only vice. Glory to predilections!

I was stunned by the insightful and desperate words of the young woman poet who committed suicide somewhere in England: she discovered that one paid a heavy price for every drop of joy. When I was still very young, before I met Osip, I knew that love was not all blue skies. I wanted to escape the common fate; i.e., I would have liked to have the attitude of the young women of the latter half of the twentieth century. But everything fell apart when I had my first serious encounter—with Osip Mandelshtam. I became a wife and everything went as usual, except that we had the additional difficulties of the times. Anna made me a gift of Osip's love.* I succumbed to the temptation and did not try to persuade her to relinquish her place.

When two people surrounded by hoodlums hold hands, can this be love? Everyday life, not extreme situations, is the greatest test of love. I don't know if our love would have withstood that test. How could I? We hardly experienced a single normal year—under the incredible circumstances in which we lived, each period brought severe tribulations. But I have to say that we lived well, really first-class. As for the suffering, I swear, we didn't invent it.

● ● ●

We often spoke of death in those years. One day in 1938, when Osip and Lev were already imprisoned, Anna and I were climbing the staircase in the big house on Nikolayevskaya Street. I believe it is now called Marat Street. There, in a tiny, dark room of the large apartment, my sister Anya was dying of cancer. "What a long time to die," Anna noted. She was envious of Anya, who was already approaching the other side, while we still had a long road to travel. If we had known the length of that road back then, we might have swerved aside—into a river, a bog, an early death. It's

---

*In her reminiscences, Akhmatova wrote that "Osip was unquestionably and incredibly in love with Nadia."—ed.

a good thing that man does not know his future; no one would fare better for it.

Several days later Anna accompanied me to the train station after Anya's funeral. Once again we witnessed the overcrowded halls, the harried people sitting on sacks. The scene resembled a disturbed human antbed—the result of dekulakization. "This is what it will be like from now on," Anna said. She could see a part of the road ahead, but I preferred to live for the moment—sending parcels to prison, going to funerals, receiving returned parcels, trying not to starve. There were many bitter misfortunes. And along with this, I never ceased trying to disseminate [Osip's] poems—taking them from one house and bringing them to another, and knowing them all by heart: how many lines in this one, how many in that one; perhaps I made a mistake here, I have to check it. And then my residential permit—would the militia register me here or not? Where was I to go with my treasure of poetry? The important thing was to know them by heart. If I forgot them, what would be left for me in a prison camp?

If I look back on it all, my head begins to swim—how did we endure? But we did endure; we lived through it, we survived. . . . Anna often remarked, "Who would have thought we would live to see this?"

She is no longer here, and I ask myself: "What else will I live to see? Perhaps the best is already behind me? God knows. . . ." But I did my duty and could not care less about anything else. Well, not quite. I'm ready to accept anything, but I cannot bear to see how they torment other people: I don't want to hear any more about prisons, prison camps, interrogations, trials, and other misfortunes. I well remember Hertzen's words, that deeds considered crimes in Russia were considered such nowhere else in the world.

We are now living in a new world where newly awakened people—we were "early risers" or perhaps we never went to sleep at all—are beginning to think and live our thoughts, our grief, our joy, and, most important, our values. Anna once said to others: "Your children will curse you on my account." She was mistaken in only one thing: it was not the children of our contemporaries but their grandchildren that accepted us. Anna and I used to say that old age would have been completely different under normal circumstances; i.e., under those we could imagine in the early twentieth century. Literary passion would have seethed all around us; young people would have met in circles, societies, and groups; they would have published manifestos and quite forgotten the celebrated and universally acknowledged poets of long ago: what use could they be when nothing was more important than the present day? Offended, prosperous—she would not have had a place in these new schools and would not have known what to do with herself.

But life turned out differently. Not only we but our grandchildren as well now feel the liberating force of poetry. It was no mere circumstance that thousands of people came to her funeral. Nor was it mere circumstance that hand-copies of Mandelshtam's poems were distributed around the country and created the consciousness of a new, just-emerging cultural stratum—a new intelligentsia of grandchildren. It is clear that we did not live in vain. And it is our fortune that we survived to be able to peer into the future. What occurred here is irreversible; the epoch of the superman is over; the epoch of arbitrary rule is finished. A qualitative leap in consciousness occurred, and we witnessed it. This does not mean that old customs will be replaced by new ones: our grandchildren will still pay a heavy price for freedom of thought and for everything they will have to achieve once again. But what was most important has been accomplished; we did not live in vain.

What else can I say about my friend? She used to give me a hard look and suddenly say something. From the startled look in my eyes she would understand my thought and answer it. Then there were the times when I would say to her: "Anna, someone is coming." And she would reply: "So, it's time to make myself pretty?" And at once she would obediently make herself pretty. Once she read in someone's memoirs (a woman's, of course) published abroad that she was not pretty and that Gumilev did not love her. "Nadia," she said to me, "explain to me why I should be pretty. Was Walter Scott handsome? Or Dostoyevsky? Who would even think about asking such a thing?" I thought she would forget about these memoirs, but nothing of the sort. From that day on she began to collect photographs. All her friends brought her pictures and she collected those where she looked pretty and pasted them in an album. She collected heaps of pictures, so many it was impossible to count them all. . . . But she did not find the time to write down poetry. Large numbers of poems remained not written down.

I also recall how she feared a fight over her works after she died. It upset her to think that her humble notebooks would become the object of buying and selling. She showed me the handwritten instructions she had made indicating which folders and notebooks were to go to which archives. I mistrusted archives; sometimes they would destroy manuscripts according to a list—the papers of this and that person must go. . . . They even burned books. But Anna Andreyevna had firmly decided to give her papers to the archives. It was out of the question to give them to Lev, who lived alone in a communal apartment. Everything had to be given to the archives. I made no further objections. [. . .]

She had no home when she grew old. Only in the summer, living in the ugly little "hut"* that belonged to the Literary Fund, was there the illusion of a home. And, fortunately, the young Leningrad poets—Brodsky, Naiman, and others—did not foresake her. They came to visit, shared her friendship, and did everything for her. [. . .] She remained a homeless and lonely wanderer to the end of her life. Apparently, this is the fate of poets. She never ceased to be amazed at her fate: everyone has at least someone or something—a husband, children, work. "Why is it I have nothing at all?"

Still, we stood our ground and did everything we could. Thank God, we had the strength and the perseverence. We will remember the unwritten poems, we will collect them, and we will not forget them.

Lydia Ginzburg
BRIEF REMINISCENCES
ON ANNA AKHMATOVA

Lydia Ginzburg, writer and literary critic, met Akhmatova in 1926. The following are excerpts from her notes on Akhmatova, published in various editions.

Most of the recollections about Anna Andreyevna Akhmatova being published today refer to the latter period of her life. Several people could

---

* Anna's name for the small summer cottage in Komarova.—ed.

speak about the Akhmatova of the *Rosary* and *A Flock of White Birds*
periods. My recollections of Anna Andreyevna are connected with the
relatively early period of her writing. I met her at the home of the
Gukovskys in the winter of 1926–27. Akhmatova was a frequent visitor
there. Natalia Victorovna Rykova, the wife of Grigory Alexandrovich
Gukovsky, was one of her closest friends in the twenties.

In 1926 Eikhenbam and Tynyanov edited a collection of their students'
articles and published them as a book entitled *Russian Prose*. My first article,
"Vyazemsky as a writer," was included. Apprehensively, I gave a reprint to
Natalia Victorovna and asked her to pass it on to Anna Andreyevna. Soon
afterwards we met at the Gukovskys and Natalia Victorovna introduced me
with the words: "This is the young woman whose article. . . ."

"It was a very good article," Anna Andreyevna said.

These were the first words I heard Akhmatova speak, and I took pride
in them. We saw each other for another forty years, until the very end. We
met frequently in the thirties and after the war—during the latter half of
the forties—then less often in the fifties and sixties when Anna Andreyevna
was spending a good deal of time in Moscow. For this reason I recall with
most clarity the image of the Akhmatova of the late twenties, when she
was thirty-seven and thirty-eight, and the poet of the thirties and forties.
I remember Akhmatova when she was still young and slender, as she was
in the portrait by Altman. She was incredibly beautiful, with a sharp wit
and majestic manner.

Akhmatova's movements and intonation were organized and purposeful. She possessed an extraordinary system of gestures which, generally speaking, was uncharacteristic of people living in non–ritualistic times
such as ours. In others this would seem affected or theatrical; in Akhmatova
it blended harmoniously with her image.

I have always had an interest in determining whether or not a poet was
like or unlike the verse. The perfect example of *likeness* was, of course,
Mayakovsky, with his distinctive vocal manner and his height. Akhmatova
was different. Her poetry of the 1910s and 1920s did not at all reflect her
interest in history or literature or her sharp, sometimes merciless, wit. In
life, Anna Akhmatova did not resemble her heroines. But with her sober,
observant, and rational mind, she did in some ways resemble her poetic
method. There was the correlation.

Akhmatova devised one of the most remarkable lyrical systems in the history of poetry; she never thought of lyricism as the spontaneous outpouring of one's soul. She needed poetic discipline, compulsion, and restrictions in her work. Pushkin liked to say that what a poet did was labor. The same was true of Akhmatova; it was a Pushkin tradition she followed. For her, writing was a kind of physical labor.

One day, for example, one of Akhmatova's readers came to see her when she was ill. She complained of feeling weak and said that for several days she had been all alone resting quietly in bed.

"Then you've probably been writing . . ."

"Of course not! How can you write poetry in such a condition? You need all your physical strength for that."

Akhmatova took a very objective approach to her own work. Once I mentioned to her something about those who wrote "viscerally."

"You can't do that for long," Anna Andreyevna replied. "Only sometimes and for very short periods."

"What about Pasternak? There are a lot of irrational aspects to his work."

"Pasternak is different."

For Akhmatova, lyricism was not raw emotion but a profound transformation of inner experience, a transference of emotion to another mode, to the realm of *language* where there was no shame and secrets were known to all. Readers of lyrical poetry want to understand not so much the poet as themselves. Hence the paradox: the most subjective type of literature, lyricism, brings us to a common understanding better than anything else.

This was what Anna Andreyevna had in mind when she said: "Poetry has no room for shame." The laws of poetic transformation allow the poet to speak about the most personal concerns, for the personal then becomes common.

Akhmatova had an intense feeling for culture. The theme is an important one—lyricism and culture—but it is not appropriate to delve into it here. I would like to note, simply, that culture provides lyricism with the necessary scope and richness of association.

Culture was always present in Akhmatova's work, of course, but in different forms. In her later poetry it's on the surface; in her earlier verse it's concealed but still felt through subtle, almost hidden mentions of the work of earlier writers.

I will speak here of Akhmatova's two creative periods—the first lasting from 1910 into the 1930s and the second from 1940 into the 1960s—
only in relative terms and make no attempt to discuss the complexity of the
evolution of her creativity. Anyway, the most important changes in her
poetic method are evident. The first period is characterized by specifics.
Words are not reorganized by the use of metaphor but are sharply altered
by context. A thing remains itself, a concrete object, but it acquires a more
generalized and broader meaning. In this, Akhmatova's poetry reveals a
peculiar reflection of the late writings of Pushkin.

> And yet we would not trade it for the world,
> This city of great fame and greater woes,
> All granite and wide rivers' sparkling floes,
> The sunless gardens' silent, gloomy rows
> Of trees; the Muse's whisper barely heard.

Grigory Gukovsky at one time made an apt comment about this
poem: "Poems about St. Petersburg have always mentioned the *river*—the
Neva. But Akhmatova saw *rivers*, a delta, in St. Petersburg and wrote:
'Wide rivers' sparkling floes . . .'"*

This poem was written in 1915. Abstract thought came to dominate
her later work as the symbolic import of words was stressed. For long-time
readers of Akhmatova (including myself) who grew up on her first books,
these remain very special. We saw for the first time Akhmatova's unique
and encompassing view of the world. She was remarkably accurate in
describing concrete objects, psychological, and even abstract concepts. In
his poem "To Anna Akhmatova" (1928), Boris Pasternak wrote:

> An eye may be acute in different ways,
> And variously apt, a word or phrase . . .

This is not an attempt to make a comparative historical evaluation of
Akhmatova's creative periods. Anna Andreyevna understood what her
readers preferred, even if they remained silent. She let them know this
when she recalled the words of Mayakovsky: "Say whatever you will about
my poems; only do not say that the preceding was better than the last."

Akhmatova's later poetry is characterized by symbolism, then, and a
new function for culture. Historical and literary associations can be found

---

* From "There is somewhere plain life and light . . ."—ed.

in the text. This is especially evident in *Poem Without a Hero,* with its masks, reminiscences, and complex epigraphs.

Akhmatova altered the way she used culture in her work, but she remained immersed in it. She had a special gift for *reading*. We are voracious readers until we become adults. We re-read, sort out what we have read, and memorize. Gradually this kind of reading changes into professional and purposeful reading aimed at our own particular ideas and interests. Anna Andreyevna never lost her ability to read voraciously. That is why she knew her favorite books as no one else did.

Preparing comments on different publications, I would often come across uncited passages from Dante, Shakespeare, and Byron. The experts I phoned would not be able to pinpoint the quotes. As a last recourse I would call Anna Andreyevna. She loved such questions (I was not the only one to ask them) and said she was her own information bureau. Sometimes she would immediately identify the quote without hanging up the phone. Now and then she would need a certain amount of time to find it. I don't recall a single case when a quote remained unidentified.

Akhmatova read Dante, Shakespeare, and Pushkin extensively. But she read many others, including modern writers. In the mid-thirties she showed me a thin book and said, "You must read this. It is very interesting."

It was *A Farewell to Arms*. At that time Hemingway was not known in our country and his novel had just been translated.

Pushkin occupied a unique place in Akhmatova's world. Russian writers in general have a special feeling for Pushkin. You may or may not like the other classics, depending on your literary point of view, but Pushkin is different. Everyone understands that Pushkin is the bond that holds together the past and the future of Russian literature. Without it, the tie is severed.

Anna Andreyevna had a personal relationship with Pushkin and his circle that bordered on the idiosyncratic. She judged, loved, and hated these people as if they were still on the scene. She had a peculiar jealousy of Natalia Nikolaevna and of all the women in Pushkin's life. This made her judgments biased and undeservedly cruel, something she is chided for today.

Anna Andreyevna's own character allowed her to have a personal, prejudiced opinion even about literary characters. Once I found her reading Shakespeare.

"You know, Desdemona is charming, but Ophelia is a hysteric with paper flowers. She resembles Natalia Nikolaevna."

Speaking of a woman she knew, Akhmatova said, "If you were to start flying around the room as you were talking to her she would not be surprised in the least. She would say: 'How well you fly.' This is because she's always in a dream. Everything is possible in a dream; only surprise is out of the question."

This shows the intimate and personal basis upon which Akhmatova formed her associations. In her speech they were freely entwined with real life, with her evaluations of her surroundings and her specific observations.

Akhmatova is invariably remembered in connection with the themes of culture, tradition, and legacy. Her work is also understood in terms of these categories. Much has already been said and written about the influence of the Russian classics on her poetry, the works of Pushkin and the poets of his time, the Russian psychological novel, and Nekrasov. Still left to be studied is the significance of Nekrasov's love lyrics, which she liked for their emotion, urban conflicts, and the conversational speech of the intelligentsia.

But these correlations are by no means linear. Critics sometimes view the "classicism" of some twentieth-century poets, even today's poets, as repetition and duplication. But the Russian poetry that emerged after the symbolists, and in conflict with the symbolists, could not forget what they had discovered: the strong linkage between words, new multiple meanings and multiple strata. Akhmatova is a poet of the twentieth century. She learned from the classic writers and their words may be found in her poetry, but the relationship between words is different.

Akhmatova's poetry combines the concrete meaning of a word with a sharply altered poetic context and with vivid conceptual conflicts. This is great poetry, a modern reworking of two centuries of Russian verse.

With remarkable clarity, we perceive through a personal communication the legacy of a culture from the nineteenth and twentieth centuries. And nothing sounds archaic or foreign. Anna Andreyevna always had the ability to speak in the language of those generations of culture with which time bound her throughout her long life.   1977

FROM THE NOTES OF LYDIA GINZBURG (1950–1980)

. . . The bodies of the Writers' Union,★ including the Literary Fund,★★ know very well that Akhmatova has worldwide fame, that her name will go down in history, and so on. They also know that not only must they accept her, they are obliged to protect her. They know that, for example, "X" or "Z" isn't really anyone and the prizes he won were third-rate. And they know, or to be more precise, they feel with the very fiber of their being, that while Anna Andreyevna can live in terrible conditions, "X" or "Y" cannot; he has to be provided for. When "X" becomes ill no one will put him in a six-bed ward in a regional hospital. But they can put Akhmatova in one. And they did. . . .   1957

• • •

"My stay in the sanatorium was completely ruined," Anna Andre-yevna said. "Every day they came—everyone: academicians, elderly ladies, and young girls. They took my hand and said: 'We are very happy you are doing so well.' What is so well? What, I should have liked to ask them, is so well? Do you know what it is? Disregard: they see a writer who is not published, who is not being discussed anywhere at any time. What is so well about that? It is the height of disregard."

"No, it is understandable, and it's good that no one is writing about you."

This was true. That same day an acquaintance announced:

"You know, Zoshchenko is doing very well."

"What happened?"

"They were told that nothing much was the matter, that they should leave him alone and give him work. But he said . . ."

"What? What did he say?"

"They were told, 'Let them see that one can say what he wants.' And they offered him some work, some translation. He told them he felt ill and was unable to work."

★ The Union of Soviet Writers exercised control over literary life in the USSR.—ed.

★★ The Literary Fund (*Litfond*) distributed state benefits to writers through the Union.—ed.

On the whole, Zoshchenko was doing very well.

Akhmatova is right, just as the academicians, young girls, and elderly ladies who congratulated her are right. Of course, it isn't very polite to tell a writer that everything is fine when she isn't writing. But there was a sense of reality in the conversation, because it was a conversation about being allowed to exist. Guided by a sense of reality, they were assuming that there is probably no writer who would rather write than live.

· · ·

Ata and [Konstantin] Simonov studied together at the Literary Institute and were married in 1935. Simonov was a poor young man (nineteen years old) without prospects. Other institutes had rejected him because he came from the gentry. He worked at a plant to earn money. He imitated Kipling in his writing. He showed me his poems and we both decided they were not for print. Already then he was incredibly industrious, and he said he was going to win his place. "I might not be the most talented, but I will achieve what I want."

Later, after they had separated, Ata said: "Kostya is not a man, he is an institution," referring to his relentless desire to organize everything.

In the latter half of the 1930s Simonov began to gain his place. Not only was he being published, he had received his first medal. It was at this point in his life that he asked me to introduce him to Anna Andreyevna. She agreed to see him.

While we were climbing the steep and dark staircase to the Punin apartment* in one of the wings of the Fontanka house (undoubtedly this was where the Sheremetyev's privileged servants lived), Simonov asked:

"Do you think I could kiss her hand?"

"Most definitely."

A strip of tin had been attached to the worn spot on the door next to the bell. Nikolai Nikolaevich (Punin), perhaps intentionally, had used a piece of metal from a tin of canned meat that still bore the label "pork."

Before we rang the bell Simonov quickly removed the new medal from his jacket lapel and put it in his pocket.

---

* The apartment of Nikolai Punin, where Akhmatova lived from 1928 until 1962, located in a wing of the palace of Count Sheremetyev on the Fontanka River in Leningrad; the Fontanka house.—ed.

In the 1920s Mandelshtam wrote some orthodox critical reviews. They weren't so much subterfuge as self-educating. The same is true of his "Ode to Stalin" in 1937, which, unfortunately, represents the best of his poetry. The poem corresponded to one of those uncoordinated twists in Mandelshtam's mind.

The poem Akhmatova wrote about Stalin for *Ogonyok* was completely different. She brought the work to the Tomashevskys, with whom she had a friendly relationship, and asked if it could be sent to Moscow. Irina Nikolaevna told me that Boris Victorovich [Tomashevsky] did not respond but sat silently at his typewriter and retyped the poem so it could be sent to Moscow. And, without asking Anna Andreyevna, he permitted himself to correct what he considered the more flagrant errors in language and poetic style.

When poets say what they do not think, it is not they who are speaking.

On Symbols:

The Akhmatova People's Museum* is a part of the Zhdanov Factory's vocational school. This farce has been noted more than once. It is an ideal example of an inappropriate program being inserted into a well-preserved mechanism.

Emma Gershtein
THE THIRTIES

Emma Gershtein, one of the best Soviet literary critics, a student of nineteenth-century Russian poetry and a writer of reminiscences on Mandelshtam and Akhmatova. After Akhmatova's death, Gershtein prepared and published the poet's manuscript on Pushkin.

I first met Anna Andreyevna Akhmatova in January or February of 1935 at the home of the Mandelshtams. In honor of her arrival, Osip Emilyevich

* Opened in 1986 in space made available in a factory.—ed.

had prepared a lengthy welcome speech that contained such phrases as: "If you feel dizzy lean on the ruling class," and "You will talk, and we will listen, listen and understand, listen and understand. . . ."

In Moscow, Anna Andreyevna recalled how she said good-bye to Nikolai Nikolaevich [Punin] in Leningrad. He was standing on the platform in front of the train car window. But the window was covered with frost, so he tapped against the glass. She answered him, and they continued to tap to each other until the train began to move.

She brought with her to Moscow Punin's bright red pajamas, which accentuated her height and linear figure. Her Matisse coloring, Renoir bangs, and black hair made her look Japanese, except for the diminutiveness of Japanese women. But my life was so humdrum, and Akhmatova's image was so extraordinary, that it evoked vague and often false associations.

Her face was tired, no longer young; her complexion sallow. Her delicate mouth and aquiline nose were lovely, but her smile did not flatter her.

Nadia introduced me to Akhmatova, who was stretched out on an ottoman wearing her red trousers. She made a face, adopting an arrogant and affected manner. I was offended; after all, I wasn't like those who, according to Nadia, she derided by saying: "They are trying to turn me into a monument." For a long time I was uncomfortable in her presence.

Later I often noticed that when she was with women Anna Andreyevna was given to posturing. She would look aloof, speak in clipped phrases, and oppress those around her with her profound silences. But when I saw her in the company of men, especially if they were illustrious men, I was always astonished by her unpretentious, intelligent, and sad expression. With men she was able to joke freely and in a friendly way.

I gradually grew accustomed to her and even began to accompany her on visits to her Moscow friends. The conversations we had as we walked down the streets were unrestrained and interesting. On one such trip I asked her what the friend she was going to visit was suffering from. "Madness and heart sickness," she replied immediately, "like most of our friends."

Once I went with her to visit Chulkov in a one-story house on Smolensky Boulevard. It was an old-style Moscow writer's apartment crammed into one room: bookshelves and tables against the walls, a dining table in front of a couch backed against windows, a bed in the far corner away from the windows, an upholstered chair at the corner of a desk standing against bookshelves, a thick column of dust visible in the sunlight. Several years later after Chulkov died, Anna Andreyevna continued to visit his widow, Nadezhda Grigoryevna Chulkova, whose name was included in the list of friends she regularly called when she came to Moscow.

Once it seemed to me that Anna Andreyevna had been in Moscow several days without calling me. When I met her I asked her about it. "Really?" she asked in sincere surprise. When I met Punin in Leningrad, he stared at me from across the table and raised his glass: "Let's drink to your silence. I thought you were Madam Recamier." Such moments revealed a great deal to me about the closeness of their guarded approach to anyone new to them.

Anna Andreyevna played a significant role in the lives of her friends. On one of her trips to Moscow she told this story: "I called N. N. He said, 'You have come in time.' His voice was so gloomy one would have thought that he had picked up the phone with one hand while holding a loaded pistol to his temple with the other."

I know through my own experience of Anna Andreyevna's ability to arrive in time. There were times when I thought: no, I can't stand it anymore; my life is over. Then a voice over the phone would say: "It's Akhmatova." It was the voice of salvation.

Sometimes Anna Andreyevna would stay with her friend Vera Fyodorovna Rumyantseva, a bibliographer who worked her entire life in the Tretyakov Gallery. After she died in 1970, some of Akhmatova's autographs were found among her papers, including a photo with the valuable inscription: ". . . in memory of simple and friendly relationships . . ." This unpretentious woman lived in a communal apartment on Bolshaya Yakimanka Street. If Anna Andreyevna stayed long in Moscow she tried to find other accommodations; she was embarrassed to have Vera Fyodorovna give up her own bed and sleep on the floor.

Back in the 1930s I visited Anna Andreyevna at N. I. Khardzhiev's apartment in Marina Roshcha; at the empty (in summer) apartment of the Oleshas* in Kamergersky Lane; at S. A. Tolstaya-Yesenina's home in one of the Ostozhensky lanes; at the Osmerkins on Kirov Street; at the

---

* Of the writer Yuri Olesh (1899–1960).—ed.

Mandelshtams (even when Osip Emilyevich was in Voronezh, Nadia's mother stayed there); and, rarely by that time, at the Ardovs.* Once in the last days of September 1941 I met Akhmatova, who had been evacuated from besieged Leningrad, at the home of S. Ya. Marshak. Anna Andreyevna also sometimes stayed with the Shervinskys in the city but mostly at the dacha in Starki.

For twenty years Anna Andreyevna traveled with the same suitcase that, not having a lock, was tied with a strap.

In both winter and spring Akhmatova wore the same shapeless hat, a felt cap of undetermined color. In winter she wore a fur coat given her by the dying V. V. Shchegoleva back in 1931; in spring, a blue raincoat with a frayed collar. Osmerkin once told me, "You are mistaken; she is very elegant. Her height, her carriage, and then those tattered clothes—you can't help but notice her. People on the streets turn to look." Speaking about the 1910s, Anna Andreyevna said in a joking manner: "That was when I had my hats made."

On that same visit to Moscow when she was staying at the Mandelshtams, S. M. Bondi came to take her to a meeting of the Pushkin commission. Anna Andreyevna's research article "Pushkin's Last Fairy Tale" had already been published in *Zvezda*. Bondi treated her personally with great respect but even so there was with just the slightest hint of condescension: she might be Akhmatova, but the Pushkin scholars weren't exactly born yesterday.

I once told Anna Andreyevna that I intended to suggest an article to a magazine, though at that time I had no experience as a writer. "Write it before you suggest it," she told me in a concerned voice. "You have no idea how difficult it is to write articles. Poems are easy, but articles are so hard!"

Akhmatova's research article on Pushkin's *Golden Cockerel* was written with the assistance of N. I. Khardzhiev. "I was ill," Anna Andreyevna liked to recall, "and Nikolai Ivanovich sat facing me and asked: 'What do you want to say?' and then wrote it down for me himself." It was a matter of urgency because Khardzhiev and his friend Tsezar Volpe, who worked at *Zvezda*, could arrange for Akhmatova's article to be published

* Family of Akhmatova's close friend Nina Olshevskaya-Ardova.—ed.

there. It was included in the first issue printed in 1933. Earlier the same magazine had printed Zabolotsky's "The Triumph of Agriculture" and Mandelshtam's "Journey to Armenia."

When I was in Leningrad in the summer of 1934 Anna Andreyevna often went to the public library's manuscript department to study Pushkin. She said it was as easy for her to work there as it was in Pushkin House, because either L. B. Modzalevsky or B. V. Tomashevsky was eager to help her decipher Pushkin's illegible text. S. Ya. Hessen and D. P. Yakubovich politely showed her the necessary sources. Yu. G. Oksman, editor of *Vremennik Pushinskoi Komissii*, published Akhmatova's new article on Benjamin Constan's *Adolphe* in the first issue (1936).

But Akhmatova did not even receive an invitation to the Pushkin commemoration ceremony. She would have spent the day, 10 February, 1937, in complete solitude had not Vera Nikolayevna Anikieva come to help cheer her up.

The art critic Vera Nikolayevna was a constant guest at the Punin and Akhmatova apartment on Fontanka. Lydia Ginzburg was a frequent visitor as well. Like Khardzhiev, she was a friend to both Nikolai Nikolayevich and Anna Andreyevna. Punin was a marvelous man who was incredibly gregarious at home (a "crazy house manager," as Khardzhiev called him). His speech was rapid and his movements were sharp and quick (traits both his daughter and granddaughter inherited). Apparently his lectures on the history of art were extremely entertaining. Even now his former students recall the lectures with admiration. Anna Andreyevna's knowledge of languages helped him prepare them. She would translate large sections of literary works for him, works that she liked to read.

As for herself, Akhmatova's creative propensity was drawn more to painting and the fine arts in general than to music. In her youth she was acquainted with many artists, and in the 1930s became friends with A. A. Osmerkin, who taught at the Academy of Arts in Leningrad and at the Surikov Institute in Moscow. Though he was a Muscovite, Osmerkin lived in both cities and had studios in each. (And since his wife, at the time Yelena Konstantinovna, had been my friend since childhood, I always heard the latest news about Akhmatova whenever Osmerkin returned to Moscow.)

Anna Andreyevna had a close friendship with Boris Victorovich Tomashevsky and his wife Irina Nikolayevna Medvedeva, and with the philosopher Boris Mikhailovich Engelgardt and his wife Lydia Mikhailovna Andreyevskaya—"Russia's best people," as Akhmatova's son, Lev, called them. She also maintained a longstanding friendship with Grigory Alexandrovich Gukovsky and his first wife Rykova (this was before I knew Akhmatova). Once, after the war, Anna Andreyevna mentioned Tomashevsky's warm relationship with his children, grand-children, and even his dog. I remarked that this was unexpectedly touch-ing since Tomashevsky was notorious for his sharpness and austerity. Yet he was so understanding with his family. "Shades of tenderness!" Anna Andreyevna commented.

In the 1930s everything was done to erase completely Akhmatova's literary fame and those years when her very appearance served as the model for elegant women in the world of the arts. At the lightest allusion to Akhmatova's stature, Nikolai Nikolayevich would make a blunt statement such as: "Anichka, go clean the herring." (Nadezhda Mandelshtam loved to tell this story.) Anna Andreyevna related, with sadness, one such episode. In 1936 or 1937 she invited Lydia Ginzburg and B. Ya. Bukhshtab to listen to her new poems. After they had arrived and Akhmatova had begun to recite, Nikolai Nikolayevich burst into the room and shouted: "Anna Andreyevna, you are a poet of local Tsarskoye Selo fame."

While Punin was surely only play-acting (it must be assumed that he understood Akhmatova's importance), his wife and adolescent daughter were quite sincere in their disdain for Akhmatova's literary name.

When Gumilev's "Blue Star"* arrived from America, she telephoned Akhmatova but did not find her at home. She asked that Anna Andreyevna be told she would like to meet her. Not one of the Punins said a word about this to Akhmatova, so she never met the woman who inspired Gumilev's great love. Anna Andreyevna was almost in tears when she told me about this.

Anna Andreyevna had no liking for the poets recognized by the Soviet authorities. Pasternak was an exception, but their relations were then distant. Still, in 1935 I had occasion to learn just how much affection he had for her. . . .

---

* Yelena Dyubushe. See "Blue Star" in the appendix.—ed.

The former acmeists M. Zenkevich and V. Narbut came to the Mandelshtams to visit Akhmatova. Narbut would not tolerate her passivity: "What are you doing lying around all day long? Why don't you get up and go outside?"

In February 1934 Eduard Bagritsky died. Narbut and Khardzhiev came to the Mandelshtams straight from the funeral. They described the ceremony and what they didn't like about it. Akhmatova's son, Lev, said: "Mama, when you die I won't bury you that way."

I was surprised to read in Akhmatova's reminiscences of Mandelshtam that "shady characters" began to gather in their apartment on Nashchokinsky Lane. What people? When? Could she have stayed there for weeks at a time and allowed Lev to live there for almost half a year if the house was unreliable? Anna Andreyevna wrote this in the late 1950s, at the time of the appearance of Nadia Mandelshtam's memoirs. Nadia states pointedly: "Many people would come in the evening; half of them were specially sent."

When Osip Emilyevich was arrested in 1934 we were so naive as to be surprised by the outlandish tales about his lifestyle that immediately began to circulate. Though it was a tragic time, waiting for the outcome of the investigation, Nadia sarcastically related what Aduyev said: "They got together. . . ." And this information spread throughout the writers' house: "They got together!" Nadia wanted to know: who "got together?" Boris Sergeyevich [Boris Kuzin]? Emma? Or perhaps Nina Nikolaevna [Nina Grin], who came to Moscow to present to the Museum the archives of her late husband, the writer Alexandr Grin? Or maybe it was Zhenya [Yevgeny Khazin], Nadia's brother? Or Shura [Aleksandr Mandelshtam], Osip's brother? Could it have been Sergei Antonovich Klychkov, with whom Osip developed a close friendship in those last years?

Those writers who were too successful, including Ardov, were looked upon with certain suspicion in our small circle. Although Nina Antonovna Ardova collected money within a few hours the day Mandelshtam was deported to Cherdyn and gave it to Akhmatova to give to Nadia, Nadia still felt no affection for Anna. Once, when Nadia had come to Moscow from Voronezh and Anna Andreyevna left her to go directly to the Pilnyaks', Nadia called out after her: "Looking for *dolce vita?*"

It's said that Boris Andreyevich Pilnyak was in love with Akhmatova and made her an official proposal of marriage. Anna Andreyevna never contradicted this. But in the 1930s Pilnyak was married to Kira Andronikova, with whom Anna Andreyevna developed a close friendship. In 1936 Anna Andreyevna and Pilnyak made an exciting trip in an open car from Leningrad to Moscow. She boasted to her acquaintances that the only thing bad that happened was that she caught a slight cold. But she later told me of an unpleasant episode on the road. Somewhere near Tver they had a slight accident and had to stop to repair the car. Workers on a collective farm came running up. Both the car and Pilnyak's suit gave him away as a Soviet bigwig. This immediately evoked their wrath. One woman turned her fury on Akhmatova: "She's a noblewoman," she yelled in a threatening voice. "Don't you see that she is? I recognized it at once."

Pilnyak lived in a secluded estate on Pravda Street. One day Anna Andreyevna asked me to accompany her to his home. We traveled down the most civilized route in Moscow—the trolleybus line along Tverskaya Street and Leningradskoye Highway. As we approached our stop, I leaned against the doors, intending to open them. "Don't!" Anna Andreyevna called out in fright, "They will open by themselves!" "You'd think they were charged with electricity," laughed a worker who was lunging across a seat. He looked at Akhmatova's tall, thin figure and her bangs and thought to himself: "She's one of them." I could read this in his desultory gaze.

We stepped down from the trolley and walked in the semi-darkness of the winter evening. We spoke about the Mandelshtams and Lev, and about the young woman Lev loved. "What is she? Some kind of a siren?" Anna Andreyevna asked peevishly. She was one of those mothers who was jealous of the women in the lives of their sons. I began to describe how I pictured Lev's life with the Mandelshtams. Osip Emilyevich and Nadezhda Yakovlevna were like his uncle and aunt. He came to stay with them in the capital. His "uncle" called him "my dear boy," and his "aunt" fed him, sent him after kerosene, entertained him with scholarly discussions, and introduced him to pretty women. He felt himself to be the center of attention; his hour had come. Osip Emilyevich would tell him, "You're on your way." Then, suddenly, "uncle" turns out to be in love with the same "siren,"* and "aunt" is jealous. No doubt the twenty-year-old and still immature Lev thought to himself: "How can old people be so passionate?" The whole affair was just an extra bother to him. Anna Andreyevna laughed, as if in agreement with me. But this was the way I felt even before Lev came to me from the Mandelshtams and said with a tired sigh: "It's all too risqué."

We walked a few more steps in the lightly falling snow. Then, apropos of nothing, Anna Andreyevna asked me: "Do you remember Ryleyev's poem?" In fact, I did not recall the lines of the Decembrist poet. Akhmatova recited:

> Where's the isle amid the sea
> Where you can feel carefree,
> > Guys?

And then she said, "Well, someone added to these lines:

> Where Yagoda, the brute,
> Wouldn't send his cronies shot
> > People
> Where Alexei Tolstoy
> Wouldn't grab such creamy spoils
> > Often . . ."**

I first reminded Anna Andreyevna of these verses in the 1960s and recited them. She calmly corrected my mistakes and added: "There were many such couplets." This was how I knew that I had been right in guessing that the "someone" was Akhmatova herself. But I never heard the other verses.

Anna Andreyevna was on friendly terms with Tolstoy after the publication of *From Six Books* (1940). She told me about her important conversation with him. He told her that neither the First World War nor the Civil War bled the Russian people as much as the cults of Yezhov and Beria.† But here we are speaking of the frightening time when Anna Andreyevna's life radically changed. Suffice it to recall *Requiem. . . .*

1970, Moscow

* See Mariya Petrovykh in the appendix.—ed.
** Tr. by Yana Glukhoded.
† NKVD chiefs Nikolai Yezhov and Lavrenty Beria, who directed the mass arrests of the 1930s. —ed.

Emma Gershtein and Nina Olshevskaya-Ardova
CONVERSATIONS

Nina Olshevskaya-Ardova, actress and wife of the writer Viktor Ardov (1900–1976). Akhmatova stayed in their apartment when she traveled to Moscow from the 1940s until the 1960s.

It has long been observed that when misfortune disrupts the normal flow of life it often brings together the most disparate people. A great shock is often followed by a new direction in life. For Anna Andreyevna Akhmatova, her two trips to Moscow in 1934 signaled such events. She and her son, Lev Gumilev, lived with the Mandelshtams in their new apartment in the writers' house on Nashchokinsky Lane. Her first stay was rather lengthy (at least a month), the second was short (we know of it from Akhmatova's reminiscences about Mandelshtam and from Nadia Mandelshtam's memoirs). Anna Andreyevna arrived on the morning of May 13, but spent only one day with Osip Mandelshtam. Sometime after midnight, "guests" arrived with a warrant for his arrest. After they took him away, they searched the apartment until morning.

Anna Andreyevna stayed with Nadia Mandelshtam until she accompanied Osip to Cherdyn, where he was sent in accordance with the sentence passed down by the OGPU.* That same evening, from another train station, Anna Andreyevna left for Leningrad.

The friends that Akhmatova made in Moscow that year would remain close to her for the rest of her life. One of the closest of the new friends was Nina Antonovna Olshevskaya, a dramatic actress and the wife of the writer and satirist Victor Yefimovich Ardov. It was to Nina Antonovna that Akhmatova, four days before she died, inscribed the following on *The Race of Time*: "To my Nina, who knows everything about me, with love, Akhmatova, 1 March 1966." Earlier she had written in her book *Poetry:* "To my fair Nina from her Akhmatova. Presented at Ordynka on 13 July 1961."

"Ordynka" is a place mentioned in almost all the Moscow recollections of Akhmatova. But before they moved to Bolshaya Ordynka (house

---

* Secret police. Foreruner to the NKVD and KGB.—ed.

17, apartment 13), the Ardovs lived on the first floor of the same writers' house on Nashchokinsky Lane where the Mandelshtams were living on the fifth floor. Nina Antonovna recalls:

"When I saw her walking up the stairs to visit the Mandelshtams, I was awestruck. I already knew the Mandelshtams, and one day Victor and I went upstairs and met Anna Andreyevna. . . . It was such an occasion in my life! Something I couldn't even imagine. . . . How lucky I was!"

The Mandelshtams kept their apartment, even after Osip's arrest, and Akhmatova sometimes stayed there when she came down from Leningrad. She was welcomed either by Nadia's mother or by Nadia herself, who sometimes came from Voronezh, to which Osip had been deported. In this way their friendship (which began back in the 1920s in Tsarskoye Selo but had waned somewhat after the Mandelshtams left Leningrad) grew even stronger. (My acquaintance with Anna Andreyevna and her son, Lev, also started here, with the Mandelshtams, in 1934.)

During this period, Anna Andreyevna also stayed with the Ardovs. Nina Antonovna recalls:

"At first Victor was so timid that he blurted out one day: 'We have to find out if she has a sense of humor; if we don't—I'll die!'"

Akhmatova, as everyone knows, had a wonderful sense of humor. She was gay in Ardov's company. A man with an artistic temperament and volatile reactions, Ardov linked his literary activity with the theater, vaude-ville, and circus. He was an amateur caricaturist as well as a man with an excellent knowledge of Russian literature and history. Akhmatova, there-fore, was not bored with him. Both were "night owls" who could sit up until three or four in the morning talking about all kinds of things. But it was several years before Anna Andreyevna developed this comfortable relationship with the Ardovs. Those first few years—when the Ardovs had only a three-leaved mirror and an ottoman in their largest room and Nina Antonovna's son from her first marriage* slept in the smaller room—

---

* To Aleksei Batalov, today a well-known actor and director.—ed.

the relationship was more formal. Though Nina Antonovna was already fond of Anna Akhmatova, she was surprised by her way of life and circle of friends. In Leningrad she was an outsider observing Akhmatova's peculiar lifestyle.

Nina Antonovna and I discussed an interesting occurrence from that trip to Leningrad. She said:

"It was there she told me, 'I think I've written all I can. The poems no longer come to me.'"

"This was probably in 1935," I said. "Soon the poems were coming one right after the other, and they never ceased until her death. She made a notation that it started in 1936. I think it all began with the poem, 'I hid my heart from you.' You know the poem."

"Yes, Punin was very cross with her about it."

"Did you ever see how Anna Andreyevna composed a poem?"

"Never. She only said, 'My head is swimming, swimming. . . .' Nothing more. Then a couple of days later she'd beckon you with her finger to read her new poem. I was always in awe and couldn't say anything. I think she read her poems to herself and corrected herself. She read slowly, listening to her voice and swaying from side to side. And her face looked like it does in this picture."

We looked at the picture that had been taken in Akhmatova's Leningrad apartment on Krasnaya Konnitsa in the 1950s. Anna Andreyevna is sitting in an armchair next to a chest of drawers. A mirror in a silver–plated frame, candles, and vases with flowers are on top of the chest. Her face is austere.

In the 1930s Akhmatova lived with other Moscow friends in addition to the Ardovs. Most of her trips from Leningrad were to try to help her son, who was being persecuted before he was even arrested. There is no need to mention her unhappiness, as it was described in *Requiem.* By this time Nina Antonovna had two more sons, and her mother had been arrested. This tragedy overshadowed everything else. Then the war separated Akhmatova from the Ardovs for a lengthy period. Anna Andreyevna, as we know, was evacuated to Tashkent in October while Nina Antonovna and her three children had been moved even earlier to Kazan and then to Chistopol. Ardov was called up and worked for the papers at the front. Anna Andreyevna and Nina Antonovna did not see each other until the spring of 1944. This meeting marked the beginning of their especially close relationship. Nina returned to Moscow in mid-May. She soon gave birth to another child, who died as an infant. On 31 May she wrote her husband Victor Ardov:

"I've just returned from seeing Anna Andreyevna off at the station. This has made me very sad—she has been a great distraction and a source of joy just like in her poem: 'I know, you are my reward for years of suffering and pain. . . .' It was very interesting, enjoyable, and, most important, intellectually stimulating to be with her. I've missed this living these past few years in solitude and wilderness. I'm going to be very sad now that our nighttime vigils, to which I had become so accustomed, are over. I'm writing you on the paper that she used yesterday to write a note."

The note was:

"Dear Victor Yefimovich, tomorrow I'm returning to Leningrad. I'm sorry to leave Nina Antonovna—we have spent a wonderful two weeks together. All is well with your family. The children are nice. Write me. Akhm."

Akhmatova described this return to Leningrad in a quatrain published for the first time only recently:

If I had only known
What I had in store
Where I was rushing headlong
I'd have buried myself before.[*]

The event that evoked these lines marked one of the most dramatic pages in Akhmatova's biography.

Anna Andreyevna was anxious to leave Tashkent to see her friend Vladimir Georgievich Garshin, who remained in besieged Leningrad. He suffered as much from their separation as Anna Andreyevna. After losing his wife during the time of the blockade, he asked Akhmatova to make a final commitment to him. In their correspondence it had been decided that he would obtain an apartment, and he had asked Anna Andreyevna to move in with him. She agreed. It even went so far that he sent her a

[*] Tr. by Yana Glukhoded.

telegram asking her to take his name. Anna Andreyevna accepted this proposal as well. This was why she spread the news in Moscow that she was getting married. But on her arrival at the Leningrad train station, Garshin suddenly turned to her and asked: "Where shall I take you?" It was a cruel practical joke. Where could Anna Andreyevna go? To her empty and deserted house at Fontanka? By herself? Her son, though he had already been released from the prison camp, was working in Turukhansk.

She was compelled to seek refuge with friends. For at least six months she lived with Lydia Yakovlevna Rybakova. For a long time her friends in Moscow knew nothing about what had happened. This was why Nina Antonovna was puzzled to receive this telegram on 14 July (i.e., six weeks after Anna Andreyevna left Moscow): "Inform me of your health. All my love. I live alone. Thanks for everything. Akhmatova."

Nina Antonovna relates:

"The sentence, 'I live alone' roused my concern, but I still couldn't guess what had happened. I was uncertain for another three weeks, until 6 August, when I received another telegram: 'Garshin seriously mentally ill. Left me. You are the only one I have told. Anna.' Afterwards I received a postcard written three days later, on 9 August:

'My dear, thank you for your touching letter. It reminded me of you and what I was like in May. Did you receive my telegram? Do you know my news? I'm still not living at Fontanka. There is no water, electricity, or gas, and it's uncertain when there will be. I was in Terioki* for two days reading poems to the wounded. All my love to you and your children. Greetings to your mother. I think about her suffering. And tell Nikolai Ivanovich to write me. Yours, Anna.

'I received a nice letter from Ardov.

'I have a cold and am staying in bed. Something is wrong with my heart.'"

"What a reserved postcard," Nina Antonovna remarked. "And what an incredible ability to sympathize and feel the sorrow and woes of others."

This is true. The message written on this postcard reflects the power of the word for Akhmatova. She had acquired anew her dignity as a poet

---

* A military hospital near Leningrad.—ed.

and citizen. She was capable of feeling another's grief—thinking of Nina's mother, who was released from prison camp because of her fatal illness to die in the arms of her daughter. She wanted contact with her friends, asking both Nina and her old friend Nikolai Ivanovich Khardzhiev to write. Only one short sentence reveals the suffering she endured the previous two months. Now it was all over—she was no longer the woman she was in May.

Nina and I discussed the distasteful episode with Garshin.

Nina repeated the same version that I have already related and continued the story:

"But that wasn't all. You no doubt remember that afterwards Garshin came to see her several times, until she forbade it."

"I even know how this came about," I said. "Anna Andreyevna told me it was like this. He came to see her at the Rybakovs and explained the situation. Anna Andreyevna pointed out the awkward position in which he had placed her. 'I didn't think about that,' he said. This infuriated Akhmatova, and she never forgave him for it. Do you know, Nina, that in the 1950s, when he had a stroke, Garshin asked someone to beg Akhmatova's pardon for him. Akhmatova did not answer, but someone said she had forgiven him. Later Anna Andreyevna told me with contempt: 'He began to cry and took to his bed.' After a pause she added: 'And who dared speak in my name?!'"

Nina: "I don't think she loved Garshin. It was merely an attraction between two elderly people."

"Whom do you think she loved most of all?"

"I asked her that one day. After a long pause she said, as if speaking to herself: 'Well, I lived with Punin two years.' That was her answer."

"What did it mean?"

"That she should have left him, but she remained another two years. So, she loved him."

Nina continued: "Punin was very much in love with her. I'm not even speaking about his letter from Samarkand, the one she was so proud of and showed to so many people. But what happened to the note he sent her from prison camp? I saw it myself. Anna Andreyevna showed it to me. It was on a scrap of wrapping paper. He wrote that she was his greatest love. I remember one sentence especially: 'We had the same opinion about everything.'

"Punin had two sides to his character. He could be elegant in a black suit with a tie (sometimes he wore a bow tie). This was his image with his students. One girl student told me she had never heard a more interesting and witty lecturer. At home, when he was in a good mood, he was equally charming and polite to me. But sometimes he would just sit in his robe and slippers playing solitaire, barely acknowledging my presence and not saying a word. Once I said to A. G. Gabrichevsky: 'You know everything about literature and art.' And he replied, 'No, but Punin does!'"

Lydia Korneyevna Chukovskaya describes in her *Notes** how Punin once refused to allow Anna Andreyevna to use the shed for firewood, claiming it was already filled with his firewood. But Lydia Korneyevna did not understand. Nina Antonovna tells the story this way: "I was there. He was just teasing Anna Andreyevna. She listened to him and smiled. The next day all the firewood was chopped and put away. By that time they had already separated, but Punin would often go to her room. He called her 'Anna Andreyevna.'"

Nina Antonovna and I began to discuss Modigliani. Nina recalls:

"Anna Andreyevna always smiled when she spoke of Modigliani, as if the subject brought back fond memories. She told me: 'When I saw him for the first time in Paris I thought at once, "What an interesting Jew." And he said (maybe he was fibbing) that when he saw me he thought, "What an interesting Frenchwoman.'"

"Showing me the drawing by Modigliani that hung in her room when she was still living with Nikolai Nikolayevich, she said: 'Perhaps he will be the most famous artist among them all.' This was evidently during the first years of our friendship, because I had not yet heard the name Modigliani.

"Anna saw a similarity between Tolya Naiman and Modigliani.

"I heard about Sudeikina from Anna Andreyevna even before the war, when she read 'You came from nowhere to Russia.' She spoke about Olga, saying that she was very beautiful, but she never said anything about her intelligence or her ability as an actress. 'I was indifferent to the theater,'

* The reference is to a book by Akhmatova's friend Lydia Chukovskaya entitled *Notes on Anna Akhmatova.*—ed.

she explained to me. She was fascinated by Sudeikina because she was what is now called a 'sex bomb.' 'We were in love with the same man,' she added, but did not mention the name of Artur Lurye. They could never determine which of them he really loved.

"She said nothing about the others; she never spoke to me of Nedobrovo or Anrep.

"I asked her once: 'During the time of acmeism, which poet among your circle do you esteem the most?'

'Gumilev.'

I was surprised: 'Not Mandelshtam?'

She answered with a laugh: 'Well, apparently for me it's a personal matter—to love Gumilev.'

"Another time I asked her, 'Whose poetry had the greatest influence on you?'

'Nekrasov's *Who Lives Well in Russia*,' she said. 'I don't like him now; I don't like his poems about peasants because they don't reflect the truth. But he was a poet.'

"She began to recite *Father Frost—the Red Nose*. 'The second poet is Mayakovsky. He, of course, is my contemporary. His is a new voice, and he's a real poet.' And she began to recite his poems on love. I can't remember now which ones she quoted. Then she told how she was once walking down a street in Leningrad and for some reason thought: 'I'm going to meet Mayakovsky now.' And there he was. He told her he had been thinking: 'I'm going to meet Akhmatova now.' He kissed both her hands and said, 'Don't tell anyone.'"

Nina: "I could never talk to Mayakovsky. I was so afraid of him, I would leave whenever he was present. I met him with Nora Polonskaya. Not long before his death I heard him say, 'I should write love poems. I would really like to do that.'"

Veronika Vitoldovna Polonskaya, whom Mayakovsky acknowledged in his suicide note to be a member of his family, had been a friend of Nina Antonovna since the early days of their life in the Arts Theater. Anna Andreyevna often met her on Ordynka and would frequently speak with Nina Antonovna about her. It was no coincidence that Akhmatova initially dedicated her poem "Mayakovsky in 1913" to "N. A. Olshevskaya," and dated it "1940 March 3–10." Anna Andreyevna intended then to write a separate essay about Polonskaya.

• • •

"Nina, what about Tsvetayeva? Were you home when she came to see Anna Andreyevna?"

"Ardov knew Tsvetayeva from the Writer's Guest House in Golitsyno. He told Anna Andreyevna that Marina Ivanovna wanted to meet her. After a long pause, Akhmatova, in a regal voice, said flatly: 'She may come.'

"Tsvetayeva came in the afternoon. I made the tea and tried to fix myself up a little, putting on a blouse of some sort. Marina Ivanovna walked timidly into the dining room, and she looked tense all the while we were drinking our tea. Soon Anna Andreyevna led her into her room. They were there for a long time—two or three hours. When they came out, they did not look at each other. But I could tell by looking at Anna Andreyevna that she was upset, that Tsvetayeva's misfortune had touched her.

"Ardov saw Tsvetayeva home. Anna Andreyevna did not say a word to me about her guest and what they discussed, not then and not ever."

• • •

When things were going bad for Pasternak—when he had a quarrel with his wife or something of the sort—he would leave for Leningrad and go to stay with Anna Andreyevna. He would place his coat on the floor and go to sleep, and she would not disturb him. I know of this happening three times.

AFTER THE VICTORY

In early June of 1945 I received a postcard from Anna Andreyevna. She congratulated us on the Victory and, as always, touched upon many topics in a small amount of time. One aside was: "I'm living a very isolated life; I see very few people." She suggested that she would see me soon in Moscow: "The Ardovs have asked me to come to their summer cottage." But she didn't come. Apparently she was waiting for her son to be demobilized. Lev had volunteered for the front when he was in Turukhansk and had ended up in Berlin.

On 2 August 1945 Anna Andreyevna wrote to N. A. Olshevskaya: "Dear Nina Antonovna, I am much ashamed for not answering your wonderful telegram and for not having thanked you and Victor Yefimovich for your unceasing kindness and friendly concern for me. Honestly, I do not merit all this.

"I think of you both often and with tenderness. I hope you are well and happy. Love to your little boys. Write me a few words.

"Yours, Akhmatova."

She did not come to Moscow until the spring of 1946. This was the time when her public recitals were not merely successful but triumphant. She brought with her *Poem Without a Hero* and presented a typewritten copy to "Ordynka," inscribed, "To the Ardov home. 27 April 1946. Moscow. Anna Akhmatova." She talked constantly about Lev, who, since his return in autumn to Leningrad, had been living with her. There was something else on her mind—meeting the man* that for so many years had occupied an important place in her thoughts about lyricism, beginning with the *Cinque* cycle. Anna Andreyevna presented this cycle of five poems to Nina Antonovna with the following inscription: 'To N.A.O. in memory of many late-night conversations. A. 27 April 1946. Moscow.'"

"What connection does this cycle of poems have with your late-night conversations?" I asked Nina Antonovna, though the answer was clear.

Nina Antonovna: "It was like this. She gave me her handwritten poems without saying a word. I read them. Later she read them to me, and I was stunned. Then she wrote that inscription. Later she told me: 'I gave you *Cinque*, but there should be something else that I will definitely write about.'

"I told her everything about myself during those late-night hours—about my first marriage, about my family life with Ardov. Anna Andreyevna would listen to all this and say: 'Yes, yes.' And we never spoke of it again. It was incredible, the way she could get into someone's life and understand everything."

"Did you go to her readings when she came to Moscow that time?"

"Yes. When she was giving a reading in the Hall of Columns some people in the audience asked her to read from *Rosary* and *A Flock of White*

---

* British philosopher Isaiah Berlin, who came to Leningrad as a member of Great Britain's diplomatic corps. Akhmatova met him in late 1945.—ed.

Birds, calling out the titles of the most famous poems. She made a negative motion with her hand, frowned, and then gave a sly smile."

"Did you immediately like *Poem Without a Hero?*"

"I was glad that she had brought it. Like all her poems, it moved me
deeply. But I heard it as remnant of the past."

"Did you hear about *Requiem* as a poem?"

"I never heard of that title. I only knew a few individual poems, for
example, 'Happy New Year! New grief for all.' When reading, Anna
Andreyevna would often wave her hand in disgust—she still wasn't
satisfied with it."

Nina goes on: "I was with my boys in Koktebel, and writing Victor
letters and telegrams. I asked about Anna Andreyevna, if she had come to
Moscow or was planning to come. I received a telegram from Victor
saying, 'Fool, read the papers.' And then I read the resolution (on Zoshchenko and Akhmatova and the journals *Zvezda* and *Leningrad*). I immediately prepared to go home, though it was difficult to get tickets for
myself and the children. Once in Moscow, I tried to get to Leningrad (one
still needed a permit to travel there). It was not until several days later that
I managed to see Anna Andreyevna. I stayed with her a few days and then
brought her to Moscow. When we walked down Klimentovsky Lane, the
writers we would meet would cross to the other side of the street.*

"Surkov told me: 'I am so grateful that you brought her to stay with
you.'

"Then Lev returned and they both went back to Leningrad.

"It was not until 18 February 1947 that I received this note from her:
'Dear Nina, it's been so long since I've heard from you. I've missed you.
I was seriously ill in autumn, then I got better and felt like I had never
been sick. Now I am once again not well. I'm studying Pushkin—*Small
Tragedies* and *Belkin's Stories*. All my love and greetings to your nice family.
Yours, Akhmatova.'"

It's remarkable to note that in the first months following the August
resolution that made her an outcast, Akhmatova wrote her best critical

---

* Because of the charges made against her in the Central Committee Resolution "On the Magazines
Zvezda and *Leningrad*."—ed.

article (on Pushkin's *The Stone Guest*). The finished article is dated 20 April 1947. In all probability this was also the time when she wrote the still undiscovered, or perhaps uncompleted, article concerning another of Pushkin's *Small Tragedies*—"Mozart and Salieri." As for *Belkin's Stories*, Akhmatova returned to this work only ten years later, after her article on *The Stone Guest* was published. Immediately after the publication, Anna Andreyevna wanted to add to the work. Specifically, she wanted to include her unique appraisal of Pushkin's psychological creativity in writing *Belkin Stories*. The addendum was published posthumously.

As is well known, Akhmatova was expelled from the Writers' Union in 1946. Consequently, she was deprived of bread- and food-ration cards. An entry in the diary of artist A. V. Lyubimova on 29 November 1947 states that Anna Andreyevna had shown Lyubimova her "permission to receive ration cards."

(Nina Antonovna remarked, upon reading this, "It was arranged here. Fadeyev arranged it.")

Nonetheless, Nina Antonovna continued to send Akhmatova each month a sum of money contributed by her Moscow friends, who, of course, remained anonymous. In Leningrad, Irina Nikolaevna Tomashevskaya-Medvedeva organized the same help.

Anna Andreyevna was living with her son. In the same apartment, Punin's growing family continued to live. His first wife, Anna Yevgenieva, had died in Samarkand during the war, and he now had another wife. His daughter, Irina, had married a second time and was raising her daughter by her first marriage (Anna Kaminskaya). Naturally, the Akhmatova family and the Punin family were two separate units.

Meanwhile, things were looking worse and worse for Lev Gumilev. He was expelled from graduate school and was forced to take a number of unusual jobs. But he never gave up and eventually won the right to defend his dissertation. Afterwards, he attained his degree as a candidate in Historical Science and began to work as a researcher in the Museum of Ethnography. The situation seemed to have improved. But misfortune was to touch Anna Andreyevna once more. In August of 1949 Nikolai Nikolaevich Punin was arrested. Three months later, Lev Gumilev was taken and brought to Moscow.

Akhmatova now did something she had never, under any circumstances, done before: she wrote a cycle of poems entitled *Glory to Peace*, which included a paean to Stalin. She sent the work from Leningrad to Nina Antonovna, who contacted A. A. Fadeyev and then A. A. Surkov, then editor-in-chief of *Ogonyok.*

Nina: "Surkov was very fond of Akhmatova: 'I will print anything she writes,' he once said."

But for years, aside from *Glory to Peace,* published in *Ogonyok* in 1950, we read nothing by Akhmatova in the Soviet press. They did, however, allow her to become a professional translator; i.e., to earn money and suppress her great talent as a poet.

Anna Andreyevna began to travel to Moscow in order to send the allowed sum of money each month to Lefortovo Prison. This was how she made sure her son was still alive. The investigation dragged on, and Lev was finally sentenced to ten years in a special regime prison camp. He did not return until 1956, when he was rehabilitated for "lack of corpus delicti."

After Lev was sent to the camp, Anna Andreyevna's life changed drastically: she began to live in two cities.

After the resolution, while she was still living with her son, Anna Andreyevna was often seriously ill. Lev was selfless in his care for her. Now, despite the attempts of the Ardovs to ease her mind, she languished and suffered. The result was a severe heart attack that put her in the hospital. When she left, she was a semi-invalid requiring constant care. Nina Antonovna took on this responsibility and skillfully and lovingly cared for her sick friend.

Attempts were made to convince Anna Andreyevna to move to Moscow, but she did not want to leave Leningrad under any circumstances. Yet there were difficulties.

After Punin and Gumilev were arrested, the administration of the Arctic Institute began to try to evict Akhmatova and Punin's daughter from the Fontanka house, which was at the disposal of the Institute. This served to bring these two women very close together. The struggle with the Institute lasted a long time, until February 1952, when Anna Andreyevna and Irina Nikolaevna, together with her husband and daughter, moved to a communal apartment on Krasnaya Konnitsa Street.

In this way the solitary Akhmatova gained two families at once. Both had children, which always brings life and happiness into the life of an elderly person. In 1950 Irina had ten-year-old Anya, and Nina had thirteen-year-old Misha and ten-year-old Borya.

So Anna Andreyevna lived in both homes, and soon she was offered a Literary Fund summer cottage in Komarovo. Now there was a third home, where she stayed during the summer months.

I did not discuss this latter period of Akhmatova's life with Nina Antonovna. For one thing, I was now firmly involved and did not need to ask information of Nina; for another, the Ardovs had taken to family squabbling. Anna Andreyevna lost her affection for Victor Yefimovich; he had somehow changed, becoming neurotic and erratic in his behavior toward his family. In the end, Anna Andreyevna lost confidence in him. But she never ceased to love Nina Antonovna. This can be seen in her letters.

The following is a letter from Akhmatova on 6 February 1955:

"My dear, I acquired a lower berth when the train began to pull out. I slept well and arrived in good spirits. Yesterday I received a Korean poem and 'The Fisherman' to translate. They are wonderful, but almost impossible to render into Russian. I still have the 'Moscow symphony' in my head—Lapa [the Ardovs' dog], telephones, radio, 'maz' [an element of play in a card game], etc.

"All is quiet here. Anyutka was happy to see me—both girls love their presents. All my love and thank you and everyone. Yours, Akhmatova."

And here is a letter written in Moscow when Nina Antonovna was on tour somewhere with the theater:

"28 January '57. Dear Nina, yesterday Marina phoned and said she had received your letter. I am jealous; write to me as well. Margarita took five of my poems for Literaturnaya Moskva (No. 3). We'll see what happens. Everything is pretty much the same. I will probably leave for Leningrad on 15 February to turn in my work. My book continues to perplex me. I have made a friend of Misha Ardov. Natalya Ilyinichna Ignatova died. I am waiting for a letter from you and send you my love. Yours, Akhmatova, Moscow."

This letter reflects the tumultuous time that was later called the "thaw." Margarita Iosifovna Aliger had taken Akhmatova's poems for the third issue of Literaturnaya Moskva, which in the end was not published. Concerning her new book of poems, plans and promises were made and then broken. As we see, she intended to spend her name day, 16 February, with the Punins in Leningrad. Akhmatova's new friend, Natalya Ignatova, had died prematurely (Anna Andreyevna developed close ties with Natalya and with her sister Tatiana Konshina in Bolshyevo in 1952).

The following is an excerpt from a 4 July letter (the year is unknown):

"Dear, it is very lonely and boring in Moscow without you. You no doubt know all the news about home from Victor Yefimovich. Misha is quite grown up and is very kind and cheerful. We are friends. I have no news. Don't be bored. Call and don't forget me. Yours, Akhmatova."

Among Akhmatova's many new acquaintances and readers in the early 1960s was a group of young poets that included Joseph Brodsky and Anatoly Naiman (to whom Akhmatova offered a job as her secretary).

Akhmatova's growing world fame and popularity was reflected in the literary prize she was awarded in Italy. She was to have received it in the city of Taormin in 1964, and Nina Antonovna was to have accompanied her. But, while working that summer in the Minsk Theater, Nina Antonovna became seriously ill, and Irina Punina took her place as Akhmatova's companion. On 13 October 1964 Anna Andreyevna wrote from Komarovo to Nina Antonovna in the hospital:

"Nina, I probably don't need to tell you that I am always with you. I can well imagine the four-bed ward, the doctor's calls, the taking of temperature, etc. The only thing that seems strange is that it is you there and not me.

"After my second heart attack, when I was staying in your small room, my only joy was hearing your dry smoker's cough in the morning. You suffered so many sleepless nights on my behalf! And then you fainted right on New Year's Eve. . . . I wrote several poems, then, and it seems that two will survive.

"I'm sending you a photograph of myself reading *The Heiress* while Tolya listens.

"I'm sure that one way or another I will be writing you this winter— if Anatoly Genrikhovich will be so kind as to continue typing the letters.

"My best regards to the one who is with you now.

"All my love. Yours, Anna."

Some time later Nina Antonovna was brought from Minsk to Moscow's privileged hospital. She received the following telegram:

"Belatedly, but from the bottom of our hearts, we congratulate our dearest Nina on her nameday. Akhmatova, Naiman."

A letter written in Leningrad on 5 January 1965 says:

"I will soon be coming to Moscow. . . . I will tell you what happened in Italy when I see you, though it wasn't that interesting. I love you, Nina, and it's hard to live without you. All my love. Yours, Anna."

The next letter:

"You no doubt already know that I have been elected to the Union Board. This was very unexpected for me. Tolya [Naiman] wrote a character portrait of me for *Moscow News*.* I would very much like for you to read it. I think you're the only one who can judge some of it. At any rate, such a portrait has never before been written about me and, no doubt, never will be again. One way or another we will see that you get it.

"On 10 February at the Pushkin recital** I will be reading two poems while Volodya Retsepter will read my short essay "Pushkin and Children." Did you receive our telegram on St. Nina Day? How many times did we spend this day together? All my love."

In autumn 1964, before her trip to Oxford, Anna Andreyevna wrote to Nina Antonovna:

"Nina, I feel just awful that I have not written to you for so long. This was only because my secretary has been gone. Apparently I will need to go to Moscow in November. There, of course, I will learn all the news. But it won't be enough for me. With all my heart, I want to see you.

"Nadezhda Yakovlevna [Mandelshtam] has been visiting these past few days and has told me some of the news from Moscow.

"You will laugh to learn that I received a telegram from Oxford yesterday saying that I'm invited to receive an honorary doctorate of literature. How about that?"

And the last letter, written in the summer of 1965:

". . . Ninochka, in my mind I am always talking to you. We have so much to talk about, don't we? I don't think I've told you enough about London and Paris. Perhaps I will write you about this when I feel like myself again."

---

* It was not published.—ed.

** The program, shown on Moscow television, 9 February 1965, featured a recording of Akhmatova's voice reading the essay as well as her poems about Pushkin.—ed.

That autumn Anna Andreyevna came to Moscow for the last time. She had another heart attack there and remained in Botkin Hospital for four months. After being discharged and in a very weakened state, she went with Nina Antonovna to a sanatorium in Domodedovo. She died there three days later, on 5 March 1966.   1983–84, 1987

Natalia Roskina

GOOD-BYE AGAIN

Natalia Roskina (1928–1989), historian of Russian literature and writer. Roskina met Akhmatova in 1945 and remained her friend. She wrote of this friendship in October and November, 1966, at the request of E. T. Gershtein.

I met Anna Andreyevna in the summer of 1945. I was seventeen at the time, and my age shaped the nature of our acquaintance. I simply phoned her and said I was a student from Moscow who had come to spend my summer vacation in Leningrad. I told her I wrote poetry and would very much like to show her my work.

"Please, come tomorrow at four," she said, and hung up the phone without bothering to ask if I knew her address. At that time she was living in Sheremetyev Palace on Fontanka Street and no doubt assumed this was common knowledge.

I will, of course, never forget the moment when she opened the door and stepped back to let me in. This was the year that she quit wearing her hair in bangs. She combed it back into an ordinary little grey bun at the nape of her neck. She was no longer the thin woman familiar to me from her portraits. Instead I saw a heavy-set, elderly woman dressed in a cheap housecoat and wearing slippers on her bare feet. But I was impressed more than I could have imagined by her bearing and posture (she held a cigarette in her bent hand) and by the beauty and inexpressible nobility of her appearance. (She later told me that sculptors had no desire to sculpt her because she wasn't interesting to them: nature had already done it all.)

The circumstances in which Akhmatova was then living could not be described as impoverished, for poverty implies having a little of something. She had nothing. There was a small, old desk in her room and an iron bed covered with a shabby blanket. The bed was obviously hard and it was obvious that the blanket provided no warmth. I had entered the door eager to offer her my affection. Now I was overcome with melancholy and a sense of impending doom.

Akhmatova asked me to sit in the only chair while she reclined on the bed with her arms crossed behind her head (her favorite pose). "Read your poetry," she said. It seems strange now to recall that I began to read without embarrassment. She nodded her head approvingly. I learned later that she was not capable of hurting anyone's feelings; she would tell me: "If I don't like it I don't say anything, or I say something insipid but kind." At this first meeting she did not keep silent, but several years later, when my poetry really bored her, she would drawl: "Oh, come on, now. . . ." It was then that I stopped writing in rhyme.

Anna Andreyevna asked me kind questions about who was teaching at Moscow University and what teaching methods were used. N. L. Brodsky was the only teacher of mine whose name she knew. Someone rang the doorbell and she sent me to answer it. "Ask who it is and if it's a robber don't open it." I fiddled with the unfamiliar lock and then opened the door for a woman who had come for the garbage. When I returned, Anna Andreyevna asked: "Would you like me to read my new poem for you?" Did she have to ask!?

Few people had then read *Poem Without a Hero,* and I had never even heard about it. Anna Andreyevna read me the old "Tashkent" version, which was later much altered.★ She read from her notebook, and for the first time I saw her unique, slanted, and round handwriting with the lines

★ I have a typewritten copy of the poem with Akhmatova's corrections that she gave me on 20 February 1958. On the cover she wrote: "Final text replacing *all* previous copies. Akhmatova. 13 February 1958. Moscow." In the third part, the author inserted a six-stanza verse to replace the series of dots. There are other changes as well. Much was altered from the Tashkent version and, in my opinion, for the worse. Akhmatova was very receptive to the opinions of her friends. For example, the editor Ignatova might tell her it was impossible to say "Unseeing eyes look at the execution," because, in her opinion, unseeing eyes don't look. Akhmatova would change the words: "Our former, clear eyes." With today's absurd studies in textual accuracy, this is the way the poem will remain. But my copy of the six-stanza verse, a wonderful poetic device, was not totally altered, as it was in the last publication in Akhmatova's lifetime. There were some changes made in the books she gave to me. In the collection *Poetry,* one page was covered and another glued on top of it—a new version of "Music."

ascending upward like a winding plant rising toward the sunlight. Her deep voice resounded loudly in the empty room, like in a church. I was extraordinarily moved by the poem, and still am to this day.

Naturally I asked her if I could copy the poem, but she refused.

"What did you think of it?"

I told her it was unlike anything else she had written and that I felt I had met not only Anna Andreyevna that day but a new and great Russian poet.

It is difficult to flatter someone in person, and I was nervous. I never realized how much she needed to hear precisely these words. For many people she remained the author of verses that she herself liked to chant to the tune of "The Brave Merchant." But at this time and until the day she died, Akhmatova was concentrating all her interest, all aspects of her personal life as a poet, on this work. "Tomashevsky told me he could write a book about my poem." The opinion of Tomashevsky meant a great deal to her. She greatly esteemed the Pushkin scholars and considered it an honor to be counted among them. To her I represented a young woman of the war years, a Soviet student. I was open to everything; I listened to the poetry of my friends in literary clubs. And so my instantaneous reaction to her poem as a work that placed her among a group of major poets was of great importance to her. I learned this all much later. That day I was simply intoxicated with emotion.

Soon, friends we had in common related Akhmatova's opinion of me: "An independent girl, not like those who start crawling as soon as they come in the door." And: "Her poems are unlike those of young literary critics like the early Eikhenbaum." I had forbidden my friends to say anything about me beforehand, and so when she told them: "A girl student from Moscow came to see me yesterday" (at that time this was a rare occurrence for her), they owned that they knew me. "Tell her she can come to see me again," Akhmatova said as they were leaving. So I began to visit her often, two to three times a week during the months of July and August. I would call her on the phone and she would answer briefly: "You may come" (she was always laconic on the phone; I think she hated it). I walked to her unpalatial room in the palace where she lived. (I was living with relatives in a horrible communal apartment blackened with soot from twenty-five years of socialism, cluttered and stinking with the smell of kerosene stoves.) Anna Andreyevna always asked if I had written anything new, and it is only now that I can appreciate her impeccable manners. At that time I thought my work was really interesting to her. Her criticism was always short and to the point. Then she would read me her new poems, always adding: "Don't remember them. I know you have one hell of a memory, but forget them." When she finished a poem you could tell by her voice, and we would walk into the kitchen where she would serve up bowls of boiled potatoes and sauerkraut. I don't ever recall there being anything else. One day a disheveled young woman was in the kitchen. She was rude and treated Akhmatova with undue familiarity.★ "Pig," Anna Andreyevna said quietly. We returned to her room to eat the potatoes and sauerkraut, she reclining on the bed, I sitting with my bowl on my knees. Her life was so incredibly difficult! For hours the phone never rang; weeks would pass without anyone coming to call. . . .

Akhmatova suffered greatly from loneliness. I realized this when I once complained to her of being lonely. I was orphaned at an early age and by the time I was sixteen I was living alone in Moscow in the room that once belonged to my father. "There is solitude and there is loneliness," Akhmatova told me. "We search for solitude but flee from loneliness. It is terrible when no one is connected with your room, when no one breathes there, and no one awaits your return."

In her solitude and loneliness, Akhmatova was unprepared for the outpouring of love and admiration Muscovites demonstrated that famous night in the Hall of Columns in 1946 when she and Pasternak read their poetry. Many people have described that night (for example, Nadia Mandelshtam in *The Second Book* and Ilya Ehrenburg). Of course I was among those who wouldn't stop applauding and demanding she go on reading. I even sent her a little note. She easily caught my eye, smiled, and shook her head.

Akhmatova was wearing a black dress with a white tasseled shawl thrown around her shoulders. She had great stage presence, but she was noticeably tense and nervous. Finally, she had to stand and address the audience: "I don't know my poems by heart and I have no more with me." The audience knew this was what she felt compelled to say. The

---

★ Irina Nikilayevna Punina, the daughter of Akhmatova's former husband. At the time I thought she shared Akhmatova's communal apartment.

ovation continued. Akhmatova, perceptive and by no means politically naive, suddenly realized that the ovation did not bode well. This evening would soon turn out to be a fateful one for her.

Akhmatova's life became more interesting, for a short time, when her son, Lev Nikolayevich Gumilev, returned from Berlin after the war. One day she opened the door wearing an expensive Japanese robe with a dragon. "My son brought it to me from Germany."

She always enjoyed such simple, feminine pleasures. She was very happy that day, but on the whole mother and son did not live together peacefully. One sensed a crack in their deep and mutual love. Lev would tell his mother with biting scorn: "You know nothing about this." Or, "Of course, they didn't have this in school in your day." Once he was questioning me about Moscow University and asked me something about linguistics. When I couldn't answer, he scowled and said: "What do they teach you, then?" "Stop it," Anna Andreyevna said. "Don't hurt the girl's feelings."

But she could never take up for herself.

I was upset and complained about Lev to my relatives. "She is Anna Akhmatova to you," they told me, "but she is his mother. That's something altogether different." But in fact it represented the terrible drama of her tragic motherhood and her son's alienation. I had only a glimpse of this drama.

Sometimes Anna Andreyevna would suggest going for a walk. She knew everything about Leningrad and its architecture (she said that architecture was her favorite art). She knew the designer and history of each building with the thorough and expert knowledge she applied to everything that interested her. She liked to take different routes to lead me to a pretty spot, so that it would suddenly pop into view. She called my attention to every architectural detail and was moved by my admiration.

Each place we saw together cries out to me now that she is no more, and fills me with sadness. Once she showed me a museum tower: "It's beautiful, isn't it?"

"Yes," I said, and then added: "It's so nice to agree with you."

She gave me a sly grin: "What do you mean? You could have said: 'The tower should be just a tiny bit taller.'"

I vividly recall one of our trips to Engineer Castle. She loved the pretty and well-tended flower beds. Bread was still rationed, along with all other food products, and the war was still being fought against Japan. But the Leningraders who survived the blockade were beautifying their weary city and this delighted Akhmatova. She kept repeating: "What fine people they are!" It was a beautiful, sunny day, and she seemed almost a harmonious part of the architectural landscape. How happy she was, squinting in the sun! She filled up my seventeen-year-old life. It would be ten years before I saw her happy again.

In later years Anna Andreyevna would often talk about how she learned of the Central Committee resolution passed concerning her and Zoshchenko. In repetition the story seemed less and less frightening, though the first time I heard it I broke into a cold sweat. Anna Andreyevna did not subscribe to newspapers and had no radio. She knew nothing of what had happened. Someone called and asked how she was doing. Someone else called to ask the same thing, and then someone else. She had no presentiment of disaster and did not quite comprehend. "I'm fine, thank you. Yes, everything is well," she said to all who called. Then she went outside and, standing on tip-toes, peered over the heads of people in front of her to read the newspaper posted on the wall with Zhdanov's report.

Her life stopped. Ten days later I arrived in Leningrad and called her. She told me she was fine but that she wouldn't be able to see me. Her voice was lifeless.

For the next two months the only information I had about Akhmatova was that she had not been arrested. When I next came to Leningrad I was more insistent and pleaded with her to see me. She agreed to meet me at the Russian Museum. It was November and the weather was bad. Sitting on a cold bench I nervously waited for her. Akhmatova walked up and sat down. She began to tell me I should not try to see her, that all her personal contacts were being watched, that she was under surveillance, that her room was bugged, and that my meeting with her could have dreadful consequences. We were both shivering. Anna Andreyevna looked aside, not at me. But as soon as I realized that she was concerned only for me, I immediately felt better and told her that I would not be bothered with thinking about that. Akhmatova continued to talk about the need to exercise caution, but I understood that she was speaking only out of a sense of duty. In fact, she was very glad to see me. Suddenly she ceased trying to hide this, turned to me, and with tender emotion said: "Darling!" A terrifying circle of doom existed at that time, and inside that circle was this entire beautiful city, our integrity, and truth. I myself was inside the circle, but I forgot this completely, so happy was I to be sitting next to her and to know that she cared for me as well.

I walked Anna Andreyevna home and extracted a promise that she would not try to prevent me from seeing her. But when we came to say good-bye in front of the house on Fontanka Street, her face changed to stone, and she barely nodded to me as she walked in through the front door.

This was no ordinary house. It was the premises of the North Sea Route Agency. A watchman sat at the entrance and asked to see passes. He always had some comment to make to Akhmatova's guests, asking why they stayed so long or something along those lines. Anna Andreyevna had to show him a picture identification card. In the space marked "profession," the word "tenant" was written. Shortly before she died she took the card out of her purse and, with a laugh, showed it to me: "Remember?" But seeing those frightened wide eyes staring at me from the photograph, I couldn't laugh.

Akhmatova's uncomfortable, cold room took on the feel of a prison cell. She rarely spoke when she was home, always pointing toward the ceiling. One day she returned home and found flecks of lime on her pillow and floor. She was convinced a microphone had been installed in the ceiling. Usually we would wander around deserted areas exchanging short remarks. The nightmare of her existence only got worse. In the autumn of 1949 Lev Nikolayevich Gumilev was arrested. Akhmatova never spoke to me of her grief. When I came to Leningrad and, suspecting nothing, asked: "Where's Lev?" she half-moaned, half-shrieked, half-whispered the words: "He's been arrested." I will never forget the sound of her voice.

It was his third arrest. The first had occurred in the early thirties, the second late in the same decade. He had been sentenced to be shot. It was Anna Andreyevna's fate to suffer the same grief over and over. My aunt, my mother's sister, was married to M. I. Grinberg, technical director of the Leningrad metal plant. Since both names, Grinberg and Gumilev, started with the same letter, my aunt often saw Akhmatova in the endless lines described in *Requiem*. Everyone was put into some kind of line by this horrible alphabet. By 1949 there were no more such lines, but everything seemed even more hopeless and final.

After the Central Committee resolution was passed and Akhmatova was expelled from the Writers' Union, she was deprived of her food ration coupons. (At approximately the same time the death penalty was abolished in our country. Why? Because, after all, there were other ways to torture people to death.) It was impossible to live on the meager pension she received, and her friends, with true heroism, organized a secret assistance fund. Anna Andreyevna told me about this much later and sadly commented: "They bought oranges and chocolates for me, as if I were a convalescent. But I was simply hungry."

In the summer of 1950 Anna Andreyevna asked me to bring her to Moscow. She had difficulty traveling and never took trips alone anymore. I now realize that her major reason for going was to try to help her son. She was so nervous about the trip that she wouldn't allow me to leave her for a second. I was unable even to say good-bye to my friends. Neither Anna Andreyevna nor I slept the entire night; we quietly conversed to the noise of our unknown fellow-travelers' snores. The trip from Petersburg to Moscow reminded her of Blok and their chance meeting. I remember what she said, word for word: "Blok was a little strange. Everything he said was a bit queer. Once when I was traveling from Kiev, the train stopped at Podsolnechnaya Station. I walked out to the car platform to smoke. Suddenly I saw Blok on the station platform in front of me. He asked: 'Who are you with?' Somewhat surprised, I answered: 'I'm alone.' And then the train pulled away. The last time I saw him was at that Pushkin evening, you know, the famous one not long before Blok's death. We were all hungry, cold, and wearing whatever we had. Blok came up to me then and asked: 'Where's your Spanish shawl?'"

I also remember talking about Freud that night. I had just read something by him, and Akhmatova commented that the whole notorious Oedipus complex was nothing more than heir envy and bourgeois psychology.

Anna Andreyevna was a remarkable conversationalist, both tolerant and kind. I don't recall her ever causing me to realize my ignorance, though I know now she had plenty of opportunities to do so.

Today I recall that evening with Akhmatova in the dirty, uncomfortable train car as a happy and at the same time terrible gift of fate. The dawn was softly breaking and we were both slightly heady from lack of sleep. An incident shortly before we left had increased Anna Andreyevna's nervousness. It was virtually impossible to get train tickets in those days. But as the daughter of a writer* who had been killed at the battle front, I was able to buy them in my own name from the Literary Fund. It was there I heard that Flit was traveling to Moscow. I knew of him only as a funny parodist and didn't think anything of the news. When we were standing on the station platform I casually mentioned to Akhmatova that Flit would be riding with us in the same compartment. She turned pale and answered curtly: "I will not travel with Flit." It was unthinkable to ask her why, especially considering the look on her face. But what was I to do? We were standing on the platform with our suitcases, a telegram had already been sent to Moscow, and here was Akhmatova, relentless in her resolve. I didn't know what to make of it all. Fortunately, the journalist Yevgeny Vorobyov came to my rescue. He helped me change the tickets and everything turned out all right. Soon I was no longer associating the name of Flit with satire but with odious functions in the literary world.

At the train station in Moscow Anna Andreyevna was met by Nina Olshevskaya, a pretty and friendly woman who was the wife of the writer Victor Ardov. She told me she had known and liked my father and invited me to visit her. "Of course, she will come," Anna Andreyevna answered for me. From then on I visited Akhmatova on Ordynka Street in Moscow. Sometimes she felt like getting out of the house and would come to see me.

Once when I was sitting in her tiny room on Ordynka Street I reminded her that I had dedicated a cycle of poems to her. She said nothing and did not ask me, as she usually did, to read them. A few days later she called and said she wanted to come see me. She came into my room, sat down in a chair, and, in an authoritative, crisp voice, said: "Let's see your poems." I obediently handed her my notebook. She began to read my poems about her, from time to time sadly shaking her head. When she was finished she said: "Bring me an ashtray." I didn't understand because she wasn't smoking. "Is there some kind of ashtray here?" she asked again. I pointed to a large glass ashtray. "We won't be discussing *these* poems," she said and then tore my notebook into four sections. She placed the pieces in the ashtray, took some matches out of her purse, and lit the paper. I watched her in stunned silence. Though I knew what was happening in our society, I was still too young to realize the danger in writing

* Aleksandr Roskin died at Smolensk in 1941.—ed.

such poems. The glass cracked and Anna Andreyevna, shaken by the loud noise, asked: "Was it your father's ashtray?" I nodded. She paused a moment and then said: "I hope you never do such a thing again."

I have completely forgotten those poems. The only thing I remember is that one was about the sufferings and courage of the Virgin. I can't even recall the subjects of the others.

After a short silence Anna Andreyevna said: "There's a beauty shop close by. Why don't we go get a manicure?"

She loved the word "apocalypse" and used it often: "This is apocalyptic." When I recall that gloomy day in 1950, this is the word that comes to mind: apocalypse. Everything was all mixed together—the commonplace and the terrible. Terror became a way of life, and, looking back, it's hard to believe that we actually lived through it.

Anna Andreyevna had remarkably beautiful hands, and she loved to show them off with a manicure or rings. I realized that her smoking was a ritual in itself, so beautiful were the movements of her hands. So we went to have a manicure at the neighborhood manicurist. When we left our building Akhmatova called my attention to a man and woman standing nearby. "Do you think they're tailing us? Did you notice if they're talking?" If they did not talk, she believed they had been sent to follow her. If they did talk, perhaps they were just a couple with no place to go. I don't know whether this was a subtle psychological observance or mere naiveté. We discussed the matter for a long time and with a certain degree of anxiety, but we nonetheless walked to the manicurist. There was, after all, nothing criminal in the poems Akhmatova had burned. They simply expressed my admiration for her courage.

Much later, when times were considerably better, I wrote another poem dedicated to Akhmatova. After listening to it she said: "Hm, not bad." A couple of years passed. One day she pointed to a sheet of paper on a table and said: "I remember that you wrote a poem to me. May I have it, please?" I was nonplussed, for by this time I knew I was not meant to be a poet. But I didn't dare refuse her. This is the poem:

On the Neva

Water speckled with light,
Lions' bared teeth, a true
and great poet nearby,
Seeks solitude.

The sun wanders the sky
Hiding among stones;
Nature welcomes its warmth,
It eludes me alone.

Anna Andreyevna took the sheet of paper from my hand and placed it in a folder. With a touch of irony she showed me the other poems she kept there. All were dedicated to her, and some were by great poets. I noticed the signatures of Blok and Gumilev. Apparently I was blushing furiously because Akhmatova began to laugh. She titled the folder "In One Hundred Mirrors"; it's now in the Leningrad Public Library.

• • •

Akhmatova began to stay in Moscow for months at a time. She stayed to try to help her son and because life was a little easier in Moscow. This was why, in the end, many Leningraders moved to Moscow. And Anna Andreyevna liked living with the Ardovs: they had a servant who cooked and three young boys who eagerly carried out whatever task she gave them. By all appearances she was wanted and loved in their home, but she never for a minute let her purse out of her sight. She kept it with her always, tucking it under her arm when she ate and placing it under her pillow when she slept. She was never at ease, not at any moment, not for any amount of time. And she lived like this for decades!

Later, when she was operated on for appendicitis and her doctor commended her on her stamina, she replied: "I've developed nerves of steel under Soviet power."

A wide diversity of people visited the Ardovs, and it was clear that some of them could not be trusted. Akhmatova was surrounded by uncertainty. As soon as anyone (including Ardov) came into the dining room, she led me away. She never talked except in private, and the conversations she had in her tiny room (there was barely enough room for a bed and a chair) were conducted almost in a whisper.

Anna Andreyevna often called me and asked me to come to see her. I would grab a taxi with the last money I had and race like a maniac to join her: more often than not such a call meant she had news too important to tell me over the telephone. Once she used an endearing word to address me over the phone, something she had not done before, and I understood that a tragedy had struck close to me. I ran to her as quickly as I could, all the while thinking: what is it? Who is it? It turned out that Pasternak had just paid Akhmatova a visit. His wife had recently returned from Leningrad where she had witnessed the arrest of Sergei Spassky. This was a terrible blow to me, but in Akhmatova's presence I held back my tears. After all, I had never seen *her* cry. "You're very pale," she told me, "would you like some coffee?"

That summer I came to Leningrad and, just as before, we spent a lot of time strolling down streets and through gardens and sometimes eating lunch in a cafe. One day we ran into Mikhail Zoshchenko who immediately grabbed her hands and kissed them. It was clear that the meeting affected her deeply as well. After he had walked away she softly spoke his name: "Mishenka . . ." Then she laughed and turned to me: "You know, Natasha, I think I've done everything I could for you. In what other city could you witness Akhmatova and Zoshchenko meet." We continued to talk about him for a long time. Anna Andreyevna greatly admired him as a writer and described *The Blue Book* as a "masterpiece."

Zoshchenko was less nervous now: he had received "high-level" permission to work as a translator. Two years before that meeting he had been the topic of conversation between Akhmatova and myself. A short story he had written had been allowed publication, and this, of course, indicated that the political campaign against him was easing. But the story was not good; everyone took note of this, including me: "It's a bad story!" Anna Andreyevna was very angry. "That's all I hear: Zoshchenko has written a bad story. And will you please tell me why they think he should write them a good story? Are they good people? What have *they* done?" I said nothing but felt thankful to her for the lesson. Anyway, this topic was a painful one for Akhmatova. She, after all, had been forced to send a poem about Stalin to *Ogonyok* when her son was a hostage in a prison camp, but the poem did not help him. I can imagine how she suffered, she who was so proud and confident. She endured much for her son, while her detractors called her a bad mother. But she would never have fought so hard for herself!

She was absolutely fearless and a faithful Christian.

The price is dear
For those who fear.
There is no reason for it. . . .

Luckily, I learned this poem early. All my life it has been one of my favorites.

I felt Anna Andreyevna's wrath another time. In 1953 Em. Kazakevich published his story "The Heart of a Friend," including the phrase: "The young girls . . . liked to read the poetry of Anna Andreyevna Akhmatova." Akhmatova was furious: "How dare he call me Anna Andreyevna! I do not have the honor of being acquainted with that gentlemen! I am Anna Akhmatova and how dare he call me anything else!" Trying to calm her, I clumsily attempted to defend Kazakevich: "He didn't mean it. . . ." But Akhmatova could not tolerate such vague presumption and screamed at me: "So you think someone has the right to act this way? He doesn't! If you don't understand this you will never be a writer!"

I said nothing and she kept silent, too. Then after a long pause she said: "Tell me something about your daughter."

I don't remember what started our argument about Stanislavsky. My father was a theater critic and an admirer of the Moscow Art Theater. Out of respect for my father's memory I considered it my duty to object when Akhmatova began to lambast this theater and its director, accusing Stanislavsky of consciously destroying the art of the theater generally. Anna Andreyevna did not like to be contradicted, but our argument had its humorous side. We were in the house on Ordynka Street in the room of Alyosha Batalov, who later became a well-known actor. His uncle Batalov was a famous actor with the Moscow Art Theater, and Alyosha himself was an ardent admirer of Stanislavsky and his method. A portrait of the director hung in his room, and this allowed Anna Andreyevna to avoid even speaking the odious name. She would merely point to the portrait saying: "This gentleman," "this charlatan." I never did find out why she disliked him so much.

Once when I was working at Literaturnoye Nasledstvo [Literary Legacy], an elderly woman came in with her memoirs of the turn of the century. She had not been personally acquainted with famous people, but she had taken hearsay and written short and interesting stories about them. For example, she quoted Gumilev: "If you want to be a poet exaggerate your emotions tenfold." She also attributed the following words to Gumilev: "For some reason I was thought to be a jealous husband, but I gave Anechka complete freedom. If she was late for a tryst I put her in a carriage and drove her there myself." I thought this a bit flippant but nonetheless poetic and endearing, and a reflection of the times.

I imagined telling Anna Andreyevna about it and how she would smile and say: yes, that really did happen. But when I actually told her the story she did not find it at all endearing or poetic. "What insolence!" she exclaimed. "Gumilev was a real man! He would never have taken his wife to meet her lover!"

This conversation took place in 1957. It was at this time that Akhmatova began to show a growing interest in what was being written and said about her. Where did her sense of humor go? Not too long before she had laughed in telling me about all the affairs she was rumored to have had and how people used to ask such tactless questions: "Is it really all over between you and Pasternak?" But now any such incident roused her lasting anger. The next time I went to see her she was still livid. "Give me the address of that woman," she demanded. "Lev will go and straighten her out." (Her son had recently returned from prison camp, and Anna Andreyevna liked having a man around to defend her honor. She apparently had no desire to question how a son who had spent his child-hood with his Grandmother Gumileva while his parents tried to work out their relationship might defend her.)

I managed to dissuade her from taking action only by convincing her that my career might suffer as a result.

No one likes to be lied about, but Akhmatova began to take offense whenever some new fact about her came to light, even if it were true. Even the truth loses its veracity when it passes through the mouths of strangers, and one can only imagine how tiring it was for Akhmatova to hear her life story as told by outsiders.

Once I told her that she would have made a good Englishwoman, alluding to the fact that England still had family castles and family secrets. She laughed and said, "But I have more terrible secrets than the English."

Still there were times when she threw off her secrecy and spoke frankly about her life. Unfortunately, in her last years she generally spoke to affirm her own conception of her life, the major role in this conception having been played by Gumilev.

I, of course, would never presume to judge who was Akhmatova's greatest love and who played the most important role in her life. I can only share my personal impressions gained from my friendship with her. It always seemed to me that her feelings for Gumilev endured despite all her other tragic loves and marriages. He was the father of her child, after all, and was at her side when she first became famous. "All of Russia was imitating Gumilev," she told me, "but not I." She told me of one argument they had: "We had this spat, like all people. And I told him, 'But I still write better poetry than you.'"

Both as a poet and as a woman, she jealously cherished Gumilev's memory, to the point that she would become incensed whenever she read anything written about him, even praise.

As she grew older, the most insignificant things could evoke her anger. Often she was irritated without any reason. Once I visited her in the hospital after her first heart attack and asked her what I should bring the next time I came. "Borzhom [mineral water]," she said. On my next visit I dragged a heavy bag filled with bottles to her room. "You brought Borzhom? I don't want it. Take it back." But the people who were fond of her did not take offense at this sort of thing. She was capable of overcoming her own bad humor, for she was by nature a kind, tactful, and compassionate woman. One could tell her anything. After her death N. Ya. Berkovsky told me: "I lost my best conversation partner when Anna Andreyevna died. There were things I could tell only her."

In general, though, it was best not to speak to her at length. She understood everything after the first few words. Once when I was telling her something she interrupted me with the words: "Child, I know all about men."

She said about women: "The key to a happy marriage is the total submissiveness of the wife." And, "Orgasm is a function of the intellect."

When I was going through a serious crisis in my life she told me: "I have heard much about this from different people but I haven't said anything. I think in such situations friends should keep quiet." And when the matter was being discussed from the point of view of the other woman, I was told that she said: "I am on Natasha's side." She then asked me a surprisingly direct question: "Do you love him?" I said nothing, for I wasn't sure in my heart if I did. "You don't even know yourself," she said, and this was precisely what someone who knew everything would say.

She was nobility itself, exhibiting sincere interest but no idle curiosity! This was why it was possible to be so open with her about anything. For a long time I could tell no one about the nightmares that tormented me. Finally I told Anna Andreyevna: "I think I'm losing my mind. I'm having hallucinations." She guessed what was wrong and interrupted: "You hear sounds at night? Don't worry, everyone does." And I was immediately cured. Everyone, it seemed, thought they heard the ring of the telephone or doorbell or imagined they were being followed. Including her.

In general Anna Andreyevna had great compassion for the victims of the Stalinist terror. She would not have been able to write *Requiem* had she not. After she learned that my uncle Grigory Roskin and his wife N. G. Klyueva had been judged in a court of honor (held at the Hall of Columns where two years previously Akhmatova and Pasternak had given their triumphant poetry recital) on charges that they had given the Americans their studies on cancer biotherapy, she always asked me to give them her regards, though she was not personally acquainted with them. In 1948 they found themselves in the same situation as Akhmatova—under open surveillance and virtual house arrest, with no idea as to what the future held. I thanked her for her concern, but it was a painful situation for me: it had never occurred to Akhmatova that not only did my uncle and his wife feel no kinship with the other victims of the general system of destruction but, on the contrary, strongly denounced them. They knew they themselves were completely innocent, but as for the others: "The government knows best," "He has only himself to blame after talking such nonsense," and so on.

Akhmatova never backed away from anyone, and this only served to make her stronger. She asked me to convey her regards and an invitation to Vasily Grossman, whom she had never met and whose books didn't interest her, but the author was too proud to accept.

I know of several incidents that reveal how popular "Anna of all Rus" was among the downtrodden and oppressed. After Khrushchev kicked up such a ruckus at the artists' exhibit in the Manezh and it was learned that Serov had goaded him into it, Anna Andreyevna told me the following story (she told it to me in confidence, but now that both she and Serov are dead there is no need for secrecy). Serov used to hire private models before the war. One young man who posed for him treated him as a confidant. When it came time to pay the model, Serov decided to save some money and informed on him. The young man tried to comfort his elderly and lonely mother by writing her brave letters from the prison camp. He wrote and told her to find out Akhmatova's address and to visit her. He did not know Anna Andreyevna personally, and both women surmised he had heard of her from his fellow prisoners. Or perhaps her poems made him think of her as some kind of protector. The young man's mother visited Akhmatova several times before the war, and then all traces of both her and her son disappeared.

Akhmatova also had unexpected admirers in the Kremlin. Once she asked me to show my hospitality to her adopted granddaughter, Anya, who needed a place to stay for a week. Anya stayed with me in my one-room apartment and slept in the kitchen. Every other minute she asked for paper, ink, or an envelope. She was writing her husband, a young artist who had been conscripted and sent to far-off Karelia. A month later Anna Andreyevna told me that Anya had come from Leningrad to Moscow to plead with her: "Akuma! You can do anything! Please get Leonid back for me!"

The young girl knew what she was doing in flattering Akuma (everyone, it seemed, now knew the nickname Shileiko had given Akhmatova). Akhmatova found the idea of omnipotence in the face of total impotence intriguing. She turned to Marshal Konev, who, she had heard, liked poetry and admired her work. The young artist was later transferred to an army unit close to Leningrad so that he could visit his wife on Sundays. (This, of course, took place in the post–Stalin period.)

Anna Andreyevna wrote little in those years. She was given the opportunity to earn money by translating and this saved her from hunger. But she told me more than once that it was pointless to try to translate and compose one's own verse at the same time. Akhmatova was not very industrious. She had been born for art and to engage in discussions about it, which she did for hours at a time. She did not like any other kind of work, including what was customarily considered "women's work." It was impossible to imagine her sewing, embroidering, or cooking. She could prepare a pretty dish of herring, and that was about the extent of her culinary talent. Given the choice, she would never have agreed to translate poetry. But in the thirties she did like to translate prose (Reubens, the letters of Radishchev, and Pushkin's prose from the French). "I love translating prose," she told me, "and I'm good at it." Some time earlier she categorically refused to translate poetry. Professor N. Ya. Berkovsky, who was in charge of a publication of Heine, told me how he had called her before even meeting her and asked her to translate something for the publication. She retorted, "*I* don't translate poetry."

Times changed, though, and the situation was such that no one could refuse work. Anna Andreyevna began to accept poems to translate and to distribute them among writers in need of money. She had to spend an enormous amount of time in co-authoring and editing them, however, and I was unable to conceal my sorrow at this; who knew what she might have done with that time? One day I came to see her and saw the poems of Usenko lying on the table. I slammed the papers down and swore. Anna Andreyevna said in a mild voice: "You shouldn't feel that way. It's nothing. Look, Shengeli translated Byron and everyone gasped: 'Just see what Shengeli had done to Byron!' As if he had broken a statue, as if no one could read Byron in the original any longer. At least no one is saying about me: 'Just see what Akhmatova had done to Usenko!' Isn't that right?"

I don't think Akhmatova could have liked Shengeli's translation of Byron, but she was always very tactful with people who were kind to her, and the Shengelis had shown her their hospitality. She used to live in their apartment in Moscow, and it was no small deed to have Akhmatova as a guest. But there was no real need for her to read Shengeli: she was able to read European literature in the original. She had read Ovid and Horatio in the Latin as a young girl, and knew French, German, and Italian.

She told me that when she was around thirty years old she suddenly thought: "How stupid to live one's life and never read Shakespeare in the original." Shakespeare was her favorite non-Russian writer (Pushkin and Dostoyevsky, her favorite Russian authors). So she began to learn English. Marshak gave her a few lessons to begin with, and then she started to read grammar and self-teaching books as much as eight hours a day. "In six months I was reading Shakespeare without difficulty."*

★ The last time Anna Andreyevna came to visit me, in the winter of 1964, she asked my daughter's teacher, E. S. Turkova: "How long do you think it would take to learn English?" Turkova replied: "About five years." "Five years? I learned it in six months." It should be noted, however, that while she could read book English, she did not know the spoken language. A young Englishman who witnessed the ceremony where she was awarded an honorary doctorate of Oxford told me that she understood perfectly the Latin part of the ceremony but could not follow the English. In her low voice she loudly asked Anya Kaminskaya (Punin's daughter, who had accompanied her to England): "Where do I go?" One further comment: one can just imagine how wonderful she looked in that gown. God created her for grand ceremonies!

She also followed contemporary literature. As a matter of fact, she enjoyed detective novels ("It's wonderful to spend an evening reading a detective novel"), but this was probably the only kind of "bad" literature she read. Most often she read masterpieces; this was where her real interest lay. She read Dante in the Italian, and when Pasternak's translation of *Faust* was published she remarked: "I've always read it in the original. This is the first time I've been able to read a translation." When Pasternak invited her to the premier of *Mary Stuart* at the Moscow Art Theater (I don't recall if she put aside her dislike of the theater for the sake of Pasternak and attended the performance), she remarked: "I could never understand what anyone saw in that woman, that husband-killer. Why has she been so idealized? Remember the beginning, when she refers to her terrible sin and her chambermaid tells her: 'Never mind. You were very young then.'" Akhmatova laughed.

About Kafka's *The Trial* she had this to say: "I felt as if someone had grabbed me by the hand and dragged me into my worst nightmares." She told Andrei Sergeyev: "You mean you haven't read *The Trial*? You must, by all means!"

About Byron's *Don Juan*: "Wonderful! But *Onegin* emerged from it like a butterfly." About *Tom Sawyer*: "A great book, like *Don Quixote*."

Overall she was an incredibly educated woman. She was an excellent student at the gymnasium and, thanks to her remarkable memory, retained everything she learned. "I remember my physics," she said, "but in my time this was only up to the invention of the telephone." She had a great interest in all forms of learning, especially if formulated concisely and effectively. Her comments about politics always reflected her independent views. For example, when the Japanese attacked Pearl Harbor and sunk American ships she commented: "The Americans are simple-hearted children. But the Japanese will turn them into beasts with this beastly deed." She remembered these words and repeated them to me when the Americans dropped the atomic bomb on Japan. We forget now that only a very few perceptive people had misgivings about this; most wanted the end of the war whatever the cost.

In 1945 she talked to me about the growing role of women in the modern world: "Soon men will not be doing anything themselves. They will announce one day, 'War is not a man's business,' and then they will control from a few centers detachments of Amazons."

Anna Andreyevna believed she had the gift of prophesy and was proud of it. She liked to tell the story of how she once overheard a conversation about a talented young girl. Akhmatova, quite young herself, was reclining on a sofa with a book, not taking part in the conversation. When someone said that the young girl had a great future, Akhmatova surprised even herself by remarking: "Yes, if she doesn't die of consumption in Nice at the age of sixteen." Everyone was amazed when the prediction came true.

"Everything that I curse flourishes," she liked to say about her book. "I cursed it and that's the only reason it was published."

She liked to relate a funny story about how she once met a graphologist and, along with everyone else, anonymously gave him a sample of her handwriting to decipher. He described Akhmatova's writing as that of a woman who ran a household and kept household accounts. Another time another graphologist told her: "You have a spark of talent!"

Akhmatova loved short stories with aphoristic content that offended no one. She herself did not like to judge people and rarely spoke badly of anyone, known to her or not. Once I complained to her about a mutual acquaintance who was a sharp-tongued gossiper. She raised her eyebrows and said: "Really? That's what everyone says, but he's an angel with me."

Of course, knowing Anna Andreyevna as long as I did, I occasionally saw her angry with someone and knew some of her dislikes. But there was always something substantial behind them: "N. N. is an awful woman. When they arrested her husband I did everything I could, but when Lev was arrested and I went to Moscow to try to help she said she was too afraid to receive me"; "The N. family is horrible—the daughter hates the mother, the father despises the son, and everyone humiliates the unhappy orphan"; "If you are ever attacked by robbers on a highway and they bring you to their leader, that leader will be N" (here she named a well-known translator); "What is there to be said about N.? He was under Stalin's wing his whole life"; "N. is a church elder, and everyone knows they work two jobs."

She had the ability to simplify the most complicated situations. In 1961 I presented her with a copy of the newly published American edition of *Ethereal Roads*, where some of Mandelshtam's poetry from *Voronezh Notebooks* and *New Poems* had been printed for the first time. The publication had been undertaken by non-professionals, a group of American admirers of Russian poetry. The publisher, R. N. Greenberg, made nothing from the book; on the contrary, his company lost money. It was quickly evident that the poems had been set from a bad copy and were filled with misprints and inaccuracies. The copy had been spirited abroad without the knowledge of the poet's widow and had not been checked against the author's sources. At least it was published, but Nadezhda Mandelshtam took another view of it. She told me she intended to write an open letter to the editor of *Ethereal Roads* and have it printed in *Literaturnaya Gazeta*. I immediately ran to Anna Andreyevna and launched into a lengthy discourse expressing my indignation. She cut me short with a gesture of her hand: "I have already spoken to Nadia. I told her she couldn't belong to two parties at the same time."

Akhmatova kept her positive opinions about people to herself as well. I knew of her friendship with Professor N. Ya. Berkovsky, and when his wonderful collection of articles was published I tried, and failed, to get her to tell me what kind of man he was. Finally I asked her: "What about his wife?" "His wife . . . her name is Yelena Alexandrovna," she replied.

Once when I was criticizing someone she said simply, "I like her very much." Her rule was never to divulge details about anyone close to her.

There were a few exceptions. After Alexei Batalov, still a young man at the height of his fame, returned from Paris after the triumphant showing of his film *Flight of the Cranes,* he decided to travel right away to Sakhalin. He was not in very good health, and his mother, Nina Antonovna, was concerned. She asked Anna Andreyevna to try to dissuade him from going. Akhmatova took Alyosha aside and asked: "Why are you going to such a harsh climate? It's penal servitude." Alexei replied: "I had a wonderful time in Paris and I must atone for it."

Akhmatova was deeply moved by his answer. Her religious belief was a very important aspect of her character, and her courage and patriotism were based on her faith. It was a contemporary faith that encompassed philosophical perceptions and those of the Orthodox Church.

She never hid her religious beliefs but she didn't advertise them and rarely spoke of them. Frida Vigdorova told me a story that perhaps Akhmatova herself originated: when an anti-religious magazine called her and asked for some poems she told them, "That's not my line."

She had the same broad views on ethnic relations. She was a true internationalist and told me she had never been able to distinguish between Jews and Russians. "In my time the intelligentsia was raised like that. Look at Irochka Punina. She had already married Roman Albertovich before she found out he was a Jew." "How could that be?" I asked in surprise, "his surname is Rubinstein." "She didn't know that was a Jewish name. She simply thought some people have names like Ivanov and others had names like Rubinstein. That's just the way it was back then."

Akhmatova had another important character trait: her aristocratic nature. She had extraordinary nobility in her appearance and in her soul, and this imbued everything she did or said with grandeur. Even children noticed this. She told me that once little Lev had said to her: "Mama, stop acting so regal!" Even her closest friends felt uneasy around her for fear of appearing diminished in her presence. She realized this and often suffered because of it.

During her affair with Gumilev (their relationship lasted much longer than their marriage) she went to the Crimea. Gumilev, wanting to see her, followed. He went to their dacha and looked over the fence into the garden. Dressed in white, she was sitting on a bench, reading a book. Gumilev hesitated, decided not to distract her, and returned to Petersburg. She related the story to me not without sadness but also not without pride, for to her mind this demonstrated the true love of a poet.

Anna Andreyevna, of course, had her faults, but they were not destructive. She was strong and explicit, like her poetry.

• • •

I never recorded any of my conversations with Anna Andreyevna, though I recognized their value to others besides myself. She never said anything that wasn't purposeful—gossip, idle chatter, and tattling were foreign to her nature. If she had nothing interesting to say she kept silent. And her comments were so laconic and witty that it would seem they would be all the more easy to put down on paper. Now, when I think back on the way she spoke, I realize I'm using too many words.

She never used contemporary slang or, if she did, it was always ironically, prefacing her remark with the words: "You know what they say these days. . . ."★ Yet neither did she use old-fashioned expressions. And

★One day I commented on something by saying "It's awful!" Anna Andreyevna observed: "Nowadays they say: 'Awful is not the word.'" In general this grande-dame, capable of and with a penchant for lofty discussions, had a keen perception for everything connected with Soviet everyday life. She once remarked: "Do you know what kind of people come to call now? They come in, look at the walls, and say, 'You must have had your bed-bugs exterminated!'"

she was tolerant of how other people spoke. Only once do I recall her lips curling into a slight smile when I mispronounced an old Slavic church term. She was not shocked by swearing, and it seems to me the Ardovs took pleasure in saying whatever came into their heads in her presence. But when she met the elderly Ignatov sisters (daughters of the publisher of *Russkiye Vedomosti* ["The Russian Gazette"] in Bolshevo, she was enchanted listening to their old-style speech, characteristic of the Moscow intelligentsia.

Anna Andreyevna had no desire to have her words recorded. In the dark times she considered this dangerous to others, for she thought her name had the power of a curse. The day that she burned my poems I asked her to autograph her picture for me. "That's impossible," she said. When I insisted, she placed her sign, the initial "A" with a bar through the center, on the back. In the mid-fifties she willingly began to autograph her books and photographs, no longer concerned about her "curse," but she continued to reject anyone she suspected of recording her words. After all, she herself wrote wonderful prose and could have written what she wanted without anyone's help. I also think that superstition played a role. I realized this when I saw Anna Andreyevna shiver and turn pale when someone told her that her autograph was being sold for fifty rubles on the black market.

But the major reason I never recorded our conversations was because of the nature of our relationship. Her demands were not always easy to understand. On the one hand, it was assumed that one knew and loved her poetry; on the other, she disliked having someone hang on her every word, never having the courage to disagree with her. Admiration, after all, can become tiring. Sometimes she grew weary of her own fame and wanted nothing more than ordinary human companionship. Once Antonina Oksman told her: "How beautiful you are!" Anna Andreyevna replied: "That's something I haven't heard." She told me how she had been invited or, to be more precise, had been entreated to spend New Year's Eve somewhere. Afterward, she learned that the actress Olga Zhizneva had said: "Anna Akhmatova was here and didn't even open her mouth." Anna Andreyevna was furious: "What did she expect me to do? Turn somersaults?"

Once she asked me to accompany her somewhere and, knowing I was very busy, apologized by saying: "I could have asked . . . (she named two nice young women) but I didn't want to; they are both so . . . silly."

She frequently chastised me for my sharp tongue, sometimes reproaching me for specific phrases. For example, Anna Andreyevna despised Olga Ivinskaya, Pasternak's great love. She believed the woman was deserving of social opprobrium. When I attempted to defend her, Akhmatova lashed out: "She is a horrible woman. She beat her own mother!" "Really? What for?" I asked. Akhmatova castigated me again and again saying: "Only you could say something like that. Sometimes you are hopeless."

But it did seem that Anna Andreyevna felt comfortable with me in a certain sense. She would read me her translations and say: "Don't think I'm trying to entertain you. I know it's all very boring, but I need your opinion. You have a habit of speaking the truth."*

For all that, in her presence, I never lost the feeling that being with her was something extraordinary; I don't think anyone ever did. But at home, I couldn't imagine myself playing Eckermann to her Goethe.

Now, of course, I regret [not putting her words on paper], and I always knew that I would. Nonetheless, I did manage to write down a few accounts. From 1950 to 1952 I frequently wrote about Akhmatova to our mutual friend in Leningrad.

"Once I told Anna Andreyevna that I bemoaned Pushkin's early death. She replied that everything in history was timely: 'Pushkin would have been out of place in the 1840s. He would have been forgotten, and that would have been terrible.'"

"Anna Andreyevna says that Volkonskaya went to Siberia for the sake of her lover, not her husband. I asked her: 'Is it less heroic to go to Siberia for the sake of a lover than for a husband?' But that, she says, is not the point. [. . .] In general she talks about history like a woman of the world: 'Pushkin was well-bred.' She is feeling sick and lonely. . . ."

"Anna Andreyevna says: 'I don't like Chekhov and I know why. "Story of an Unknown Man" is phony and contrived. Chekhov did not know anything about the Socialist Revolutionaries. You cannot imagine, my child, how ludicrous they were. When Grand Prince Vladimir Alexandrovich

---

* I believe these were someone else's translations that she was supposed to pass off as her own. Perhaps that is why she would ask me to be especially critical.

died they pulled out their hair because they themselves hadn't killed him. And he was just an old debaucher, but they couldn't forgive themselves for letting him die a natural death. And was she the kind of woman for whom someone would sacrifice anything? All she did was run around shops all day and speak nonsense, utter nonsense. And what about Chekhov's understanding of the civil service? He takes high-level Petersburg bureau-crats and describes them as if they were lowly policemen from Tsarevo-Kokshaisk [a provincial town]. They walk around in their bedrooms giggling over their slippers. Who ever heard of such a thing! It's ridiculous. I also read "A Hopper." One shouldn't write such symmetrical stories. Symmetry is to be avoided in all the arts except architecture.'

"'What about poetry?' I asked her.

"'In poetry as well. Asymmetrical things are much more pleasant. That is elementary here.'

"'I thought "The Bride" was overemotional. All this desire to live. To live, live, live! What does this mean? A person shouldn't desire life, that comes in and of itself. Nadya is so cruel; she feels no pity for anyone, nei-ther her mother nor her grandmother. She just wants to live. Petersburg was filled with young girls like that who wanted to live. They went to classes and nothing good came of it.'

"'I think Chekhov was affected by his illness. It shows in "Black Monk" and "The Bride." His consumption played a large role.'

"'And Chekhov did not see much. He was short-sighted in his view of Russia. If one looks too closely all one sees are cockroaches in the cabbage soup. Right now I'm reading Pushkin's material on the history of Peter [the Great]. Russia is such a vast expanse of land! The only water the Russians ever saw was when they washed their faces in a river. But what about the Swedes, the Vikings? Yet the Russians engaged them in battle and defeated them at will. And the remarkable thing is that they defeated them at sea!'

"'How was that possible?'

"'I don't know. But one should know it. Pushkin knew it, but Chekhov didn't. No, no, he didn't. I know you like him, but you have to agree he was very short-sighted . . . wearing a pince-nez. . . .'"

"Yesterday Anna Andreyevna told me about her break-up with Garshin: 'I had a wonderful time in Tashkent. Everyone loved me and took care of me. I received a telegram from him asking me to be his wife. I answered that I would. Then he sent me another telegram asking me to change my name to "Garshina." Strange to think of me changing my name, isn't it? But I agreed to this as well. I made the trip to the hungry and cold city of post-blockade Leningrad. He met me on the train platform and I immediately felt that something was wrong. As we walked away from the station he asked: "Where shall I take you?" I told him I was going to my apartment.* He took me there, said good-bye at the entrance, and kissed my hand. We never saw each other again. What do you say to that? I know very well how relationships are ended, and thank God, I've done it myself a thousand times. But this was simply incomprehensible.'"

"We talked about Pushkin. Anna Andreyevna has this theory that we are all in love with him. That's why we find everything about him so interesting and why there is even a society called 'Friends of Pushkin.' But there is no 'Friends of Dostoyevsky.'

"'Dostoyevsky is most important to me. In general, he is the most important. I've just finished re-reading *Crime and Punishment*. And, you know, it seems to me that the entire Marmeladov plot is superfluous. It is something left over from *The Drunkards*; it's a weakness in his writing that one doesn't find in his later works. We want to be with him [Raskolnikov], to suffer together with him, but we have to listen to something about the Marmeladovs. He needed Sonya, but a mother, father, and three children should not have been attached to her.

"'It was ingenious that Raskolnikov later came to hate his mother and sister. They were connected with "the deed," and he couldn't bear them. . . .

"'You know, Tomashevsky found the house where the old woman lived. There is only one such house that fits the description. He asked me to come and see it but I didn't go.' With a sly smile she added, 'It's dangerous for me to climb stairs. . . . Yes, Dostoyevsky is the most important. Tomashevsky told me that foreigners come to see the house where Dostoyevsky lived and the house where the old woman lived. They *beg* him not to show them anything else and then leave.'"

• • •

* Akhamtova's room in the house on Fontanka where her former husband, N. N. Punin, lived with his daughter.—ed.

Immediately after Stalin's death Akhmatova's life became easier, at least financially. Her translation of the play *Marion Delorme* was published in a collection of the works of Victor Hugo, and she received her first large sum of money. This made her very happy. She did not, however, change her lifestyle or try to improve her living conditions. She had never had a home of her own, and now, in her old age, she had no desire to acquire one. Once I asked her: "If I were to become rich how long would I derive pleasure from it?" She answered with characteristic clarity: "Not long. Maybe ten days." When I did acquire some money and asked her what I should do with it, she said: "Build a place to live. That is the most important thing." But she continued to seek refuge with others, just as before. When the Ardovs had no room, she lived with the Zapadovs, with Nika Glen, M. S. Petrovykh, L. D. Bolshintsova, M. I. Aliger, or the Shengelis.* And her room in Leningrad and later the Komarovo dacha where she sometimes stayed reflected her vagabond existence. . . .

Lev Gumilev returned from the prison camp in 1956, later than almost everyone else. Anna Andreyevna wore herself out petitioning for his release. All the others were returning while her pleas remained unanswered. I think she was just about on the verge of collapse when Lev was finally released. His outstanding contributions to science were immediately recognized, and Anna Andreyevna was very proud of him. She loved to talk about his success. She admired scientific erudition in general, and all the more so in her own son, who had spent half his life in penal servitude. But in the end the lack of understanding between them so destroyed their relationship that they ceased to see each other altogether. This caused Akhmatova a great deal of grief in the final years of her life.

Lev Gumilev was included in the last wave of rehabilitation. Anna Andreyevna began to call herself a "Khrushchevite" and a member of the "Khrushchev Party." For years she was steadfast in her support, saying that Khrushchev could be forgiven a great deal for having released innocent people from prison. It was probably only the trial of Joseph Brodsky that made her change her mind about Khrushchev. She was very fond of Brodsky and greatly admired his poetry. I think he was the only young poet whom she considered to be a kindred spirit. She liked him for his

* Akhmatova's Moscow friends, besides Nika Glen, were Aleksandr Zapadov, Mariya Petrovykh, Lyubov Bolshintsova, Margarita Aliger, and Nina Shengeli.—ed.

learning and his spirituality. Anna Andreyevna rarely read the poetry of others aloud, but Brodsky was an exception. Some of his lines she constantly recalled, as for example: "You will write about us slantwise." She used this line (referring to her slanted handwriting) as an epigram for her poem "Last Rose."

Brodsky's arrest and trial caused Akhmatova much sorrow in her final years. And, of course, she also suffered over the events that occurred when Boris Pasternak was awarded the Nobel Prize. Everyone thought that the Central Committee resolution on Zoshchenko and Akhmatova was in the past. Then once again there was another campaign of public vilification and persecution; shameless speeches were given by people who had themselves only recently suffered from persecution. These were dark days, when no one wanted to look anyone in the eyes. . . .

Akhmatova put off reading *Doctor Zhivago* for a long time, even though the manuscript was passed from hand to hand before it was published abroad. Pasternak himself was eager to have it read and allowed it to be circulated and retyped. No one had any idea that this would soon be a criminal offense. When I went to see Anna Andreyevna to discuss the work with her, she surprised me by saying she had not yet acquired a copy. I took her words at face value and tried to find her a copy as quickly as possible. I brought her a package containing both volumes of the work, happy with myself for so quickly having fulfilled her wish. She grabbed her head with her hands: "Do you mean to tell me you really believed I couldn't get the manuscript? Boris himself offered it to me several times and many other people as well. But I did everything I could to keep from getting a copy. I'm not sure I will like it." I was ready to take the manuscript back, but she stopped me: "Don't take it back. This is fate. Now I will read it." But her presentiment turned out to be true; she did not like the novel. Only the descriptive passages, especially the description of the shrubbery, did she consider really fine.

Of course, she already knew and loved the poems in the novel. But Pasternak's later poetry often disappointed her. One day she showed me a typewritten copy of a long poem and asked: "Who do you think wrote it?" I read it and said: "It's some kind of parody of Pasternak." "That's what I thought," she said. "But Boris himself wrote it. Look, here's his signature," and she handed me the text of *Bacchanalia*.

When Pasternak wrote his confession ("I am writing in *Pravda* because I love the truth"), she said softly: "He shouldn't have given the manuscript to the Italians if he were going to have to write such letters later. In our country only those who know they are made of iron may do such things. And Boris knew that he wasn't made of iron."

When I asked her about Stalin's call to Pasternak about Mandelshtam, she answered: "Nadia and I discussed this at length at the time and decided that Boris deserved a B+ for his behavior." Akhmatova was very fond of Pasternak, often calling him "Borisik." She enjoyed his company very much, and it pained her that Zinaida Pasternak did not approve of their meetings.

There is a wonderful photograph taken on that famous evening in 1946. Akhmatova is in a black dress with her white tasseled shawl and Pasternak is beside her. It's a good photograph of both of them. They are looking straight ahead, at the viewer, and the solitude of each is evident. At the same time, their inner similarity is also plain. Zinaida Pasternak was unlike either of them. One day Akhmatova wanted to give something to Pasternak and asked me to accompany her. While we were riding the elevator to their apartment, Akhmatova said: "If Zina opens the door, you will witness a scene." Zina opened the door; the scene was short: she treated Akhmatova as if she were a messenger from the publishing house, reaching across the threshold to take the package from Akhmatova's hand and then slamming the door. Akhmatova did not try to conceal her hurt: "Did you see that?" she asked.

In the late fifties the country was caught up in a wave of poetry fever. Young people discovered the verse of Tsvetayeva, Mandelshtam, and Zabolotsky that had been banned for decades.

Akhmatova described Tsvetayeva as a "powerful poet" and Mandelshtam as "the first twentieth-century poet." When I compared Mandelshtam to Boratynsky she objected: "Mandelshtam surpasses Boratynsky." She respected but did not love Zabolotsky's work; she did hold some of his poems in high regard. For example, she described "The Cranes" as a "genuine classic," and after I gave her a copy of "Confession" to read she pronounced: "A wonderful poem, but very masculine." But she was not impressed with the Zabolotsky of the *Columns* epoch and did not at all like such poems as "The ugly girl" and "The old actress." Her comment: "For some reason everyone compares this poetry to that of

Nekrasov, but it resembles that of Apukhtin." One day someone told her that at a particular gathering a toast to her had been proposed and that Zabolotsky had set his glass on the table, saying: "I will not drink to Akhmatova." She could not forgive this, though if the poet had asked her pardon she would have told him: "God forgives."

Anna Andreyevna gave me a notebook with the unpublished poetry of Arseny Tarkovsky, a poet she much admired. And then there was Blok. Akhmatova was hurt when she read his personal notebooks and discovered she was not mentioned at all. More than once I heard her make comments such as: "As Blok's notebooks shows, I occupied no place in his life. . . ."

Young poets also rose to fame during this wave of poetry revival: Andrei Voznesenksy, Robert Rozhdestvensky, Yevgeny Yevtushenko, and Bella Akhmadulina. Akhmatova called them "pop poets." She did not care for their noise and sensationalism or their hunger for publicity. She and her circle found this incongruous with the image of a poet. Anna Andreyevna told me that Bella Akhmadulina had been to see her three times hoping to read her poetry. But each time Akhmatova suffered an angina attack. Bulat Okudzhava also visited her, and she liked his poems and songs (but for some reason not those of Novella Matveyeva). She found him, as well as the secret of his success, interesting. She had loved song writing since the time of Vertinsky. "Vertinsky was an era," she would say. Later she was captivated by Aleksandr Galich. I remember going to see her in 1965 or thereabouts and instead of saying "hello" she said: "They've arrested the song-writer." "What songwriter?" I asked. "Galich." This rumor was freely circulating around Moscow but, fortunately, it proved unfounded.

As for the young poets, in general, she thought their poems were too long.

So many people came to visit her in those years: young poets, elderly ladies, and all kinds of foreigners. Everyone seemed to see it as a duty to meet Akhmatova. I was responsible for opening the flood of foreigners: in 1960 my uncle, Eugene Rabinovich, an American professor of biophysics and biochemistry, came to the Soviet Union, and I brought him to see Akhmatova. He had admired her his entire life and had long dreamed of meeting her. He told her how as an émigré in the 1930s, when it seemed that the end was at hand and no voice would be heard cither in America

or in Russia, he and his friends wrote down from memory a complete collection of Akhmatova's poetry. Anna Andreyevna was deeply touched.

When the Ardovs were preparing to receive this first foreign guest,
they took me aside and asked what they should serve. But receiving
foreigners soon became routine. They were everywhere, and some turned
out to be real bores. I remember how back during the Stalinist era a close
friend had asked me to take her to meet Akhmatova. I didn't like to refuse
her, but I couldn't imagine showing up with a stranger.* Now I myself
brought an ignorant fool of a foreigner to meet her. He had pestered me
constantly, saying he absolutely had to see Akhmatova. He asked her for
her autograph to give his wife and then added: "Because she has a heart of
gold." When he left I turned to Akhmatova and said: "Anna Andreyevna,
please forgive me." She laughed and said: "I didn't know what to say. I felt
like asking, 'What else does she have that's gold? Her teeth?'"

But foreigners were also sometimes disappointed after meeting
Akhmatova. She liked to talk about herself, or more precisely, about what
was being written about her in the foreign press. She was displeased with
everything that was published about her and Gumilev, and demanded that
her visitors set about rebutting this information and publishing her version
of the facts. Several of the foreign Slavonic specialists I knew complained
to me of this. They couldn't even understand what she wanted of them:
they didn't think the information she objected to deserved to be rebutted.
I do remember, however, one young Englishwoman who was writing a
thesis on the theme "the image of Akhmatova in Gumilev's poetry." Anna
Andreyevna liked both the theme and the young woman.

Konstantin Paustovsky also came to see Akhmatova but it was not a
successful visit. He greeted her with the words: "I was coming to see you
and didn't know what pants to put on." Akhmatova froze. Embarrassed,
Paustovsky hastened to explain he was quoting Bunin's recollections of
Chekhov, how Chekhov felt when he was going to meet Lev Tolstoy. But
this explanation did not help matters. Akhmatova strongly disliked Bunin,
who had written a nasty epigram about her. ("In my time everyone knew

---

* Not long before Anna Andreyevna died I did take a woman, a close friend, to meet her. Akhmatova
had heard from others as well as myself that the woman was a brilliant scientist. My friend later
reminded me of how Anna Andreyevna had looked at her kindly and asked: "Do you also write
poetry?" When she answered, "No," Akhmatova had sighed with relief and smiled.

who the most evil person was—Bunin"; "Bunin had a grudge against humanity because he never completed the gymnasium"; "Bunin had never even sat next to poets.") I have already described how she felt about Chekhov, and she didn't care much for Tolstoy, either. Unfortunately, I never wrote down her comments about Tolstoy, but her views were well known to many people. Paustovsky, however, considered himself to be a student of Bunin and could not imagine that Akhmatova would think his little joke crude. When she described the episode to me she shrugged her shoulders and gave an ironical smile: the sensitive Paustovsky must have been devastated!

Much earlier Akhmatova had read Paustovsky's first book, *A Story about Life*. She told me she thought the first few pages were wonderful: "Remember how he arrives because his father has died but he can't cross the river, and his mother is running to and fro on the other bank?" But she didn't like the rest of it.

Akhmatova was perceptive in her high esteem of Solzhenitsyn. After "A Day in the Life of Ivan Denisovich" was published in *Novy Mir* and the author had become incredibly well known, he expressed the desire to see Akhmatova. Anna Andreyevna was happy to receive him. She talked about this meeting in an unusual way. After all, she was used to people coming to admire her, yet here was a man whom she wished to admire. He read her his poetry, and when I asked her if it was good she answered evasively: "You can tell by his poetry that he loves nature." Nor was she pleased with Solzhentisyn's comment about her work. She read him *Requiem,* and he said: "It was a national tragedy but you have made it only the tragedy of a mother and son." She repeated these words to me with her usual shrug of the shoulders and a slight grimace.

Solzhenitsyn himself impressed her. She asked him: "Do you understand that in a few days you will be the most famous man in the world and this will perhaps be the most difficult thing you will ever have to endure?" She told me he answered that he was ready to endure his future fame, but it is not so much his answer as her question that is interesting.* Akhmatova was a true Christian and despite the fame that surrounded

---

* I have been told another version: that Solzhenitsyn laughed after hearing Akhmatova's question. But she never told me this.

her, the cornerstone of her consciousness was that everyone was equal before God, that she was but one of many. It is difficult to explain how she rationalized this with her belief in her uniqueness, but this was what made her so attractive to so many different people.

Akhmatova thought highly of Solzhenitsyn's story "Matryona's Yard." She gave me the manuscript to read, saying; "I want to give you a present." But she liked his other stories much less. "For the Good of the Matter" she did not like at all, nor his play ("How medieval!"). But on the whole Solzhenitsyn was the single contemporary Soviet prose writer (with the exception of Zoshchenko) whom she found really interesting.

In September 1965 I went to see Akhmatova at the Ardovs to relate the news about the arrests of Sinyavsky and Daniel.* She had already heard about the arrests, but I told her the accusations. She didn't believe it when I said that Sinyavsky had been published abroad under the pseudonym of Abram Terts: "They brought me the books of this Terts when I was in Paris and I told them to take the trash away. I will never believe that Sinyavsky wrote that. He came to see me and I liked him very much. Sinyavsky is goodness incarnate while Abram Terts is evil incarnate. No, there is no way a Muscovite could have written that. It is clear from the very start that the gentleman has not been in Moscow for years. You can tell from the details. Perhaps he completed the gymnasium here, but he hasn't been in Moscow since then." When I asked her why he was being touted as a Soviet citizen in the West, she answered: "My God, they are a dime a dozen there. They had to say it was a Soviet citizen and not an émigré or else no one would have read him." Nadezhda Mandelshtam, who was sitting with us, acrimoniously observed, "They are spreading these rumors on purpose. We have already seen it happen. Sinyavsky has nothing to do with it."

Akhmatova was extremely interested in anything contemporary. She read everything new, everything that people were talking about, and she liked to attend art exhibits and the cinema. After her heart attack she could not get around so easily. She had become very heavy, and even though she ate little, she could not lose weight. She had difficulty in walking (stairs presented a special problem) and had to be accompanied in a taxi everywhere

---

* Andrei Sinyavsky and Juli Daniel. See also the reminiscence by Nadezhda Mandelshtam.—ed.

she went. But before she had her first heart attack she never missed a good movie. She found Italian neo-realism as interesting as the young people did. She told me that she had fallen in love with the cinema at an early age, attending a small movie theater before films were even considered to be an art. It was in such a theater that she saw an "introductory clip" to painting. She went into peals of laughter when she recalled the subtitle under the famous painting by Repin: "Pushkin is reading, Derzhavin is listening."

Anna Andreyevna found modern criticism too verbose. It is difficult to believe some of the things that were written about her, and I am not speaking now of the "resolution" period. I remember paying a visit to Akhmatova at the Ardovs in 1960 and finding her suffering from an attack of angina. That morning, it turned out, she had read a typed copy of an article by Aleksei Surkov that was supposed to be the afterword to her collection of verse, *Poetry,* being published by Goslitizdat. She told me that Surkov had said such things as, "Akhmatova did not have the intelligence. . . ." These phrases were deleted from the printed text of the afterword, but still it was full of banalities. And this was a man who "had the intelligence" and, one might add, the cynicism to head the commission on the study of her literary works after her death.

But Akhmatova always found even the best examples of literary criticism too detailed. She liked everything to be laconic. I was present when she received a letter from a prisoner who was by no means well read in poetry and was in general poorly educated. He had seen Akhmatova's name for the first time when he read some of her poems published in *Moskva* magazine and had sent an unusual letter to the editors in which he described her poetry as "a coolness flowing from the wounded feeling of simplicity." Akhmatova was delighted with this observation, saying: "No critic has said anything like that about me."

One day Anna Andreyevna discovered that my eighth-grade daughter had written a composition on Pushkin for her class and had started the paper with the words: "One always expects the impossible from poetry, and Pushkin provides us with the impossible." Akhmatova liked the phrase so much that she told me to bring my daughter to see her. She gave the girl her gold pen and her large bound notebook and said: "Write it here and I will use it as an epigraph for my article about Pushkin." She used the formal "you" with my Ira, though she had known her since birth. She also used the formal address with Alyosha Batalov, though she had known him quite well since he was six years old. The first day she had gone to the Ardovs the boy was misbehaving. He began to toss his cutlet round the table and his parents could not stop him. But Akhmatova had said, "Don't you like cutlets?" using the formal "you," and the boy was dumbfounded and began to eat.

Once Anna Andreyevna and I were speaking about Hemingway's new novel. She did not like the book, nor did I. "My child," she said, "bloody steaks and maimed arms are awful." I added: "Love was always understated in Hemingway, but here it is straightforward: I love you, you love me. We all know how to do that." She thought this was very funny and afterwards would frequently apply my words to different occasions: "We all know how to do that."

Anna Andreyevna did not like popular literary criticism, especially the "Biographie romancee" genre that became so widely read in the mid-twentieth century. What she found interesting was strict research based on documentation. This material she read thoroughly and kept in her memory. Her own interest in the field of literary criticism lay in the study of the works of Pushkin. When L. Lansky, my colleague at *Literaturnoye Nasledstvo*, decided to send Akhmatova his article concerning the publication of the letters of Natalia Hertzen to her lover Georg Hervegh, I was doubtful of her interest. I thought it was old-fashioned to show her something like this, as if she were an international expert on women's feeling. But I was wrong. Anna Andreyevna liked the article and asked me to convey her thanks to the author. She said about Natalia Hertzen: "Say what you will, it is an honorable thing to die for love."

Judging by her poems, Anna Andreyevna died many times for love. But in reality she died after suffering angina and a series of heart attacks, which, like everything else in her hard life, she bore with courage. I visited her in a number of hospitals in Moscow and Leningrad, and everywhere I saw how people loved her. This pleased Anna Andreyevna very much. She told me how a nurse who was combing her hair kept repeating: "Nyura, the snackbar waitress, says you write good poetry."

Anna Andreyevna was always tolerant and unpretentious. Once Antonina Oksman walked into her room without phoning beforehand and woke her. Antonina was abashed and began to apologize, but Anna

Andreyevna simply said: "Don't worry. It's all right." She was even more tolerant when she was in the hospital. And under what conditions! She laughed when she recalled the hospital in Tashkent where she lay with typhus and a high temperature. She saw a bed-bug crawling up the wall and told the nurse to get rid of it. "That's not a bed-bug," the nurse had replied, "it's just a small cockroach." In the last hospital, the bed next to hers was occupied by the mother-in-law of the *Izvestia* editor. The woman was constantly whining and complaining and never gave Anna Andreyevna a moment's peace. As soon as someone would come to visit Akhmatova she would loudly call for the nurse to bring the bedpan.

Anna Andreyevna's father died young from a first attack of angina. When she asked the doctor about the cause of death he had told her: "This disease is nothing for you to worry about. In the first place, it is not hereditary, and in the second, it rarely affects women." But fate decided differently.

Anna Andreyevna loved to travel to new places. She told me once: "There is nothing better for the nerves than to visit a place you have never been to before." It is wonderful that late in her life she was able to make a triumphant tour of Europe.

The last time I saw Anna Andreyevna was in mid–February of 1966 when she was in Botkin Hospital. She was sitting in a chair in the hall waiting to see if someone would come to visit. One day she would have a number of visitors and the next, none at all. That day I was the only one to come. I stayed with her more than two hours. She was overjoyed at the news coming from Sovetsky Pisatel [Soviet Writer] Publishing House concerning a new edition of her book. She liked the idea of the artist V. Medvedev to use only the profile of her portrait by Modigliani on the dust cover. It made her happy when I told her that speculators were selling her book at ten times the cover price. She asked about the Daniel and Sinyavsky trial and then told me that the taxi driver who brought Anechka Kaminskaya to the hospital to see her had said: "We will be praying for Akhmatova." She asked about my own health (I had not been well), and advised me not to be afraid of hospitals; one got used to them and they weren't so bad.

We walked to her ward, and I took something out of my bag. Anna Andreyevna smiled: "Juice! Wonderful! For some reason everyone brings me apples." (They were hard for her to chew.) I opened the bottle and

Anna Andreyevna drank the juice. Sitting on her high hospital bed with
slippers on her feet and holding a cup of juice in her hand, this old, cor-
pulent woman still looked regal. Close to the bed was the beautiful
narcissus plant Koma Ivanov had brought the day before. "Cherry—my
favorite." Hearing these words, I left in a happy mood. I had no presentiment that I would never see her again.

In the last book she gave me, she wrote: "My dear Natasha Roskina,
for all the memories. Anna Akhmatova. 10 December 1965. Moscow."

Vyacheslav Vsevolodovich Ivanov
MEETINGS WITH AKHMATOVA

*Vyacheslav Vsevolodovich Ivanov (born 1929), philologist, author of two
books of memoirs on Pasternak and Akhmatova and the son of Vsevolod
Ivanov (1895–1963).*

I

Though I had known Anna Andreyevna Akhmatova and had occasion
to see her at the apartments of mutual friends (including Boris Leonidovich
Pasternak) and in my own home, it was not until the autumn of 1958 that
we began to have private conversations. In late November of that year—
when the persecution against Pasternak began and I was the object of a
similar campaign at Moscow University—I was told that Anna Andreyevna
wished me to call on her. The Ardovs' apartment, where she usually stayed
and where I frequently visited her later, was undergoing repairs. They
were now living somewhere else. It seemed to me that it was a remote area
(but also in the Zamoskvorechye district or perhaps farther to the south-
west). In a strange room she still seemed at home. This would happen
again and again—I saw her in many such strange rooms—but one soon
forgot the happenstance of the location.

At this first *tête-à-tête* (we were to have many) she immediately estab-
lished the order of things, and it never changed: she read her poems,
mostly those she had just written (this time it was a mischievous quatrain:

"For such a buffoon") or something from the distant past, which at times would remind her of episodes in her life. On this occasion she spoke of her meeting with Marina Tsvetayeva. She did not trust the walls of the Ardovs' apartment, where the meeting (or, as she put it "non-meeting") took place. Talking about this apartment, she would often make a gesture signifying someone was listening. (Her concern was evoked by a mixture of real experience and almost phobic paranoia: "They like it when I stay there.") And it was out of fear, perhaps more for her guest than for herself, that she did not read what she wanted to read to Tsvetayeva.

I asked Anna Andreyevna about my long-held assumption (since the time I was a student reading Blake) that Gumilev's line "The heart will be scorched by flames" was a loose translation of Blake. Akhmatova replied that she was not living with Gumilev when he wrote that poem, but that he was studying English at that time and therefore my assumption seemed plausible.

In memory of our conversation concerning her critique on Pushkin's *The Stone Guest*, Anna Andreyevna gave me a copy of the article with the inscription: "To V. V. Ivanov, the first to praise my prose. Gratefully, Akhmatova. 22 November 1958. Moscow."

II

After I was fired from Moscow University in January 1959 I went to Leningrad to attend to certain affairs and called on Anna Andreyevna. She was still living on Krasnaya Kommuna Street. I saw an old chest of drawers and bookshelves in her room. This was probably the only time (except in the "hut"—the dacha in Komarovo) that her surroundings seemed to be her own. She began to ask me about my affairs and I answered her in as much detail as possible (at the inexperienced age of twenty-nine, believing that my misfortune at that time was really serious). She entertained me by parodying some of the words from my stories, intimating by her tone that she did not find the matter at all serious: "Yes, you know I already heard all this from Kholodovich. He stayed with me for a week. He talked about you and used the same phrases—'save' and 'cybernetics.'" And, in fact, why should she, who had witnessed the arrests and deaths of so many friends and relatives, take to heart my being fired (nothing more) from

Moscow University and the magazine *Voprosy Yazykoznaniya* [*Problems of Linguistics*]? Her ironic observations were more helpful to me than all the condolences I was hearing from half of Moscow. That same evening Akhmatova read to me many of the poems from *Requiem* and others on the same theme written at approximately the same time.

III

My life became somewhat settled. I was working at the Institute of Exact Mechanics and Computer Technology and had begun to study Chinese (the computer translating group I headed was involved with the translation of Chinese). At a dinner we gave for Akhmatova in our home, I or someone else mentioned this fact. Anna Andreyevna responded enthusiastically: "You should be put on exhibit: you are studying Chinese hieroglyphs and still manage to write poetry." It was evident that she wanted to try to cheer me up at the time, immediately after my misfortune.

I was supposed to call for her at the Ardovs', who were living on Ordynka, and accompany her to my apartment. It was only two blocks away, but it took us a long time to cover it. She had difficulty in breathing and needed to stop every few minutes. I noticed that she also had a psychological problem in crossing the street, even in the absence of cars.

IV

Akhmatova was in the hospital when they buried Pasternak (she saw him for the last time at my birthday celebration in August of 1959). The day after the funeral I went to visit her. She left the ward with me and we walked into the corridor, where we found a place to talk. Akhmatova listened to what I had to say and then commented: "I feel like it's a ceremonious event, a great religious holiday. This was how it was when Blok died." She told me how she had visited Pasternak in the same Botkin hospital Blok had been in and had recited for Pasternak from a poem to Blok's memory:

> And one linden tree, out of its mind,
> Was blooming that mournful May,
> Near the window where he said one time
> That he saw before him a golden hill,

With a winged road that he would climb,
Protected by the highest will.*

V

In 1960 the third volume of Blok's works was published, and Akhmatova for the first time discovered several versions of a poem and outlines of a poem devoted to her. That day at the Ardovs' this was all she could talk about. She discussed the various interpretations of the line: "But I am not so simple/Nor so complex. . . ."**

Evidently she had always wanted to know what was behind Blok's poem of 1913. A half-century later, each line in his notebooks helped her in her favorite endeavor—deciphering the meaning of that poem.

Akhmatova was always interested in what people said and wrote about her, even unknown people, let alone Blok. She was never indifferent to this. Nor was she always pleased with praise. Once, when showing me a flattering letter from a young woman of a literary family, Akhmatova said, "Doesn't it seem odd to you? She's like a snake crawling toward me."

Akhmatova approved of observations comparing her early poetry with the prose of Hemingway and describing it as "novella-like."

In the late 1950s, when she was constantly editing and adding to *Poem Without a Hero,* Akhmatova asked the opinion of everyone who read it. Later she would take the criticisms and compare them. At one time she thoroughly agreed with the reader who saw her as the exact representation of Petersburg's "Silver Age"—that glorious, short-lived flourishing of art, literature, and all spheres of culture: the compressed reflection of the beginning of the century that held such promise for Russia.

VI

In 1961 I. S. Shklovsky's book on astrophysics—*Universe, Life, Reason*— was published. I read it avidly in one night and then told Akhmatova about it when I saw her at the Ardovs'. She was intrigued and immediately said: "I would like to read such a book." The next time I saw her she had already read it and liked it very much.

* From Akhmatova's poem "As the daughter of blind Oedipus."
** From Blok's poem "Beauty's fearsome, they tell you. . . ."

Once, before I went to see Akhmatova in her old Leningrad apartment, she told me that while looking through some old books she found something on the theory of relativity. She talked knowledgeably about the subject; such topics were always of interest to her.

Another time, when I was reading her a poem, she recognized the exposition of modern theories of physics. In a learned way, she related in a clear and precise manner what had been unclear and vague in the poem: "Is it about the flow of particles . . . ?"

I had frequent occasion to observe how she could untangle a strange poem and relate its meaning in prose. And if she liked a poem but found something unclear in it, she would try to change the line.

VII

One day I had to leave Anna Andreyevna early in order to see the imminent philologist and Academician Viktor Vladimirovich Vinogradov, who had once written an article about her. A few years before I had worked as his assistant at a journal, but now we rarely saw each other. On this occasion it was imperative that I see him: our meeting would determine whether or not he would join in the campaign to help free mathematician V. I. Pimenov from prison. Knowing that Anna Andreyevna had been acquainted with the Vinogradovs for years in Leningrad and maintained contact with them, I told her the purpose of my visit to him. She listened to me very attentively and then expressed her wish, hope, and prayer: that Vinogradov would have the courage to do a good deed (she knew how difficult this was for Vinogradov himself, who had been arrested and exiled so many times and then rehabilitated under Stalin). Her benediction helped—if only by giving me more strength and conviction in my conversation with Vinogradov. A few months later, when Pimenov was thanking those who had helped win his unexpected release, he had no idea that Anna Andreyevna was among that number.

VIII

If Akhmatova happened to be in Moscow on the day of an Orthodox Church holiday she never failed to call me in the morning to congratulate me on the occasion. Orthodox Church holidays were very important to her. We never spoke specifically on this topic; like many other things it was simply understood.

IX

Most of what I write here is based on my recollections of the years gone by. But sometimes I rely on my notes, which I began to keep in the winter of 1964 when Anna Andreyevna was living in Margarita Aliger's apartment on the same floor as we were, in the Writers' House on Lavrushinsky Lane. During that time we saw each other almost every day.

The following are some excerpts from my diary.

On 24 January 1964 we were with Anna Andreyevna at the home of Ivan Dmitrievich Rozhansky, a physicist and a broadly educated man to whom we are indebted for the best quality recordings of Akhmatova reciting her poetry. Akhmatova began to talk about a poem ("The last one" from *Songs*) that she had written that day. She said that she herself did not know where it had come from. Then she turned to me and asked: "Does this happen to you?" After I answered she continued: "There are some poems that I know how I wrote—with the usual human endeavor. And then there are those like this one." When we met a couple of days later (on Lavrushinsky), Anna Andreyevna told me she wanted to read the poem to me again, adding: "I think you were drunk at the Rozhanskys'." I tried to convince her otherwise (once before I had called upon her in an intoxicated state and had become notorious throughout Moscow because of it; for my own edification Akhmatova told me that when Churchill's son was in Russia and wanted to see her, he sent someone to tell her this but did not come himself, because *he* was drunk). In response to my protestations against my guilt: "Oh yes, of course! You were only drinking juice. I was the one who was drunk. . . ." And then, without further ado, she read her poem.

On 1 February I was leaving for Maleyevka and called on Anna Andreyevna the day before to tell her good-bye. She was not quite her usual self. She joked about her upcoming trip to Italy. For some reason she was sorting out a number of her own photographs, the photo portraits. Looking at the photograph made of her and Pasternak in the Hall of Columns on the evening of the poets' recital, Akhmatova made her usual

comment: "That's how I 'earned' the resolution."[*] And she said about
one of her photos: "This one can be sent to Prague." She showed me the
letters and the poems dedicated to her. We spoke of Vasily Komarovsky,
whose poems were becoming a success in Moscow (thanks to the readings
of Roman Yakobson). I thought I heard something like poetic jealousy
in her words (she rarely expressed this). With a laugh (of indignation?)
she related how someone had once confused Komarovsky with the protagonist in *Poem Without a Hero.* We began to speak about Eikhenbaum.
Akhmatova recalled that in the 1920s he had quite a different reputation
than the one he had now, when he was considered to be the founder of
the new literary criticism. Certainly Akhmatova was not inclined to listen
to the praise of other literary figures of the first decade. We began to speak
about one of the few of Mandelshtam's articles that she strongly disliked—
the one where he praised Khlebnikov, in her opinion, at her expense. She
found things to criticize in the article—Mandelshtam's wrong choice of
words, for example. After some of the guests had left, the conversation (as
was usually the case) became more interesting. Anna Andreyevna commented that she did not like *The Fall,* a book she had just read in French.
Camus, she said, was a bad imitation of Kafka, then she added: "Good cannot be theoretically taught: one must actually try to do good deeds in
order to see how difficult it is." Concerning *The Plague,* Akhmatova said
that the beginning was good but that it got progressively worse.
Concerning her recollections of Modigliani, she admitted that she could
not write about the most important thing, the night he had stood under
her window. "I look out my window at night and still see him there."

16 March 1964. Anna Andreyevna reads from her recollections on
Modigliani. I tell her that they are recollections of the twentieth century,
to which she replies: "Yes, we can now speak about a century, but at one
time this was a sphinx." She agreed with me that Apollinaire was the last
"tolerable" French poet and added: "I think it's because the language is so
ossified; inversions are impossible. Everything has been told and retold in
every way, and this is not good for poetry." For the last few weeks Anna
Andreyevna has been reading, in English, Joyce's *Portrait of the Artist as a*

---

[*] Akhmatova believed that Central Committee's ban against her and Zoshchenko resulted in part from
Stalin's resentment of the standing oration she received. Such homage was reserved for party and
government leaders.—ed.

Young Man. The day before (when I was still in Maleyevka) we learned of the sentence handed down to Brodsky. Akhmatova commented: "Because of our uniqueness, you and I are not always aware of what is going on; this is our shortcoming." Concerning Modigliani's alleged drinking, she said that anyone involved in such arduous labor had to use stimulants, but they were destructive. As a matter of principle she was interested in the dispute as to whether Modigliani could have read Lautreamont. Ehrenburg thought not, since Lautreamont had supposedly only been discovered in the 1920s. But Khardzhiev proved him wrong. "The difference between a scholar and a journalist."

On 23 March I called on Akhmatova. She showed me her new present, a Japanese kimono. With her kimono on, Akhmatova is reflected in the cheval-glass.

March 30 was the anniversary of *Rosary.* I went to see Anna Andreyevna, having reread the collection and discovering how much of it had affected my life twenty years earlier: it contained so many intimations of the future. I asked Akhmatova to autograph two different editions (something I had not done before). On the Berlin edition, published by S. Efron, she wrote: "It is fifty years old today. 30 March 1964. Moscow." On the ninth Petersburg edition of 1923 she wrote: "To V. Ivanov in friendship."

Anna Andreyevna told stories about Kluyev that I had heard before in abbreviated form and had even tried to write down. Concerning Yesenin's fall into depravity a year before his death, Kluyev said to Akhmatova: "They should have put him in prison. Then he would have known what sunshine and the human word mean." She thought Kluyev was better than Yesenin, and believed it was Kluyev who had given Blok the idea for the image of the "bride-Rus." She recalled his plea for a pardon. A priest related how Kluyev had died—the result of a fall in the baths.

On 3 April Akhmatova told me that Mandelshtam did not like Blok because of his cosmetic beauty. She also said that there was no humility in Blok's poetry, that humility could only be found in orthodoxy. She found it strange that people had begun to forget this.

On 19 April Akhmatova said of her life, "One chapter could be entitled 'Restless Old Age.'" Concerning a particular writer who was afraid to help plead for Brodsky, she recalled what was said about another literary figure in 1937: "He changed into a poodle and hid under the couch." [. . .]

On 9 May Anna Andreyevna discussed Riva's book on Russian poetry. She laughed in remembering her meeting with Frost. They called him a "gramps" who was turning into a "granny." She gave a lively description of how actors read poetry: "It's a shame!" Then she criticized Poggioli's composition about our literature. Akhmatova is hoping to go on trips abroad and to receive the [Nobel] Prize.

On 10 May I went to see Anna Andreyevna. She was in bed, not well, and two young women were helping her. Despite her ill health, she sat up and spoke contemptuously of Vyacheslav Ivanovich Ivanov: "Fraud! As much a charlatan as those of the eighteenth century—like those who talked like they lived at the time of Christ, like Cagliostro. . . . This is what he did: brought me to his room and asked me to read. Praising me, he wiped the tears from his eyes. Then he led me out to everyone else and there began to criticize me. What a traitor. . . . I don't read his philosophy for its dullness. He was merciless to us, but then, what could we have expected?"

Anna Andreyevna spoke eloquently of St. Petersburg, which she had known almost since the time of Dostoyevsky—"since the 1890s, and a matter of ten years makes no difference. There were many signs then of carriage makers on Troitskaya (now Rubenstein). All the houses had signs. Later they organized the Komsomol *subbotnik,** and the city's architecture was discovered. It was beautiful, with carved window jambs and caryatids. But something was gone; the city grew deadly. Dostoyevsky saw it still in signs."

Then Akhmatova spoke of how they tore down the house described in *Crime and Punishment*: "Tomashevsky showed it to me. The man was there on that staircase and imagined how it could have happened—it was a back staircase, so the doomed heard nothing. The next time I went there, the house was gone." Then Petersburg, its streets and their names, led her away to Paris where "all the names—Marat and Kings—were side by side."

I had read a book of articles by the art scholar M. V. Alpatov and began to tell Anna Andreyevna about it. She commented that she didn't like what he had recently written about Aleksander Ivanov: "He got up, drank tea . . . ," etc.

* Forced Sabbath work.—ed.

I mentioned Alpatov's article on Michelangelo and his poetry (previously, Anna Andreyevna had spoken of Khardzhiev's etude on the "Night" by Michelangelo, which seemed to continue Akhmatova's etude). Akhmatova, who read Michelangelo in Italian, said: "I like what he wrote. Dense poetry, just like Rilke's." I jumped at the comparison, citing Rilke's translations of Michelangelo. "So, it's been well put. It sometimes happens to me," she said.

15 May. Anna Andreyevna recalled her conversation with Gorky in the early 1920s. She was penniless at the time, working in the Rykov's garden. They convinced her to go to Gorky and ask him for work. She went as she was—barefoot and dressed in a shift. Gorky observed: "They say you have tuberculosis and yet you are barefoot." He offered her a job translating proclamations from the Russian into Italian. Akhmatova declined.

On another day Anna Andreyevna told me in dismay that it had become acceptable to criticize Gorky. But he had helped so many people in the 1920s: "Without him many would have died from hunger."

We began to speak about Zoshchenko. Anna Andreyevna recalled how he had offered Stenich, who was translating *Ulysses,* his help with some of the unusual words (by that time Akhmatova had moved from Lavrushinsky Lane to Sokolniki to live with Lyubov Bolshinikova, Stenich's widow). According to Anna Andreyevna, Zoshchenko did not read Freud until late in life. She thought his judgments naive: "He advised his readers how to live."

The day following the jubilee ceremony in honor of Anna Andreyevna in the Mayakovsky Museum on 30 May 1964 (Akhmatova herself was unable to attend, and we could only listen to a recording of her reciting her poetry), she called me on the phone. She was especially interested in knowing how I liked the speech given by V. M. Zhirmunsky at the beginning of the evening: "He thinks you didn't like it." I assured her this was not so. "Then call him and tell him what you think about the speech because he's upset." It's remarkable that even on the occasion of the first ceremony in her honor after so many years she wanted to hear some kind words, not for herself, but for members of her close circle. This solicitude concerning others markedly distinguished her from the rest of the literary circle.

Akhmatova told me over the phone that she was tired and was going to rest. She had finished the translation of Tagore (she complained about how strange she found the East and how its literature lacked any humor) and was going to receive money for it. With respect to the speech given by Tarkovsky the evening before, she said that they had quarreled previously. "He's in a bad mood, so gloomy. Fame came to him, but it was not what he expected." He criticized her for her prose and for Modigliani the entire evening. She excommunicated him from her home and did not call him.

In late July and early August I was in Leningrad and went to see Anna Andreyevna in Komarovo. She repeated (with evident enthusiasm) a phrase she had recently heard: "A poet is someone from whom no one can take anything away and therefore no one can give anything." She began to speak about Leopardi, whose poetry and prose she admired, including his early work, just like Rimbaud. "He was born at almost the same time as Pushkin. Why is it that poets are born almost simultaneously?"

X

The campaign to help Joseph Brodsky continued. Frida Vigdorova asked me to go to see Anna Andreyevna to make another request of Fedin. I called her, and though it was still morning, she asked me to come right away. (She was staying at a new Moscow abode, not at the Ardovs'.) Several people had come to see her at once, and while she was busy with an urgent matter—either finishing reading or correcting something she had written—she gave me Mandelshtam's typed copy of *The Fourth Prose* to read. When I started to say something about how good the text was and to praise Mandelshtam's prose in general, she commented: "Osip is fine. The young read him." This was an important criterion for her: what the literary youth were reading.

XI

I went to Leningrad and learned that Akhmatova had been hospitalized under suspicion of having suffered a heart attack. I hurried to see her. Despite the inconveniences of the hospital ward (I never saw her in any tolerable, not to mention privileged, conditions—not in the hospital and not in the outside world), she was in her spiritual element, thinking about the books she had read. This time it was *The Dhammapada*, which had just been published in the excellent Russian translation of V. N. Toporov. She complained that this book, like much of the literature of the East, was alien to her, that it was dull, and that the lack of humor irked her.

She told me about a conversation with mathematician O. A. Ladyzhenskaya, who had come to visit her in the hospital. She had asked Akhmatova's opinion as to which of the arts she should study—she was interested both in poetry and painting. With the usual care and attention she gave each person interested in the arts, Anna Andreyevna spoke to me in detail about the course she had decided for Ladyzhenskaya: she should study one art at a time, not all together. She looked on this matter with great seriousness.

XII

Akhmatova had several favorite topics, and she sometimes repeated jokes and stories. She was aware of her tendency to make fun of herself: "I've got this reputation."

XIII

With respect to the poetry of a contemporary, especially one who was not successful, Anna Andreyevna took a more lenient approach, giving an early favorable opinion. Frequently, in her conversations with me, she would reproach (sometimes unjustifiably if it concerned her own poetry) Boris Pasternak for failing to give due importance to his contemporary poets. She juxtaposed Pasternak with Pushkin, reminding me that the latter always tried to find if not a good poem at least a good line from the poets of his circle. Regarding contemporary poetry, Anna Andreyevna, with small variation, repeated the names of those she considered the most gifted: [Mariya] Petrovykh, [Arseny] Tarkovsky, [Semyon] Lipkin, [David] Samoilov, and [Vladimir] Kornilov. (Akhmatova often told me that Kornilov was a poet who succeeded in introducing contemporary collo-quial speech—the language of prose—into poetry.)

Especially in the latter years of her life, Akhmatova distinguished Brodsky from among the young poets. She held him up as an example—there was so much behind his poetry: English poet-metaphysics, old chamber music. . . . When she lived in Komarovo, Brodsky and his friends used to visit her almost every day. After she moved back to Moscow, she told me how Brodsky had stopped coming to see her for several days. When he at last came and she asked him what had happened, he replied that he had nothing to bring her. This she could understand: each time he came to see her he would have a new poem or a new record of an old composer that he wanted Akhmatova to hear.

XIV

With the exception of Blok, about whom she was constantly chang-ing her opinion, she maintained an unswerving antipathy (sometimes per-sonal) against the symbolists. This included Vyacheslav Ivanov, even though he had noticed her poetic talent early. As a man as well she saw him in a black light. When we spoke about Andrei Bely, Akhmatova immediately made an exception of his last book: "*Gogol's Skill* is a remark-able book," she said with conviction.

But another time (9 April 1964) Anna Andreyevna told me: "For us, the people of St. Petersburg, *Petersburg* ★ does not reflect the city. The man was wily and deceitful. Berdyaev said this about him: 'He disappeared, but he should have waited for the flood of abuse.' All the symbolists, with the exception of Blok, were strange. The book about Gogol is both nonsense and enlightenment. He [Bely] didn't speak with me. Everything for him was divided into the initiate and the non-initiate profane, into Steinerians★★ and non-Steinerians. I could not even pretend to know anything about it. But Nikolai Stepanovich [Gumilev] read a great deal in this line, and they used to have discussions."

With time, Akhmatova's loyalty to acmeism grew. She said of her late poetry: "My work is acmeist." And, coming from her lips, this statement rang especially important and true.

XV

More than once Akhmatova expressed her negative feelings about Freud. She explained to me that, for her, childhood had nothing in com-mon with the psychoanalytical interpretation. It was not confined to home

---

★ Another book by Andrei Bely, Russian symbolist and author of *Gogol's Skill*.—ed.
★★ Followers of Rudolph Steiner (1861–1925).—ed.

and family; on the contrary, for a child the world begins outside, beyond the gate.

Another time, Akhmatova told me that she would never enter psychoanalysis, for she would then never be able to write poetry. I told her what Rilke said in his letter to Lou Andreas-Salome, who was trying to convince her friend to enter psychoanalysis on the eve of the First World War. Word for word, Rilke had said just what Akhmatova told me. Anna Andreyevna smiled and said: "So, I'm right."

Concerning the connection between madness and creativity, Anna Andreyevna often commented on Pushkin's draft of "Once again I came to call." According to Akhmatova, the draft clearly reveals the madness of the poet, who suspects everyone, even his best friend, of being an informant (I am inclined to believe that the researcher, Akhmatova, was projecting her own weakness onto Pushkin: she had the same fears herself). But later, in comparing the draft with the final version, we see that Pushkin deleted reference to this painful subject. "It was camouflaged, but it was real madness," Akhmatova observed.

XVI

Concerning Mayakovsky's suicide, Anna Andreyevna excluded the possibility that it could have been for purely personal reasons: "It could not have been because of one woman when there were so many at the same time." She believed the explanation lay in understanding the memoirs of Polonskaya. (By the way, this caused a misunderstanding between her and Roman Yakobson, when he came to Moscow in 1964.)

XVII

Akhmatova often said that wives are always terrible (at one time she made Nadezhda Yakovlevna Mandelshtam the sole exception to this rule). Concerning the woman friend of a talented poet, she said: "She looks like a divine apparition but she acts like the devil." [. . .]

XVIII

Akhmatova could passionately detest even a woman who lived a hundred and fifty years ago. Few of her contemporaries were accorded the vehemence and derision with which she spoke of Sobanskaya. Anna Andreyevna commented on the similarity of Pushkin's letter to Sobanskaya and that of Onegin's letter to Tatiana. She sympathized and commiserated with Pushkin during the time of his affair, but she was jealous of Sobanskaya.

Anna Andreyevna never lost her ability to feel passionate emotions. She became incensed upon reading the memoirs of people who alleged that she was jealous of Gumilev. One day she phoned me in Peredelkino and said that she had an urgent need for advice. An hour later she was there. My mother, who was with me to greet her on the porch, later called me aside and asked: "Is Anna Andreyevna coming to live with us? Did you invite her?" My mother did not know that by that time Anna Andreyevna never parted with her small suitcase filled with her personal manuscripts. Aside from the fact that she had already been subjected to several searches, there had been a number of occasions when circumstantial evidence indicated that someone had gone through her papers in her absence. So she always kept her suitcase with her.

Bringing the suitcase inside, she had barely sat down when she began to speak. She had just read a book that, in her opinion, distorted her relationship with Gumilev. She took this as a new offence, comparing its seriousness with the Zhdanov report against her. She never forgot Zhdanov's dirty insinuations, and was extremely upset that the date the resolution was published in *Zvezda* and *Leningrad* was taught in school.

Akhmatova believed that the books of memoirs published in the sixties did as much damage to her character and reputation as a poet as had Zhdanov and the resolution under Stalin. She positively seethed with rage and could not be calmed.

XIX

Akhmatova believed that humdrum occurrences provided grist for poetry. She said that poetry grew from such everyday expressions as, "Would you like some tea?" This represented the miracle of poetry and also the incredible difficulty of its composition.

She once admitted to me that she sometimes feared the verses would cease to come (later, Brodsky told me the same thing). I recalled the long period of time when she could not write and how she had predicted it together with the other misfortunes that befell her:

Take my child, take my friend, dispossess me
Of my secret strange talent for song.

XX

Once, when Akhmatova was our guest, she told us that when she was a young girl of sixteen she discovered she had the gift of the soothsayer. She said that a sudden insight into the future was always preceded by a feeling of lassitude bordering on sleep or fainting. That day she felt limp and in a kind of semiconscious state. Reclining on a sofa, she was listening to her older relatives talk about the young and fortunate girl who was their neighbor—how charming she was, how beautiful, and how many suitors she had. Suddenly, herself not understanding how, she blurted out: "Yes, and then she will go to Nice and die of tuberculosis six months later." And this is exactly what happened.

In the 1960s Anna Andreyevna was busy trying to rewrite the play she had written in Tashkent during the war and burned in 1944. The play was called *Enuma Elish*—the first words in a Babylonian mythological poem about the creation of the world. Shileiko translated the title as "When at the summit." Anna Andreyevna told me the story of how she wrote it. She had been ill with typhus, but the worst was over. Delirium had passed into a state of fervor that already presaged her recovery. I recall this state quite well; I was also down with typhus there and then, in Tashkent. It was while in this state that she began to look at the dirty, foam-like spots on the walls. The most important scene of the play opened up behind these spots: a trial where the author stood accused of all possible and impossible sins. After she wrote the play she had seen in her delirium Akhmatova felt that she had predicted her own misfortune and, out of fear, burned it. Later the predictions she made in the play came true.

Akhmatova herself and the few friends and acquaintances in Tashkent who read the play before she burned it recalled it as being also a literary prediction. Before Ionesco and Beckett, it contained the elements and form of the theater of the absurd. The absurdity of the delirium-induced visions began (albeit very slowly and gradually) to dissipate. Then the play's artistic innovation emerged. Beyond the ancient title and mysterious form, Akhmatova envisioned something new, something similar to the new theater of Europe.

Now she wanted to rewrite the text she had destroyed almost twenty years earlier. But she could not remember even her shortest poems, much less such a long text. And Nadezhda Mandelshtam, Ranevskaya, and others who heard the play in Tashkent could only attest that the individual parts of the play that Akhmatova rewrote had nothing in common with what she had written in Tashkent.

XXI

The last time I saw Akhmatova was in a Moscow hospital in the winter of 1966. I had to go to Leningrad to give reports and lectures and came to tell her good-bye, not knowing it was forever. The Sinyavsky and Daniel trial had just ended. We spoke of their sad fate and about the writers who had tried to defend them.

It was during this meeting that Akhmatova told me about a conversation she had had with Blok when she unexpectedly saw him on a train platform as she was leaving Moscow for St. Petersburg. She had some notes about Blok in her hand, but she didn't so much read them as tell them. She continued to be amused and shocked that Blok asked her whom she was traveling with on the train. More than anything else she liked the way a well-known American literary critic reacted when she told him this story about Blok. "Do you know what he did when he heard about that accidental meeting on the train platform?" She paused for effect: "He whistled!" Anna Andreyevna was charmed by the "cowboy's" carefree attitude.

Her good manners were legend.

Anya Gorenko, Tsarskoye Selo, 1896.

Anna Gorenko after her graduation from the gymnasium,
Kiev, 1907.

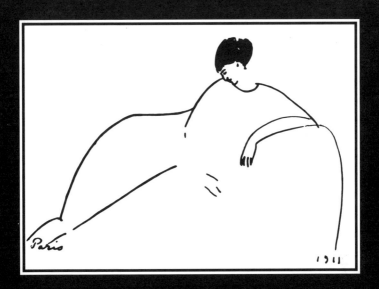

Anna Akhmatova. A drawing by Amedeo Modigliani.

Anna Akhmatova
with relatives and
friends, around 1911.

Anna Akhmatova, Tsarskoye Selo, 1914.

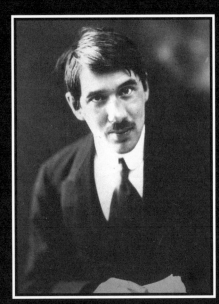

Kornei I. Chukovsky,
1915.

Nikolai Gumilev, Lev Gumilev, and Anna Akhmatova,
Petrograd, 1915.

Anna Akhmatova in the 1920s.

Anna Akhmatova and Nikolai Punin,
Leningrad, 1920s.

Anna Akhmatova's portrait by Kuzma Petrov-Vodkin, 1922.

Akhmatova's portrait by Yury Annenkov.

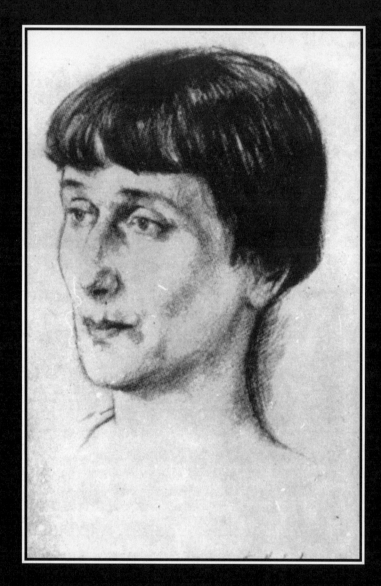

Akhmatova's portrait by Vereisky.

Lev Gumilev, Anna Akhmatova, and Anna Gumileva, 1925.

Anna Akhmatova, Tsarskoye Selo, 1925.

Anna Akhmatova, 1920s.

Left to right: Anna Akhmatova, Osip Mandelshtam,
Mariya Petrovykh, Emile Mandelshtam,
Nadezhda Mandelshtam, Aleksandr Mandelshtam.

Vyacheslav Ivanov.

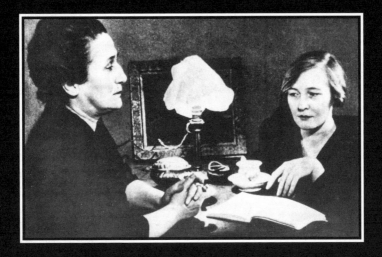

Anna Akhmatova and Olga Bergholtz, Leningrad, 1940.

Anna Akhmatova and Boris Pasternak, Moscow, 1946.

Akhmatova at ceremony awarding the International Literary Prize, Catania, Italy, December 1964.

Akhmatova at her desk, early 1960s.

Anna Akhmatova,
1964.

Anna Akhmatova
in Komarovo near
Leningrad, 1964.

Anna Akhmatova after receiving an honorary degree of
Doctor of Literature from Oxford University, June 1965.

Akhmatova's tomb
in Komarovo.

POETS' CIRCLE: ON AKHMATOVA'S FRIENDS

Boris Anrep

NIKOLAI NEDOBROVO AND ANNA AKHMATOVA

Boris Anrep wrote his recollections of the Russian critic and poet Nikolai Nedobrovo at the request of Gleb Struve, a Russian literary historian. The work was published in 1989 by Stanford University Professor Lazar Fleishman (Akhmatova Collection, Paris, 1989).

In 1899 my father, Professor Vasily Konstantinovich Anrep, was appointed administrator of the Kharkov Academic District. We moved from St. Petersburg to Kharkov, where we stayed in a wonderful, state-owned apartment located in a former palace of Catherine the Great built by Potemkin.

I was sixteen years old and had been transferred from the St. Petersburg Gymnasium to the sixth class of Kharkov Gymnasium No. 3, located on Kokoshkinskaya Street. The pupils attending Kharkov gymnasiums wore grey uniforms; we had worn black in St. Petersburg. It was a large class, and the teacher sat me in the front row of desks—a privilege. Two pupils sat at each desk. I shared mine with a boy by the name of von der Launitz, the son of the wealthy marshal of the nobility. He was a nice boy but not much inclined to scholastic endeavor. He would later become an officer and die a heroic death in the First World War.

The other boys regarded me with interest, partly because I was a newcomer from the capital of St. Petersburg, partly because I was the son of the administrator. Their curiosity made me uncomfortable and I kept to myself. Moreover, the class consisted of all types of boys.

We were having a history lesson on the liberation of Greece. I was not paying attention to what the teacher was saying, being engrossed instead in something more interesting—Shelley's *Prometheus Unbound.* At that time this English poet was one of my favorites, and I did not think the teacher, who was standing between the last row of desks and the back wall, would notice my "crime." Suddenly I heard: "Anrep, name the Greek national hero who played such a significant role in the liberation of Greece."

I stood up and was at a total loss as to what to answer. Vaguely I recalled a famous name:

"Padocordia!" I said loudly and with confidence. The class roared in laughter; the teacher frowned:

"I suggest that you listen more carefully. Nedobrovo, perhaps you can answer my question?"

A refined young man from the last desk in the first row stood up and smiled:

"Kapodistrias played an important role at the time of the Greek rebellion against the Turks. He was born in Corphus in 1776 and was the dictator of liberated Greece for a short time. In 1831 he was assassinated by his political enemies."

"Excellent!" the teacher commented. "I give you a five."*

The lesson ended and the pupils hurried out the door. Embarrassed, I remained seated and took my book out from under my desk. Nedobrovo walked up to me and smiled:

"You're clever. You gave us all a good laugh."

I blushed.

"I see you were reading a book in English. Let me have a look at it."

"I wasn't listening; I was reading Shelley. Padocordia was the best I could come up with."

---

* The highest mark in a five-point grading system.—ed.

"It was great! I also like Shelley, but I don't know English so I read it in translation. Let's go get some lunch."

An elderly lady sat in the corridor selling tea, sandwiches, pressed caviar, and meat and cabbage pastries. Nedobrovo and I began to talk.

"Why did you come to Kharkov? I just dream of going to St. Petersburg. I should be in the seventh class, but I lost an entire year when I came down with meningitis. The doctors forbade any mental work. I vegetated, but now I've been resurrected."

We began to discuss literature. In the early period of our acquaintance and during our subsequent friendship, this was our major topic of discussion. Nedobrovo charmed me right from the beginning with his refined appearance, wonderful manners, and erudition. He forced me to think and give an opinion about things I had never thought of before. For his part, he loved to analyze his own emotions and also poetry and philosophy. And if he criticized my views, he did it with great tact and skillfully obliged me to accept his logic. I was always eager to meet him, and each occasion was eventful.

The first day we met, Nedobrovo waited for me at the door of the gymnasium.

"We live in the same direction. Let's walk together."

Launitz, my desk partner, told me that Nedobrovo spoke little to anyone and considered himself to be head and shoulders above everyone else. He had reason for this. He didn't know foreign languages well enough to converse in them, but he was well-versed in foreign literature, and he astonished me with his astute observations about famous writers. I felt that I wasn't on his level and tried not to make a fool of myself. I began to seek his friendship and was flattered when I felt he also sought mine. We became inseparable, and he usually walked me home.

"Good-bye, Boris Vasilyevich."

"Good-bye, Nikolai Vladimirovich."

We always used the polite form of address and called each other by name and patronymic.

The wife of Professor Lagermark, rector of the university, became acquainted with my mother when we moved to Kharkov. One day, upon my return from the gymnasium, my mother, who was clearly upset, met me and said she wanted to speak with me on a serious matter.

"Madame Lagermark was just here and told me that you are friends with a boy named Nedobrovo. She said you were keeping bad company. She told me that last year Nedobrovo's mother (she had met her a few times) had invited her and her two sons to tea to celebrate her name day. She said that during the general conversation Nedobrovo had interrupted his mother and shouted: 'Keep quiet, you fool! You don't know anything about it.' Madame Lagermark said that she and her sons were dumbfounded and indignant. Nedobrovo's mother left the room, and they stood up and left as well. Since then she had forbidden her boys to see Nedobrovo. She wanted to warn us as well."

I was shaking with indignation:

"She's a sneak and a gossip. I don't believe that happened. Anyway, last year Nedobrovo had meningitis and he was probably in a nervous state."

"All right," my mother said, "you can see him wherever else you want, but he's not to be allowed in this house."

For the two years I lived in Kharkov I never invited Nedobrovo into my home, nor did he invite me into his.

Madame Lagermark gave my mother more information:

"Nedobrovo's mother earns a living by letting rooms to lodgers. His father, it seems, is a district police official, or something along those lines. They say he doesn't live with his wife. Nedobrovo's sister is a beautiful woman who lives somewhere as an actress. You know, Praskovya Mikhailovna, what that means!"

Perhaps it was all true. Nedobrovo never talked to me about his family. But all this gossip seemed to be insignificant if not complete rubbish. It only made me feel compassion for Nedobrovo. If what Madame Lagermark said was true, he had no doubt suffered because of it. In all that time he only once, when we were talking about ancient Russia, mentioned his family history. His ancestor, Boyar Nedobrovo, had been executed by Ivan the Terrible. The *oprichniks*★ had plundered his estates, and since then the Nedobrovo clan had been impoverished.

My friendship with Nedobrovo continued and, if anything, grew stronger. The streets were our refuge, our meeting place. After lessons we

★ Members of the special administrative elite under Ivan the Terrible.—ed.

would walk for hours or sit in the park. He would read his poetry and I would timidly read mine. He encouraged me:

"Your poems have what's best of all—simplicity, sincerity, and 'insouciance.' I've lost that."

I thought he was just making it all up and jokingly accused him of playing at being Onegin.[*]

"Not at all!" he cried with feeling. "I think I'm being too professional."

I wanted to say something kind:

"That's absurd. You're at least trying for technical perfection. I haven't reached that point yet. What you write is already filled with feeling and technical beauty."

We were waiting for the gymnasium ball—my first. It was to play an important role in my two years in Kharkov. We (Nedobrovo and I) met a charming girl by the name of Dina Zhdanova. She was the daughter of the owner of the boiler factory, and both of us fell in love with her. Nedobrovo danced beautifully, and after the dance brought Dina to me. Later, we met her at the exit of the women's gymnasium and strolled a long time together. Then we both walked her home. For the most part, it was Nedobrovo who carried the conversation. Philosophy and poetry were replaced by an analysis of her beauty and character, and what she would be ten years later. I was burning with inner fire but could only say "yes" or finish a thought for him. Mostly, I said nothing. She was reticent by nature and once asked him:

"Why are you saying all this?"

He liked to ask her questions she couldn't answer. Once I said to him:

"Why are you tormenting Dina?"

"Tormenting?" he responded. "You, Boris Vasilyevich, know little about women."

We were not jealous. One day she would express a preference for me, the next for him. People began to talk about our "romance." We were together at several gymnasium balls, and our parents found out about it. The "romance" lasted about two years.

At the end of my seventh year my parents sent me to England while Dina's parents took her to Switzerland. As always, Nedobrovo spent the

---

[*] From Pushkin's poem-as-novel, *Yevgeny Onegin*.—ed.

summer in the Crimea. My romance with Dina ended, for I never saw her again. Later Nedobrovo became enamored of a certain Lisovskaya, a girl who had attended the St. Petersburg Gymnasium and the daughter of Professor Lisovsky. Dina married. I became a balletophile and fell in love with a beautiful ballerina named Sprysinskaya, who later married Kchessinsky, the brother of the famous ballerina.

I was not fated to return to Kharkov. My father was appointed the administrator of the St. Petersburg Academic District, and I went from England directly to St. Petersburg. I received only an occasional letter from Nedobrovo.

In 1902 I entered the Imperial School of Jurisprudence.* I was over-joyed to receive a letter from Nedobrovo saying he was coming to St. Petersburg to attend the University. To my surprise, when I told this to my mother she said:

"I'll be happy to meet your old friend. Surely you'll bring him here?"

I was delighted with this turn of events and impatient to see him. I didn't have to wait long. A few days later, as I turned onto Nevsky Prospekt, I ran into him. He was already wearing the elegant frock-coat of the student (he never wore double-breasted jackets). Unable to restrain my joy, I embraced him, ignoring his embarrassment.

"Nikolai Vladimirovich! I'm so happy! Let's address each other as *ty*." [The informal second-person singular pronoun, pronounced approximately as "tĭih," with the i- of "chĭldren."]

He seemed a little nonplussed:

"Well, if you like. Let it be *ty*."

As far as I know, I was the only friend he addressed with the informal *ty*. In the future, he would even address his wife as "*Vy*, Lyubov Alexandrovna" and she would always answer, "*Vy*, Nikolai Vladimirovich." ["Vy" is the formal pronoun, pronounced "vĭih."]

It turned out that he had already been to my home and found me gone. I was happy about this: It showed that we were both grown up.

"I was just at the Lisovskys," he told me. "I went to apologize for your prank."

"I must admit I was angry with you to begin with. But when I received your 'ingenious' letter, I laughed till I dropped."

* An institution of higher learning for the especially privileged.—ed.

This was what happened. A year before Nedobrovo came to St. Petersburg he wrote and asked me to try to arrange a meeting with Mlle. Lisovskaya in order to keep burning the fire he had kindled in her heart in the Crimea. He gave me her address and told me what gymnasium she was attending. Having returned from England, where I had kept up a lively correspondence with a few English misses, I decided to write the Mlle. a nice, worldly letter stating that my friend Nedobrovo had written me about their meeting in the Crimea and that I would be very happy to call on her. I received a sharp reply from her mother, who told me that "her daughter did not meet with strangers." Period. I understood that I had made a terrible mistake and wrote Mme. Lisovskaya a letter of apology stating that I would come the next day to apologize in person. I was given a cold reception, but I covered for Nedobrovo, saying that it had been entirely my idea (Mme. Lisovskaya was especially interested in what part Nedobrovo had played in the "conspiracy"). While I was talking to Mme. Lisovskaya I heard the rustle of skirts behind the door and knew that Mlle. Lisovskaya was listening. I began to speak louder to make sure she heard every word.

I had to write Nedobrovo about the incident and received a justifiably angry response from him. But by the time he came to St. Petersburg, his affections for Mlle. Lisovskaya had cooled, so it all worked out for the best. Seeing how ashamed I was of my behavior, he thanked me for taking all the blame on myself.

Nedobrovo began to visit my home regularly once a week. Sometimes my mother invited him to lunch. His manners were flawless. He knew to kiss her hand and could conduct polite conversation. Listening to Nedobrovo, my father's interest was piqued, and I soon realized that my friend had won his approval as well. They would have political and academic discussions, in which I scarcely took part. I noticed that Nedobrovo would listen attentively to my father. He often disagreed with him, but was very polite in doing so. Nonetheless, he never surrendered his own position. My father was an "Octobrist"; Nedobrovo was a "Cadet."* Nedobrovo dreamed of a constitution similar to the British model and also believed, taking into consideration the many nationalities, in the logical necessity of a future federated Russian state.

---

* Respectively, The Union of 17 October and Constitutional Democrats, political parties in Russia from 1905 to 1917.—ed.

"Perhaps," my father said, "but I am more interested in the more urgent issue of compulsory education."

I was usually impatient for lunch to end so that I could take Nikolai Vladimirovich into my room and talk about something quite different—Tyutchev, Fet, Annensky, Blok, and other Russian poets, and also Baudelaire and Verlaine, whom we adored. Nedobrovo knew a lot of poetry by heart, and he loved to analyze a poem's content, rhyme, rhythm, and emotional aspects. Having enrolled in the philological curriculum, he was also studying Horatio and Greek poetry. He translated it for me, expounding on the individual beauty of the verses. He would always read me his own poems and asked me to read mine: "I'm interested in how you're developing. . . ."

Nedobrovo offered me friendly criticism, and I usually agreed with his every word. He was very criticial of most of the young poets and did not try to make personal contact with them. Many considered him to be a snob and ostracized him. Perhaps it was his refined nature that made him intolerant of shortcomings in education, imperfect technique, and so forth. Of course, he gave credit to Annensky, Blok, and others, and he especially valued Vyacheslav Ivanov, both as a person and a poet. For his part, Ivanov greatly appreciated the intelligence, critical articles, and literary exigencies of Nikolai Vladimirovich. The two men met frequently and became close friends.

We saw each other less frequently. We were both busy—he in the University (1902–06) and I in the Imperial School of Jurisprudence. Though he kept aloof from many of his colleagues, Nikolai Vladimirovich did seek out those people he found interesting. Evidently he met a few to whom he was attracted and with whom he enjoyed talking. Perhaps because he grew up in the provinces, Nedobrovo was attracted to the glitter of St. Petersburg society. But he avoided superficiality in people and more than anything else valued intelligence and originality. There was another, very interesting thing about him—he was a wonderful figure skater. We would sometimes go skating together, and I, with the other onlookers, would admire his skill on the ice. He also loved to dance. At the balls—for example, those sponsored by the Academy of Arts—he always drew the attention of the ladies. At one of these balls (as far as I can remember), he met one of the most beautiful and famous artists in the world—Lyubov Alexandrovna

Olkhina—and her friend, the artist Dmitry Semyonovich Stelletsky, to whom he introduced me. These new acquaintances were to play an important role in our lives. Stelletsky became like a brother to me and introduced me to entirely new interests. He persuaded me to give up my academic career and to become an artist. Nedobrovo married Lyubov Olkhina.

Until this time I had led a very quiet life. I had no desire to socialize with people and dedicated myself to my law studies. I found the theories of the imminent Professor Lev Petrazhitsky fascinating and was thinking of an academic career with the University.

After graduating from the School of Jurisprudence I was accepted into the fourth level of the University, provided I pass all my transfer exams as well as the State exam. This I did within the course of one year and was taken into Petrazhitsky's department at the University to study for the title of magistrate.

It was during this time that I fell under the influence of Stelletsky and began to paint. Stelletsky was a sculptor and he was then working on a bust of Nedobrovo. He told me I was wasting my life on "lawyerism"; he said that I was an emotional person, a poet, an artist. He took me to the Hermitage and to the Alexander III Museum.* I was incredibly impressed.

"Give it all up," he told me, "dedicate yourself to art . . ."

A new world opened before me. For one year more I tried to combine "lawyerism" with art. Then I thought I would like to have Nedobrovo's opinion. By that time Nikolai Vladimirovich had graduated from the University and was working at the State Duma Chancellery. I was happy that my father had recommended him. Nedobrovo welcomed me with particular warmth.

"You are experiencing a storm in yourself that you might not ever experience again. Your material needs are provided for, and you burn with desire. Stelletsky is right in saying you might not ever be a famous artist. But what is fame in the face of love? You will always regret not following your own awakened passion. Forget your 'lawyerism,' as Stelletsky puts it, and go to Paris"—this is what Stelletsky had recommended—"and start your new life. I give you my blessing, even though I fear that I will lose you. But let's ask Lyubov Alexandrovna."

---

* Now the Russian Museum in Leningrad.—ed.

Of course, Lyubov Alexandrovna persuaded me as well. Then they both kissed me, which moved me deeply.

Professor Petrazhitsky was suffering with smallpox and this prevented me from bidding him farewell in person. To be honest, I was glad of this. I sent him a bouquet of white lilacs, explained the change that had taken place in me, and asked him to forgive my "treachery."

Stelletsky took complete charge of me. I went with him to Italy and to Paris, where I gazed my fill of great art. I grew under his guidance and also studied at various academies of art. In 1908 I moved to Paris for good. In the summer I would return to visit my parents in Russia. Nedobrovo, however, was loyal to the Crimea, and was usually away. We corresponded. I learned of his marriage to Lyubov Olkhina. This marriage caused quite a stir in St. Petersburg, for Nikolai Vladimirovich had insisted that it take place in the State Council Church, where lackeys in livery and white stockings stood in a row along the carpeted main staircase.

As I recall, Lyubov Alexandrovna told me her father had once been exiled for political reasons. She lived with him in exile when she was a little girl, and she could remember how she loved to sit under his desk and play with her dolls as he wrote. She was a kind, saintly woman and totally devoted to Nikolai Vladimirovich. And he was deeply devoted to her. As I mentioned earlier, artists highly esteemed her stylized beauty. She attended costume balls in a Renaissance dress. This was the era she especially loved and much of the furniture in her apartment was from this period. Gossipers said it was an unsuitable marriage, that Nedobrovo was unworthy of Lyubov Alexandrovna, and that the fancy wedding showed bad taste on the part of the groom.

I was in Paris when they married and sent a congratulatory telegram. For some reason many people did not believe Nedobrovo was sincere. I detested these rumors, which went so far as to claim that "he had married Lyubov Alexandrovna for her furniture." I can swear that Nedobrovo loved no one more sincerely and deeply than Lyubov Alexandrovna.

In Paris, I received an occasional letter from him. I took them as evidence of our continuing friendship, and they cheered me up.

One day Nedobrovo and his wife came to Paris, and we spent a great deal of time together seeing the city and museums. I was already tired of this pastime, for I was absorbed in thought about my own art. Nor did I forget my verse: I wrote a long symbolic poem entitled *Fiza*.

I believe it was in 1912 when Nikolai Vladimirovich wrote that he and his wife would be traveling to Munich. I decided to meet them there. Of course, I took *Fiza* with me, for I was anxious to read it to them. I read with some trepidation. When I finished, I could tell by the expression on their faces that they were pleased.

Nikolai Vladimirovich said, "You can see for yourself that I'm speechless. I can see that Lyubov Alexandrovna feels the same way."

I knew even then that my poem had technical faults, but I also knew that it had "something." And whatever that "something" was, it had reached beyond Nedobrovo's friendly feelings for me and touched something deeper than his analytical intellect.

In 1913 I learned from one of Nedobrovo's letters that he had made the acquaintance of Anna Andreyevna Akhmatova and thought her poetry exceptionally fine.

In 1914 I returned to Russia as a reserve officer and visited Nedobrovo at his Tsarskoye Selo apartment. It was there I met Anna Akhmatova. I immediately understood that I was in the presence of a remarkable woman and poet and that her friendship was extremely important to Nikolai Vladimirovich.

Let me go back a few years: I had returned from Paris to visit St. Petersburg. Nedobrovo told me that Vyacheslav Ivanov wanted to meet me and was inviting me to a soiree in his home that would be attended by several young poets. Nedobrovo and I went together. Both the host and hostess (Vyacheslav Ivanov's stepdaughter, Mlle. Shvartselon) met us warmly. The poets read their poems, and the host asked first one guest and then another for his opinion. One poet read a sonnet filled with mythological figures: Dionysius, Pan, various muses and satyrs, nymphs and naiads.

"Boris Vasilyevich, what is your opinion of this sonnet?"

I was not expecting the question and blurted out:

"A wonderful poem. But what is the need for all those satyrs? Is it a mythological ballet?" I fell silent.

Everyone smiled and I felt embarrassed. Nedobrovo was sitting next to me, and it was evident that he had not heard the poem or my comment.

"And you, Nikolai Vladimirovich?" asked Vyacheslav Ivanov.

"Me? Oh, I always agree with Boris Vasilyevich." And he laughed. Seeing my embarrassment, Mlle. Shvartselon sat down beside me and began to ask me about my life in Paris. I have always remembered her kindness.

On another trip to St. Petersburg, Nedobrovo told me that Vyacheslav Ivanov wanted to hear *Fiza*. Nedobrovo arranged a meeting at his apartment on Konnogvardeiskaya, not far from the State Duma. The apartment was small but beautifully furnished with objects from the Renaissance period. Apparently, Nikolai Vladimirovich to a certain extent identified himself with this era. And, in truth, such exquisite surroundings were appropriate for his thin, elegant figure. Both he and his wife appeared to be completely happy there.

I arrived feeling nervous. "It's like an exam," I thought. Vyacheslav Ivanov, an important figure in the literary world, met me with a few kind words.

Nedobrovo seated me and whispered:

"Don't be nervous. Read the way you read to us."

I apologized for the length of the poem.

"No matter," Ivanov replied, "poems are always long."

My nervousness left me. I read, and when I was finished felt excited by my own work. Lyubov Alexandrovna stood up and kissed me. I heard Nedobrovo say to Vyacheslav Ivanov:

"Didn't I tell you?"

Vyacheslav Ivanov nodded.

"I am amazed that being so removed from literary circles Boris Vasilyevich could write such a poem."

Vyacheslav Ivanov and I remained in the room alone for a few minutes.

"What I like is that you remain totally 'defenseless' in your poem." I didn't understand what he meant.

"To defend oneself is to repudiate oneself," I replied.

"You are absolutely right. That is what I appreciate."

It was time to go. Nedobrovo saw me to the hall and said:

"Thank you, Boris Vasilyevich. Write me from Paris. It will be a long time before we see each other again, and I very much want to stay in contact with you."

Each expression of his friendship touched me, especially since I knew how uncomfortable it made him to put his feelings into spoken words, though he could do this skillfully and with sincerity in his letters. I knew that the reserve he showed was only superficial, that inside he was a warm and emotional individual.

These episodes I have described took place in different years before the war.

I was charmed by Anna Akhmatova when Nedobrovo introduced us in 1914. After I left for the front her image stayed in my heart, and on my leaves I saw both Nedobrovo and Akhmatova in Petrograd and in Tsarskoye Selo. [. . .]

My interest in Akhmatova's poetry grew into adoration. The conversations I had with Nedobrovo began to revolve around one theme: Akhmatova and her work.

In 1916 I was sent from the front to Britain, where I worked with the Russian Governmental Committee and where I once again met Gumilev (who had come from Paris and was working in the Committee's cryptography department).

I traveled to Petrograd several times on military matters, departing it for the last time ten days before the Bolsheviks seized power in 1917. To my deep sorrow, I learned on that last trip that Nedobrovo was suffering from tuberculosis and had been moved to the Crimea. I was utterly grieved by this news and wrote him at once. I remember only one line—a foolish, unpardonable, "defenseless," as Vyacheslav Ivanov would say, sentence: "Dear man, don't die. You and Anna Andreyevna are all of Russia to me."

I never received an answer. I returned to Britain with the British generals and later learned of Nikolai Vladimirovich's death in the Crimea and also of Lyubov Alexandrovna's demise in San Remo.

Nedobrovo's passing affected me deeply. Many years later I learned from an individual who was close to him that Nedobrovo had ceased to feel kindly about me because he was jealous over Anna Akhmatova. I never felt this change in him, which of course was totally unjustified. My admiration for Akhmatova was strictly literary and platonic.

THREE RECOLLECTIONS

One day, when I was still studying jurisprudence, Nedobrovo and I were walking down Palace Embankment, a stone's throw away from my school. Nedobrovo was deep in thought. Heavy clouds gathered and suddenly there was a peal of thunder. "The prophet Elijah goes for a ride in the sky," I said. To my surprise, instead of smiling as usual at one of my "childish observations," Nedobrovo turned to me and asked:

"Do you believe in God?"

"What a question!" I exclaimed. "What about you?"

"I look at religious philosophy as an early period of scientific knowledge that I would call the period of 'figurative' thinking and the incipient and patriarchal substantiation of moral principles. But when I think of all the beauty in art and literature that has derived from this primitive, 'figurative' philosophy, I give it due credit. But, today when we speak or sing about it, or when we paint divine subjects, it comes off false, a mere artistic method. Though I am a total disbeliever, I listen with reverence and musical satisfaction to church singing and I admire the Easter mass. Many other rational and scientific people share these feelings. Just as enjoying the fragrance of a rose has nothing to do with reason. How can you explain this?"

"You describe my own thoughts. I can't explain it."

I remembered Nedobrovo's words almost verbatim, and would later recall them frequently. The memory of them filled my soul with joy when I created mosaics on religious themes for churches. Thus I, an agnostic, could shape saintly faces with love and tenderness, and my hands and soul reach out for the icons as if toward the highest expression of the human spirit.

•   •   •

Winter. Once again we were walking down Palace Embankment and saw a beautiful sleigh coming in our direction. Small crowns were fitted around the lights, which indicated that it was the Tsar or a member of the royal family. The policemen saluted, and I, in accordance with juridical regulations, stood at attention and touched my three-corner hat. Nedobrovo asked:

"What are you doing?"

"Didn't you see? It was the Tsar's sleigh. I think it was Grand Prince Mikhail."

"You should have told me. I would have removed my cap."

"I'm sorry. I didn't have time."

"It's not important. *Ce n'est que pour la forme.*"

But I could tell that he thought it was important.

• • •

Nedobrovo was waiting for me in the vestibule of the School of Jurisprudence. He was engaged in conversation with our doorman—a tall, imposing figure dressed in the beautiful uniform of palace opulence who would lend money at interest to jurisprudence students. We walked out to Fontanka and at the door ran into a charming lady. We walked a little further on, talking about her. Suddenly Nedobrovo asked me:

"How do you plan to spend your wedding night?"

I was taken aback by the unexpected question and somewhat stupidly answered: "In the normal way."

"That's what I thought. You are a very normal person. You see your wedding night as the necessary way in which to become intimate. I, on the other hand, plan to enter into intimate relations months before I marry or else will wait six months after the wedding."

As a rule we never spoke about such things.

I saw Anna Andreyevna in Paris in 1965. She had come to the city a few days after her ceremonial reception in Oxford. We talked about Nedobrovo. . . .

"Do you remember our meeting on 13 February at Nedobrovo's apartment in Tsarskoye Selo? He read us *Judith*. I never read it myself, but I remember it."

Yes, I remembered *Judith*, and I remembered 13 February, when we met to listen to Nedobrovo's tragic poem. Despite its impressive form, I was not as impressed as I ought to have been, because I was completely overwhelmed by the presence of Anna Andreyevna and could not find the words to say something flattering. Anna Andreyevna, who was sitting next to me on the sofa, said something polite. I felt that Nedobrovo expected more. Fortunately, Lyubov Alexandrovna entered and invited us to the dining room for tea. There, among the general conversation, the poem was forgotten.

Yes, I remembered the night of 13 February 1916 we listened to *Judith*, when I received from Anna Andreyevna her book of verse *Evening* with her inscription.

Yes, I remember *Judith* and the day when for the hundredth time I read Anna Andreyevna's words:

In my mind this month will live. . . .*

In Paris in 1965 Anna Andreyevna and I had nothing to say, until finally I spoke:

"I was much saddened by Nikolai Vladimirovich's early death."
"And I," she whispered.

I never saw Anna Andreyevna again. . . .   13 February 1969

Artur Lurye

OLGA AFANASYEVNA GLEBOVA-SUDEIKINA

Artur Lurye, composer and friend of Akhmatova who emigrated in 1922. His recollections are of the actress and artist Olga Glebova-Sudeikina (1885–1945), a close friend of Akhmatova's in the 1910s–20s. In 1924 Glebova-Sudeikina emigrated to Paris. She served as the prototype of Akhmatova's heroine in Poem Without a Hero.

> . . . When at the past years you stare
> You see mirage or nightmare . . .
>   A. Blok

Long golden braids, like Melisinda's, or like Debussy's *la fille aux cheveux de laine;* large grey-green eyes that sparkle like opals; porcelain shoulders, the "bosom of Diana" virtually exposed by the sharp decollete of her

---

* Anna Akhmatova, *Selected Poems,* translated by Walter Arndt (Ann Arbor: Ardis, 1976).—ed.

bodice; a captivating smile; fleeting, soft laugh, fleeting, soft movements—who is she? A butterfly? A Colombina? Perhaps a fairy in a shimmering doll kingdom, where everything is happiness and joy, where every day is a holiday?

Olga Afanasyevna Glebova-Sudeikina, Petersburg's magical fairy, entered my life the year before the First World War. Nikolai Ivanovich Kulbin brought me to her. I brought with me two notebooks of my "Greek Songs" based on Sappho's poems as translated by Vyacheslav Ivanov. Olga Afanasyevna immediately liked the songs. In those days she would ask me to play and sing them for her every time we met.

Olga Afanasyevna adored music and art and all their possible manifestations; she immersed herself in them. Painting, sculpture, poetry, theater—all were equally important and dear to her. She lived only for art, making a cult of it. At that first meeting she spoke to us about Italy, from where she had just returned with our mutual friend, Saveli Sorin. They traveled together to Florence, and Olga Afanasyevna spoke of Saveli with great admiration. It was in Florence, incidentally, where Olga Afanasyevna became friends with a Franciscan monk, who sent her baskets of fresh figs from the abbey garden, while she brought him flowers.

When we were young, Olga Afanasyevna's life revolved around the Italian commedia dell'arte. She could talk incessantly about Carlo Gozzi's theater; all the actors in the Italian theater group were her close friends. Her passion for the mask theater pushed her off the normal path of artistic development. She was an actress with the Alexandrine Theater, and Varlamov's favorite student, when the omnipotent Suvorin took her under his wing. Enchanted by her talent, Suvorin asked Olga Afanasyevna to join his own theater. But, under the influence of Sudeikin, she went over to modernism, to Meierkhold, and gave up the brilliant career that was hers for the taking.

At that time Belyaev's plays were very popular, and Olga Afanasyevna had a part in each one—"Psyche," "The Lady from Torzhok," and "Muddle-headed lady." In the dedication of her *Poem Without a Hero*, Akhmatova speaks of her character ("Was it you, Psyche, etc."). Sudeikin painted a wonderful portrait of Olga in this role. She also played in Sheldon's play, in Skribe's "Glass of Water," and, of course, in the plays of Goldoni and Gozzi.

Olga Afanasyevna was one of the most naturally talented people I have ever known. Only in Russia could such a phenomenon occur. She was like a fairy—anything she touched was imbued with magic: the magic of people, feelings, and things. Like a fairy, Olga Afanasyevna possessed keys to magical worlds, and these keys opened doors to the unseen and unheard. Everything surrounding her glowed with the bright flame of art.

This magical fairy came from the common people, from the heart of Russia—the province of Pskov. Her grandfather was a peasant and her great-grandfather was a serf. I remember an old daguerreotype of her grandfather. He was sitting at a round table upon which sat a bouquet of flowers and his top hat. He had a beard and was wearing a long frock-coat. As was the custom in those times, he wore rubber galoshes on holidays. Olga Afanasyevna took Sergei Yuryevich Sudeikin—the hope of Russian modernism and a refined aesthete—to visit her provincial grandfather, where they lived in a hut and Sergei made sketches. Both of them were elated by the experience.

Olga Afanasyevna's father was a Petersburg office functionary, much like the poor functionaries described by Dostoyevsky. He frequently drank and, as a young girl, Olga Afanasyevna would search for him in the taverns. When she found him, she would take him by the hand and lead him home. Looking at the little girl wearing her mother's shawl, the father and his drunk friends would shed bitter tears.

Olga Afanasyevna loved to entertain her best friends in the famous Ozarovsky "theater house." This exquisite little house contained Elizabethan furniture made of Karelian birch, harpsichords, Venetian mirrors, Russian glass, portraits by Borovikovsky, and paintings of beautiful women by Venetsianov. Olga Afanasyevna reigned among these treasures like a queen. A visit to her was always like a holiday, and each visit was always commemorated in some way—either by a little present or by a tasty treat she had prepared. She could do anything: bake cookies, make jam, pickle mushrooms, sew, bead, and paint. She also knew how to make dolls, and created such masterpieces as Don Juan, Queen of the Night, Desdemona, Hamlet, and d'Artagnan. Her imagination was limitless. Olga Afanasyevna presented me with such a collection of dolls. She kept them in special boxes, taking them out when guests arrived. Everyone was enchanted by them. Olga Afanasyevna knew the style of every era, and her taste was impeccable. I remember how she used to like to walk to Alexandrovsk Market, where she knew all the sellers. She would bring back all kinds of improbable things she had uncovered among the junk: old china, snuff-boxes, miniatures, and knick-knacks.

Olga Afanasyevna was loved and admired by everyone. She grew to be so popular that she was asked to take part in what was at the time a novel event in the city: modeling clothes for Petersburg fashion houses.

Several important plays were being performed at that time, including Kuzmin's "Venetian Follies." This was staged in the home of the wealthy Nosov, and the opulence of the performance was unparalleled. Olga's costumes were based on the drawings of Sudeikin. People described the event as "exquisite."

Olga Afanasyevna was exceptionally musical; she had an extraordinary musical memory and a wonderful ear. She could sing anything at a moment's notice. She could also sing a second part. When I was composing the piano piece "Toccada" in Paris, Olga was in my studio and immediately began to sing along, improvising the words: "Here I bowed low to my mother, do not scold me, my dear." Olga Afanasyevna could "melodize" a note. I wrote down a number of old folk songs from her voice, one of which I used in writing my "Arazh." Kuzmin described Olga's musical ability in the short poem he wrote about us three (with the help of Yuri Yurkun, then the companion of Kuzmin).

Olga Afanasyevna was never interested in the theory of aesthetics; I never heard her speak of the intellectual concepts of art. In her mind and heart, everything connected with art was concrete, though she could easily grasp the intellectual concepts in every sphere of art, regardless of epoch or style.

It was all natural and convincing, as if she had always known what she heard at the moment, but all of her aesthetic knowledge was empirical; it came out of real action.

Olga Afanasyevna represented the refined epoch of Petersburg in the early twentieth century in the same way that Madame Récamier—*la divine Juliette*—represented the epoch of the early Empire style. Olga Afanas-yevna's taste was the taste of the epoch and her style was the style of the epoch—refined and fanciful.

Anna Akhmatova on Osip Mandelshtam
PAGES FROM A DIARY

Akhmatova began to write her reminiscences on Osip Mandelshtam (1891–1937) in 1957. Several drafts were made, but Akhmatova apparently did not accept any as the final text. In this book we offer the excerpt kept in the State Public Library in Leningrad.

28 JULY 1957

. . . And in some mysterious way the death of Lozinsky disrupted my train of recollections. I can no longer recall things that he is no longer able to confirm (about the Poets' Guild, acmeism, the *Giperborei* magazine, and such). Because of his illness we met only infrequently the past few years, and I was unable to finish telling him some very important things or to read him *Requiem,* my poetry from the thirties. For this reason, to a certain extent, he continued to think of me as he knew me in Tsarskoye Selo. I realized this in 1949, when we both looked at the proofs of my collection *From Six Books. . . .**

Something like this also occurred with Mandelshtam (who, of course, knew all my poetry). He was unable to remember. To be more precise, memory for him was a different kind of mental process. I don't know what to call it, but it's something akin to creativity. (As for example, Petersburg in *Noise of the Times*** is seen through the shining eyes of a five-year-old child.)

Mandelshtam was a brilliant conversationalist: he did not listen to himself speak and did not answer himself, as almost everyone does now. While conversing, he was considerate, clever, and incredibly diverse. I never heard him repeat himself or play a worn-out record. Osip Emilyevich had a great aptitude for languages. He could recite from memory whole pages of the *Divina Comedia* in Italian.

Not long before his death he asked Nadia to teach him English, which he did not know at all. He spoke with a blind passion about poetry and

---

* Akhmatova's 1940 collection, published in Leningrad.—ed.
** Mandelshtam's autobiography.—ed.

was sometimes unbelievably unjust—to Blok, for example. About Pasternak he said, "I have thought about him so much it has made me tired," and "I am certain he never read a single line I wrote."* About Marina [Tsvetayeva]: "I am an antitsvetayevist."

Osip felt at home with music, and this is a rare quality. More than anything else he feared his own inability to speak. When this happened, he went crazy and came up with outlandish reasons to explain his trouble. His second and frequent disappointment was his readers. It always seemed to him that the people who liked his work were not the right people. He knew well and remembered the poetry of others and would often have great affection for a few lines; for example: "On the earth, heated by the pounding horses / Lie the white clothes of my brother—Snow . . ." (I know these lines only from him. Who wrote them?). He easily remembered what was read to him. He liked to talk about what he called his "idolation." Sometimes, wanting to comfort me, he would tell me something silly. For example, how when he was very young he had translated Mallarmé's line, "*La jeune femme allaitant son enfant*" into "And the young mother breastfeeds her baby when she awakes." We made each other laugh so hard that we sank down on the couch with its squeaking springs. We laughed ourselves semiconscious, like the candy shop waitresses in Joyce's *Ulysses.*

I met Mandelshtam at Vyacheslav Ivanov's "Tower"** in the spring of 1911. At that time he was a thin young man who wore a lily-of-the-valley in his buttonhole, carried his head high, and had eyelashes that came half-way down his cheeks. The second time I saw him was at the Tolstoys' on Staro-Nevsky. He didn't recognize me, and A[leksei] N[ikolaevich] began to ask him what kind of wife Gumilev had. Osip spread his hands to demonstrate what a large hat I had been wearing. I became alarmed that he would say something unforgivable and told him who I was.

This was my first Mandelshtam, the author of the *Green Stone†* (Acme Publishers) with the inscription: "To Anna Akhmatova—bursts of consciousness in the forgetfulness of days. Respectfully, the author."

* Time would prove him right (see Pasternak's autobiography, in which he writes that he did not appreciate four poets of his time: Gumilev, Khlebnikov, Bagritsky, and Mandelshtam).

** The name given to the apartment of poet Vyacheslav Ivanov, a writers' and artists' gathering place from about 1900 to 1920.—ed.

† Mandelshtam's first book of verse (1912).—ed.

With his characteristic self-irony, Osip loved to tell how an elderly Jew—the owner of the printing press where *Stone* was printed—congratulated him on his book by shaking his hand and saying: "Young man, you will write better and better."

I see him as if through light smoke—the fog of Vasilyevsky Island—and in the former "Kinshy"* restaurant, where at one time, according to legend, Lomonosov sold a watch he did not own to pay for a drink and where we (Gumilev and I) sometimes came from "Tuchka"** to have breakfast.

This was Mandelshtam—the generous co-author if not author of *Anthology of Ancient Stupidity*, which was written by members of the Poets' Guild (almost all of them except me) at dinner.

Just recently Osip Emilyevich's letters to Vyacheslav Ivanov (1909) were discovered. These are the letters of the member of the (Tower) Academy. This is Mandelshtam the symbolist. There is no record that Vyacheslav Ivanov ever answered. They were written by an eighteen-year-old boy, but one could swear the author of these letters was forty. They include many poems—good poems, but lacking that which we call Mandelshtam.

The memoirs of his sister,† Adelaida Gertsyk, confirm that Vyacheslav Ivanov did not acknowledge us all. In 1911 Mandelshtam felt no reverence toward him.

When Vyacheslav Ivanov came to St. Petersburg in 1919 (?), he stayed with the [Feodor] Sologubs at Razyezhaya. It was an unusually ceremonious evening and a sumptuous dinner. Mandelshtam approached me in the parlor and said: "I think one Master is an impressive sight, but two is a little comic."

The Guild boycotted the Academy of Poetry.

In the 1910s, of course, we met each other everywhere: in the editorial offices, at the homes of friends, on Friday evenings in Giperborei; i.e.,

---

* The corner of the No. 2 line and Bolshoi Prospekt. A hairdresser shop is there now.

** There were no gatherings at "Tuchka," nor could there have been. It was Nikolai Stepanovich's modest student's room, and there wasn't even a place to sit down. The five o'clock tea described (in Georgy Ivanov's *Poets*) is a fabrication from beginning to end. N[ikolai] V[ladimirovich] N[edobrovo] never crossed the threshold of "Tuchka."

† Yevgeniya Gertsyk (1879–1944), translator, writer, friend of Vyacheslav Ivanov.—ed.

at Lozinsky's, at Stray Dog where, by the way, he [Mandelshtam] introduced me to Mayakovsky* (he related this to Khardzhiev in a humorous
way in the 1920s), in the "Academy of Poetry" (the Society of Guardians
of the Artistic Word headed by Vyacheslav Ivanov), and at the Poets'
Guild meetings that were hostile to the Academy and where Mandelshtam
soon became the first fiddle. It was then that he wrote (and not too suc-
cessfully) a mysterious poem about a black angel in the snow. Nadia claims
it refers to me.

"Black Angel" is, I believe, a complicated subject. For Mandelshtam
at that time, the poem is weak and vague. Apparently it was never published. It seems this was the result of a conversation with V. K. Shileiko,
who then said much the same thing about me. But at that time Osip still
was "incapable" (his word) of writing poems "To and About women."
"Black Angel" was probably his first attempt, and this explains its similarity to my lines:

> The wings of black angels are sharp,
> the last judgment is near
> and the crimson bonfires
> like roses flower in the snow.
>   [Rosary]

Mandelshtam never read me this poem. It's well known that his conversation with Shileiko inspired him to write "The Egyptian."

Gumilev developed an early appreciation for Mandelshtam. They met
in Paris (see the end of Mandelshtam's poem about Gumilev; it states that
N. S. wore powder and was in a top-hat).

> But in Petersburg I am fonder of the acmeist,
> Than I am of the romantic Pierot in Paris.

The symbolists never accepted him.

Osip would come to Tsarskoye. When he would fall in love, which
happened rather frequently, I was sometimes his confidante. As I recall, the
first was Anna Mikhailovna Zelmanova-Chudovskaya, a beautiful artist.
She drew his portrait, with his head held high, on a blue background (1914,

---

* Once at the Stray Dog, when everyone was eating and the dishes were clattering, Mayakovsky got
it into his head to recite. O. E. went up to him and said: "Mayakovsky, quit reciting. You're not a
Romanian orchestra." I was present. The witty Mayakovsky could think of no reply.

Alexeyevskaya Street). He didn't write poetry for her, something he seriously regretted—he was still incapable of writing love poems. The second
was Tsvetayeva, who was the subject of his Crimean and Moscow poems;
the third—Salomea Andronikova (Andreyeva, now Galpern, whom
Mandelshtam immortalized in his book *Tristia*: "Solominka, when . . .")*

Osip did in fact travel to Warsaw, and he was shocked by the ghetto
there (M. A. Z. remembers this as well). But as for his alleged attempt at
suicide reported by Georgy Ivanov, even Nadia knew nothing of it, nor
of the daughter named Lipochka whom she was said to have borne.

At the beginning of the Revolution (1920), when I was living all alone
and did not meet even with him, Osip was for a time in love with Olga
Arbenina, an actress at the Alexandrine Theater who later became the wife
of Yu. Yurkin. He wrote her poems, and though the manuscripts were said
to have been lost during the time of the blockade, I recently saw them in
the possession of Kh[ardzhiev].

Mandelshtam dedicated some beautiful poems to Olga Vaksel and to
her memory: "In the cold Stockholm grave . . ."

Many years later he would refer to all these pre-revolutionary ladies
(myself included, I'm afraid) as "Sweet European beauties":

> Oh you, sweet European beauties,
> How bitterly you made me suffer!

From 1933 to 1934 Osip Emilyevich felt a passionate but unrequited
love for Mariya Sergeyevna Petrovykh. He dedicated to her or, to be more
precise, wrote about her, a poem that I have titled "Turkish woman." In
my opinion, it is the best love poem of the twentieth century. Mariya
Sergeyevna—the "master of guilty glances"—says that there was another
magical poem about the color white. Apparently the manuscript has been
lost, but Mariya Sergeyevna remembers some lines by heart.

The lady who "looked over her shoulder" is "Byaka," who at that time
was the very close friend of S. Yu. Sudeikin and today is married to Igor
Stravinsky.

In Voronezh Osip had a friendship with Natasha Stempel. Allegations
of his infatuation with Anna Radlova are completely groundless.

---

* One of the lines: "What does a certain woman know about the hour of death?" Compare with my
line: "I do not wait for the hour of death." I remember Salomea's magnificent bedroom on Vasilyevsky
Island.

The 1910s were an important and creative time for Mandelshtam, and his work (on Villon, Chaadayev, Catholicism) provide much material for future discussion and writing. Concerning his contacts with the "Giley" group, see the recollections of Zenkevich (published?).

Osip's 1920 visit to Petersburg is recalled not only in his beautiful poems to O. Arbenina in *Tristia* [break in text] but also by the faded posters like Napoleonic banners from that era where the name of Mandelshtam is written beside that of Gumilev and Blok.

For example: [break in text]

All the old Petersburg placards were still in place, but there was nothing but dust, gloom, and gaping emptiness behind them. Typhus, hunger, shootings, darkened apartments, damp firewood, and people swollen beyond recognition. You could gather a large bouquet of wild flowers in Gostiny Dvor. The famous wooden paving blocks in Petersburg* were rotting, yet the smell of chocolate still wafted from the basement window of "Kraft" (at the corner of Sadovaya and Italyanskaya). All the cemeteries were devastated. The city did not just change, it was transformed into its opposite. But the people loved poetry (especially the young), almost as much as now; i.e., 1964.

Mandelshtam was rather diligent in attending the Guild meetings, but in the winter of 1913–14 (after the debacle of acmeism) we began to tire of the Guild. Osip and I even gave Gorodetsky and Gumilev a written request to close it. S. Gorodetsky handed down a resolution: "Hang everyone, but imprison Akhmatova." This was in the editorial office of *Severniye Zapiski*.

The Poets' Guild 1911–1914

Gumilev "Syndics"
Gorodetsky
Dm. Kuzmin-Karavayev—Attorney
O. Mandelshtam
Vl. Narbut
I. Zenkevich

---

* Into the early twentieth century the streets Bolshaya Morskaya and Millionnaya (today Khalturina) and part of Nevsky Prospekt were paved with wood.—ed.

I. Bruni
Georgy Ivanov
Adamovich
Vas. Vas. Gippius
M. Moravskaya
Yel. Kuzmina-Karavayeva
Chernayvsky
M. Lozinsky
O. Radimov
Yunger
N. Burlyuk
Vel. Khlebnikov
Akhmatova
Gr. V. Komarovsky
Kn. Gedroits

The first meeting was at Gorodetsky's apartment on Fontanka. Blok and the Frenchmen were there. The second was held at Liza's on Manezhnaya Square, and the next was at Bruni's place in the Academy of Arts. Acmeism was defined by us (in Tsarskoye Selo, Malaya 63).

By the time of the Revolution Mandelshtam was already an accomplished poet and, among a small circle, well known. He was among the first to write on political subjects and considered the Revolution to be an extremely important event. It is not coincidental that the word *narod* [people] is so prominent in his verse.

I met Mandelshtam quite frequently in 1917 and 1918, when I lived with the Sreznevskys on Vyborgskaya (Botkinskaya 9). I wasn't living in the insane asylum but in the apartment of the head physician Vyacheslav Vyacheslavovich Sreznevsky, the husband of my friend Valeria Sergeyevna.

Mandelshtam would often call on me. We would take carriage rides across the incredible bumps of the revolutionary winter and among the infamous bonfires that burned almost until May. We would hear the sound of rifles firing, but we couldn't tell where they were. This was how we rode to the recitals at the Academy of Arts. They were held for the benefit of the wounded, and we both gave several recitals. Osip was with me at the Butumo-Nezvanova concert in the conservatory where she sang Schubert. This was the period when Mandelshtam wrote his poems to me! "Time blossomed . . ." (*"To Cassandra")** "The way you speak is miraculous"; a strange prediction he wrote to me has partly come true:

> In that crazy capital on Neva,
> some Scythian holiday,
> some sickening land ball,
> they'll rip the kerchief off that lovely head . . .**

And another—"The clock-cricket singing"—that was when I lay in fever and we measured my temperature:

> That's the fever rustling,
> The dry stove hissing,
> That's the fire in red silk . . .

After some hesitation, I have decided to state in these notes that at one time I felt compelled to tell Osip that we shouldn't meet so often. I thought it would give people the wrong impression about us. Afterwards, around March, Mandelshtam disappeared. At that time everyone used to disappear and then reappear, and no one was surprised by this.

In Moscow Mandelshtam began to work full-time for *Znamya Truda*.

Again and just briefly, in autumn 1918, I saw Osip in Moscow. In 1920 he came to visit me a couple of times when I was living on Sergievskaya Street (Petersburg) and working in the library of the Institute of Agronomy. It was then that I learned he had been arrested by Whites in the Crimea and by the Mensheviks in Tiflis. And he told me that N. V. N. [Nedobrovo] had died in December of 1919.

In the summer of 1924 Osip brought his young wife to meet me (Fontanka 2). Nadia was what the French call *laide mais charmante*.

This marked the beginning of my friendship with Nadia, and it continues to this day.

---

* Four quatrains were written to me in different years:
  1) "You want to be wound like a toy" (1911)
  2) "A face twisted" (1910)
  3) "Bees get used to the bee-keeper" (1930s)
  4) "On the decline of our acquaintance . . ." (1930s)

** *Complete Poetry of Osip Emilyevich Mandelshtam*. Translated by Burton Raffel and Alla Burago. State University of New York Press. Albany, 1973, pp. 96–97.—ed.

Osip was unquestionably and incredibly in love with Nadia. When she had her appendix removed in Kiev, he slept in the small room of the hospital doorman and never left the hospital. He kept Nadia always by his side, did not permit her to work, and was insanely jealous. He also asked her advice about every word he wrote in a poem. In my entire life I never saw anything like this. Mandelshtam's letters to his wife bear it out.

In 1925 I lived on the same floor as the Mandelshtams in the Zaitsev Boarding House in Tsarskoye Selo. Both Nadia and I were very ill. We stayed in bed and checked our temperatures, which were quite high. As I recall, we never once went for a walk in the nearby park. Each day Osip would travel to Leningrad to try to settle some professional matters and obtain some money. It was there that he took me into his confidence and read the poem he had written to Olga Vaksel, which I remembered and secretly wrote down. And it was there that he dictated his recollections of Gumilev to P. N. L. [Pavel Luknitsky].

One winter, because of Nadia's health, the Mandelshtams lived in the lyceum in Tsarskoye Selo. I visited them several times and went skiing. They had wanted to live in the semicircle of Bolshoi Dvor, but the stoves were smoky or else the roofs leaked, so they moved into the lyceum. Osip did not like it there. He positively despised the so-called Tsarskoye Selo lisp of Gollerbakh and Rozhdestvensky and could not abide speculation about Pushkin. Osip had an unusually stern attitude toward Pushkin. He hated anything that was "Pushkinized." Neither Nadia nor I had any idea that the line "They carry yesterday's sun on a black stretcher" referred to Pushkin until just recently (1950s) when we read Osip's notebooks.

Mandelshtam picked up off my desk my "Last Fairy Tale"* (the article on *The Golden Cockerel*), read it and said: "It's truly like a chess game."

 . . . Did Alexander's sun hang, a hundred years ago,
 Shining on everyone? . . . (December 1917)

These words, too, (so he said) are also about Pushkin.

In the summer I also visited the Mandelshtams in Chinese Village, where they lived with the Livshitzes.** There was not a single piece of furniture in the room, and the rotting floors had gaping holes. Osip was not

---

* Akhmatova's article on Pushkin's poem was actually entitled "Pushkin's Last Story."—ed.
** The family of poet Benedikt Livshitz.

in the least impressed with the fact that at one time both Zhukovsky and Karamzin had lived there. I am certain it was intentional when he asked me to go with him to buy cigarettes or sugar and said: "Let's go to the European part of the town," as if [the Village] were Bakhchisarai or something equally exotic. His lack of awareness is also revealed in the line: "There the uhlans are smiling." There were no uhlans in Tsarskoye Selo, only hussars, yellow quivers, and convoys.

In 1923 the Mandelshtams were in the Crimea. Here is the letter he wrote me on 25 August, the day N. S.* died:

"Dear Anna Andreyevna,

"We are writing you together with P. N. Luknitsky from Yalta, where the three of us are living the difficult life of working people.

"I would like to go home; I would like to see you. You know. I am able to conduct an imaginative conversation with only two people— Nikolai Stepanovich and you. The conversation with Kolya [Nikolai] has not been disrupted and will never be disrupted.

"We have persuaded P. N. to remain in Yalta for our own selfish reasons. Write us.

Yours,

O. Mandelshtam"

He needed the south and the sea almost as much as he needed Nadia.

If I had but a droplet of sea,
Just a tiniest speck or a splinter . . . **

They were unsuccessful in their attempt to settle in Leningrad. Nadia detested everything about the city and wanted to go to Moscow, where her dear brother, Yevgeny Yakovlevich Khazin, lived. Osip believed that he was known and liked in Moscow, but the opposite was true.

For a long time I did not see either Osip or Nadia. In 1933 the Mandelshtams came to Leningrad on some kind of invitation and stayed in the Yevropeiskaya Hotel. Osip gave two readings.† He had just learned Italian and was raving about Dante. He quoted whole pages of *The Divine*

* Nikolai Gumilev, assumed to have been shot on 25 August 1921.—ed.
** From a poem by Mandelshtam.—ed.
† A remarkable occurrence in Leningrad at that time.—ed.

Comedy. We started to talk about "Purgatory," and I recited from memory a part of Canto XXX (Beatrice's appearance). Osip began to cry. "What's wrong?" I asked in alarm. "No, it's nothing. Just those words and your voice." It's not my place to recall this incident. Let Nadia do so if she likes.

Osip recited from memory some lines from N. Klyuev's poem "Slanderers of Art"* which was the cause of poor Nikolai Alexeyevich's death. At Varvara Klychkova's home I saw with my own eyes Klyuev's application (his plea for pardon from the prison camp): "I, sentenced for my poem 'Slanderers of Art' and for the crazy verses in my notebooks . . ." This was where I took two poems for the epigraph of "Tails." When I said something disapproving about Yesenin, Osip objected, saying that Yesenin could be forgiven anything for the line: "I did not shoot the wretched in the jail."**

At the same time (1933) that Osip was being greeted in Leningrad as a great poet, a *persona grata*, etc., and all the literary people of the city (Tynyanov, Eikhenbaum, Gukovsky† were coming to the Yevropeiskaya to pay him respect; his arrival and his recitals were events that are remembered to this day, 1962). In Moscow, no one wanted to know him. Here Osip's only friends were two or three young natural scientists. Pasternak avoided him, preferring the Georgians and their "beautiful wives," and the Union authorities were suspiciously cautious.

Among Leningrad literary critics, Lydia Yakovlevna Ginzburg and Boris Yakovlevich Bukhshtab always maintained faith in Mandelshtam. Here we should also remember Tsezar Volpe, who published "Journey to Armenia" in *Zvezda.*

Among contemporary writers Mandelshtam greatly respected Babel and Zoshchenko. Mikhail Mikhailovich knew this and was proud of it. For some reason Mandelshtam detested Leonov most of all.

Someone said that N. Ch. [Nikolai Chukovsky] wrote a novel, but Mandelshtam was skeptical. He commented that to write a novel one had to have at least experienced penal servitude like Dostoyevsky or, like Lev Tolstoy, have been a wealthy landowner.

---

* Akhmatova's use of a passage from this poem as an epigraph to part II of *Poem Without a Hero* exacerbated the charges against Klyuev.—ed.

** From a poem by Sergei Yesenin.—ed.

† Grigory Aleksandrovich Gukovsky also visited Mandelshtam in Moscow.

In the autumn of 1933 Mandelshtam at last obtained the apartment[*] he cherished so much on Nashchokinsky Lane, and his nomadic life seemed to come to an end. For the first time Osip began to collect books, primarily old editions of the Italian poets (Dante, Petrarch). In reality, nothing changed: there was always someone to call, something to wait for, something to hope for. And nothing ever came of it.

Osip detested poetry in translation. He said to Pasternak in my presence: "Your collected works will consist of twelve volumes of translation and one volume of your own poetry." Mandelshtam knew that creative energy was sapped by translating, and it was impossible to get him to translate. Many people, most of them shady characters and almost always unnecessary, milled around. The times were not particularly hopeful, but the shadow of trouble and doom lay especially on this house. We were walking down Prechistenka [now Kropotkinskaya Street] (February 1934), talking about something I can't remember now. We turned onto Gogol Boulevard and Osip said: "I am ready to die." For twenty-eight years now, whenever I pass this spot, I have recalled that moment. He earned practically nothing—living on half-translations, half-reviews, half-promises. Despite the ban of the censors, the final part of "Journey to Armenia" was published in *Zvezda*. His pension barely covered the cost of his apartment and food rations.

By this time Mandelshtam's outer appearance was much changed—he had grown heavy, turned grey, and had difficulty in breathing. He gave the impression of being an old man (he was forty-two), but his eyes still sparkled as before. His poetry continued to improve, as did his prose. It is only now that his prose, long unheard and forgotten, is beginning to reach readers. But I constantly hear, especially from the young, that there is nothing like his prose in the twentieth century. This is the so-called *Fourth Prose*.

I well remember one discussion of poetry. Osip, who was very distraught by what is now labeled the cult of personality, said: "Poetry should be social now," and read: "We live, not feeling the ground under our feet. . . ." It was around this time that he developed his theory on word familiarity. Much later he said that poems were written only as the result of strong emotions, both joyous and tragic. About the poems in which he praised Stalin,[**] he told me: "I realize now that it was a sickness."

---

[*] Two rooms, on the fifth floor, no elevator, no gas stove, and no bath.

[**] "I want to say not Stalin—Dzhugashvili" (1935). [Dzhugashvili was Stalin's true last name.]—ed.

When I read Osip my verses "They took you away at the dawn" (1935), he said, "Thank you." These verses are in *Requiem* and refer to the arrest of N. N. P. in 1935. Mandelshtam correctly understood that the last verse in the poem "A Little of Geography" also was written with him in mind: "He is celebrated by the first poet / By us sinners, and you."

Osip was arrested on 13 May 1934. After an avalanche of telegrams and numerous phone calls, I arrived at the Mandelshtams' on that very same day from Leningrad (where only a short time before, Osip had clashed with Tolstoy). We were all so poor then that in order to purchase a return ticket I took along with me to sell my last medal of the House of Monkeys given me by Remizov* in Russia and the statuette (by Danko, my portrait, 1924). S. Tolstaya bought them for the Writers' Union Museum. Yagoda himself signed the arrest warrant. The search was conducted all night long; they were looking for poems. Manuscripts were tossed from a trunk and walked upon. We all sat in one room. It was very quiet. The strumming of a Havana guitar sounded from behind the wall in the Kirsanov** apartment. The investigator found "The Wolf" and showed it to Osip, who nodded in silence. He kissed me good-bye. They took him away at seven in the morning; it was already light. Nadia went to her brother; I went to the Chulkovs on Smolensky Boulevard. We decided on where we would meet. Nadia and I returned home together. We cleaned up the apartment and ate breakfast. Once again came a knock on the door—another search. Yevgeny Khazin said: "If they come again, they will take you with them." Pasternak, whom I had seen that day, went to the *Izvestia* office to plead Mandelshtam's case with Bukharin. I went to see Yenukidze in the Kremlin. (At that time it was virtually impossible to get inside the Kremlin. The actor Ruslanov arranged it through Yenukidze's secretary.) Yenukidze was rather polite, but immediately asked: "Perhaps there were some poems?" Nonetheless, in this way we speeded up and, no doubt, mitigated the outcome. Osip was sentenced to three years in Cherdyn,† where he threw himself from a hospital window and broke his arm because he

* They brought it to me after Remizov's flight (1921).
** Semyon Kirsanov, a poet and a neighbor of Mandelshtam.—ed.
† After a suicide attempt at Cherdyn, in the remote Perm region, Mandelshtam was removed to Voronezh, where he served out his term of exile (to 1937).—ed.

thought they were coming to get him (see: Stanzas, verse 4). Nadia sent a telegram to the Central Committee. Stalin ordered the case reviewed and permitted the selection of another location. Then he called Pasternak.* The rest is well known to everyone.

Pasternak and I also went to see Usiyevich, where we found the Union authorities and many of the Marxist youth of the times.

Perets Markish was the only man to visit Nadia.

It was at this time that Sergei Gorodetsky, a former syndic from the Poets' Guild uttered this immortal phrase in a speech he was giving somewhere: "These lines belong to the Akhmatova who joined the counterrevolution." Even in *Literaturnaya Cazeta*, which published an account of this meeting, the words of the speaker were toned down (see: *Literaturnaya Gazeta*, May 1934).

At the end of his letter to Stalin, B[ukharin] wrote: "P[asterna]k is also worried." Stalin informed him that instructions had been given and that everything concerning Mandelshtam would be all right. He asked Pasternak why he was not trying to intercede for Mandelshtam: "If my poet friend got into trouble I would scale a mountain to try to save him." Pasternak replied that had he *not* interceded Stalin would never have known about the matter. Stalin: "Why did you not turn to me or the writers' organizations?" Pasternak: "The writers' organizations have not concerned themselves with these matters since 1927." Stalin: "But he is your friend?" Pasternak was nonplussed. After a short pause Stalin continued to question him: "After all, he is a master poet, is he not?" Pasternak replied: "That is of no importance. (Boris thought that Stalin was trying to verify if he knew about the poem, which was why his answers were so evasive.)

Stalin: "Why are we talking all the time of Mandelshtam and Mandelshtam? For a long time I have wanted to talk with *you*." Pasternak: "About what?" Stalin: "Life and death." And he hung up the phone.

In his book about Pasternak, Robert Payne offers even more astonishing information about Mandelshtam, an awful description of his outward appearance, and the telephone conversation with Stalin. All this has

---

* Everything connected with this phone call deserves special attention. Two widows, Nadia and Zina, write about it, and an entire folklore surrounds it. A certain Trioleshka [Elsa Triolet] went so far as to write (in Pasternak's days, of course) that Boris destroyed Osip. Nadia and I believe that Pasternak deserves a strong 4 [Akhmatova refers to the five-point grade system—ed.] for his behavior.

the hint of information from Zinaida Nikolaevna Pasternak, who fiercely
hated the Mandelshtams and believed they were compromising her "loyal
husband."

Nadia never went to see Boris Pasternak and never begged him for
anything, as Robert Payne wrote that she did. This information came
from Zina, who once uttered the notorious immortal phrase: "My young-
sters (sons) love Stalin first and then their mother."

Many women came. I remember that they were pretty and dressed in
new spring frocks: Sima Narbut (Zenkevich's wife), the beautiful "Captive
Turk" as we called her, still untouched by tragedy; Nina Olshevskaya,
bright-eyed, slim, and unusually composed. Meanwhile, Nadia and I sat
in our wrinkled yellow and stiff knit jackets. Emma Gershtein and Nadia's
brother kept us company.

Fifteen days later, in the early morning, someone called Nadia and told
her that if she wanted to see her husband she should go to the Kazansky
Railway Station. It was all over. Nina Olshevskaya and I went to collect
money for the departure. People were generous. Yelena Sergeyevna
Bulgakova burst into tears and pressed into my hand all that she had in her
purse.

Nadia and I went to the train station together after stopping at
Lubyanka* for the documents. It was a clear, bright day. From each win-
dow the "cockroach whiskers"** of the hero of the occasion glared at us.
We waited a long time for them to bring Osip. His condition was such that
even they [his jailers] could not seat him in a prison coach. My train was
leaving from the Leningrad Station, and I was unable to wait any longer.
The brothers, Yevgeny Yakovlevich Khazin and Aleksander Emilyevich
Mandelshtam, accompanied me. Not until they had returned to the
Kazansky Station was Osip brought. It was already forbidden to talk to him.
It was most unfortunate that I wasn't able to wait for him and that he didn't
see me. Because this was why, when he was in Cherdyn, he began to
believe that I had perished.

At this time preparations were being made for the First Congress of
Writers (1934). I was sent a questionnaire to fill out, but Osip's arrest so

---

* Lubyanka Square, location of the NKVD headquarters in Moscow.—ed.

** Portraits of Joseph Stalin; a term from a poem by Mandelshtam and the cause of his arrest.—ed.

affected me that I could not raise my hand to write. It was at this Congress that Bukharin named Pasternak First Poet (to Demyan Bedny's dismay), fulminated against me, and, no doubt, said nothing about Osip.

In February 1936 I was at the Mandelshtams in Voronezh and learned all the details about Osip's "case." He told me how in a fit of delirium he had run around Cherdyn searching for my bullet-riddled body and loudly announced to everyone he came into contact with what he was doing, and that he believed the arches erected in honor of the crew of the *Chelyuskin* were built to commemorate his arrival.

Pasternak and I regularly went to see the procurator general that happened to be in power at the given time to plead for Mandelshtam. But the terror had already begun and it was of no use.

It is amazing that it was in Voronezh, where he was by no means free, that Mandelshtam's poetry expressed great expansiveness and deepness of breath.

> And after the asthma's over
> My voice echoes the earth—a final weapon—
> The black earth's dry moisture.

After returning from visiting the Mandelshtams I wrote a poem titled *Voronezh*. This is how it ends:

> But in the room both terror and his muse
> Watch over the disgraced poet.
> And night is walking
> But will never reach dawn.

About his existence in Voronezh Mandelshtam said: "I am a waiting person by nature. That's why it's even harder for me here."

In the early 1920s [1922] Mandelshtam had twice sharply attacked my poetry in the press (*Russkoye Iskusstvo*, Nos. 1, 2). The two of us never discussed this. But nor did he mention his praise for my poetry. I read this only recently (review of "Almanac of the Muses" and "Letters on Russian Poetry," 1922, Kharkov).

Mandelshtam was forced to give a report on acmeism there (in Voronezh). We should not forget what he said in 1937: "I renounce neither the living nor the dead." In answer to the question, "What is acmeism?" Mandelshtam replied: "A yearning for world culture."

As for the cheap memoirs *Petersburg Nights*, written by Georgy Ivanov, who left Russia at the very beginning of the 1920s and knew nothing about the mature Mandelshtam, everything is superficial, vapid, and insignificant. It is not difficult to write such memoirs; there is no requirement for memory, attention, love, or sense of epoch. Everything is fair game and everything is utilized by the unscrupulous. What is most deplorable, though, is that sometimes such information makes its way into works of serious literature. This is what Leonid Shatsky (Strakhovsky) did with Mandelshtam. He took a few of the more "spicy" memoirs (*Petersburg Nights* by G. Ivanov, *The One-and-a-Half-Eyed Strelets** by Benedikt Livshitz, *Portraits of Russian Poets*, by Ilya Ehrenburg) and exploited them to the fullest. The author gleaned most of his material from an early reference book by Kozmin (*Contemporary Writers*, Moscow, 1928). Then, from Mandelshtam's collection *Poetry* (1928), he selected the poem "Music at the Train Station," which was not even the latest poem from among that collection. It is arbitrarily dated 1945; i.e., seven years after Mandelshtam's death on 27 December 1938. That a number of magazines and newspapers published Mandelshtam's poetry (at the very least the wonderful cycle *Armenia* printed in *Novy Mir* in 1930) did not interest Shatsky in the slightest. He flippantly stated that after writing "Music at the Train Station" Mandelshtam ceased to be a poet, becoming a pitiful translator, roaming around taverns, etc. This information, no doubt, came from the mouth of some kind of Parisian Georgy Ivanov.

Instead of the tragic figure of a rare poet who, even during his years of exile in Voronezh, continued to write works of indescribable beauty and strength, we are given an "urban madman," a rogue, a depraved being. And all of this in a book published under the aegis of the best, and the oldest, university in America (Harvard).

Eccentric? Of course he was eccentric. For example, he threw out a young poet who came to him to complain that he was not being published. The confused young man descended the stairs as Osip stood on the landing shouting: "And did they publish Andre Chenier? Sappho? Jesus Christ?"

---

* A book of futuristic poetry. A strelet is an archer.—ed.

Semyon Lipkin and Arseny Tarkovsky even now tell of how strongly Mandelshtam criticized their early poetry.

Artur Sergeyevich Lurye, who knew Mandelshtam very well and wrote credibly about Osip's feelings concerning music, told me (in the 1910s) about another episode. One day he was walking with Mandelshtam along Nevsky and they met an extremely beautifully dressed woman. Osip turned to him and flippantly remarked. "Let's take it all away from her and give it to Anna Andreyevna."

Mandelshtam hated it when young women said they loved *Rosary*. I am told that once he was at [Valentin] Katayev's having a pleasant conversation with the pretty hostess. As the conversation drew to an end he wanted to test the woman's taste. So he asked her: "Do you like Akhmatova?" To which the woman franky replied: "I have never read him." Osip grew livid, swore, and left in a fury. He never told me about this.

In February of 1934, when I was staying at the Mandelshtams', on Nashchokinsky, the Bulgakovs invited me to dinner. Osip expressed his concern: "They want to bring you together with the Moscow literary circle?" Unfortunately, in an effort to placate him, I said: "No, Bulgakov is an outcast himself. Probably there will be someone from the Moscow Arts Theater." Osip was furious. He ran around the room screaming: "How can we tear Akhmatova away from the Moscow Arts Theater?"

One time Nadia brought Osip with her to meet me at the train station. He had awakened early, was cold, and was in a bad mood. When I stepped out of the car, he said: "You came with the same speed as Anna Karenina."

Why do certain memoir writers (Shatsky [Strakhovsky], Mindlin, S. Makovsky, G. Ivanov, B. Livshitz) so carefully and lovingly preserve any rumor and nonsense, especially narrow-minded opinions about a poet, rather than bow their heads before such a grand and unprecedented event as the appearance of a poet whose first poems were astonishing in their perfection and uniqueness?

Mandelshtam never had a teacher. This is something that deserves attention. I know of nothing like it in the world of poetry. We know the sources of Pushkin and Blok, but who can show us the origins of this new divine harmony that we call the poetry of Osip Mandelshtam!

• • •

In May of 1937 the Mandelshtams returned "home" to the apartment on Nashchokinsky in Moscow. At that time I was staying with the Ardovs in the same building. Osip was already ill and kept to his bed most of the time. He read me all his new poems, but he wouldn't allow anyone to copy them. We spoke a great deal about Natasha [Shtempel], who became his friend in Voronezh. (Two poems are dedicated to her: "Buds smell like a sticky oath" and "Limping slightly, against her will, pressing [herself on the bare] earth. . . .")

The terror had been seething and growing for a year now. One of the Mandelshtams' two rooms was taken by a person who made false accusations against them. Soon they were unable even to go to their apartment. Osip couldn't get permission to remain in the capital. He said to Nadia: "One should have the ability to change one's profession. We are now beggars. In the summer the beggar's lot is always easier."

The last poem I heard Osip recite was "Along the streets of Kiev . . ." (1937). This is the story: the Mandelshtams had no place to sleep. I kept them in my apartment (on Fontanka). I made Osip a bed on the couch. For some reason I left and when I returned, he was already falling asleep. He woke up and read me the poem. I repeated it; he said, "Thank you," and then went on to sleep.

During this time we were both reading Joyce's *Ulysses*. Osip had a good German translation while I read the book in the original. A few times we got together intending to discuss the novel, but the circumstances were not conducive.

The Mandelshtams lived in this way for a whole year. Osip was already very ill, but he stubbornly insisted that the Writers' Union organize a reading for him. A date was set, but apparently they "forgot" to send out notices and no one came. Osip phoned Aseyev to invite him. Aseyev replied: "I'm going to see *The Snow Maiden*" and Selvinsky only gave him three rubles when Osip ran into him on the boulevard.

I saw Mandelshtam for the last time in autumn 1937 when he and Nadia came to Leningrad for a couple of days. The times were apocalyptic: trouble followed close at our heels. The two of them had no place to stay. Osip was having difficulty breathing, sucking in air between his lips.

I went somewhere to see them; I can't remember where. It was all like a bad dream. Someone who came after me told Osip that his [Osip's] father did not have any warm clothing. Osip took off the sweater he was wearing under his jacket and said it was to be given to his father. My son told me that when he was being interrogated he was read Osip's statements concerning the two of us and that they were irreproachable. Can this be said of others?

Osip was arrested a second time on 1 May 1938 in a sanatorium near Cherustye Station. It was the height of the terror. My son had been in Shpalernaya [prison] for two months (since 10 March). Everyone talked openly about the torture.

Nadia came to Leningrad. There was a terrified look about her: "I will calm down only when I know that he is dead."

• • •

In early 1939 I received a short letter from a friend in Moscow (Emma Gershtein): "Our friend Lena (Osmerkina) has had a little girl, and our friend Nadia has been widowed."

Osip wrote just one letter (to his brother Aleksander) from the place where he died. Nadia had the letter and showed it to me. "Where is my darling Nadia?" Osip wrote, and asked for warm clothing. A parcel was sent but it was returned. He was no longer alive.

Throughout these extremely difficult times Vasilisa Georgievna Shklovskaya and her daughter Varya remained faithful friends to Nadia.

Today Osip Mandelshtam is a poet of world renown. Books and dissertations are written about him. It is an honor to have been his friend; a disgrace to have been his enemy.

For me he was not just a great poet but a man who, having learned (probably from Nadia) of my difficulties living in Fontanka House, said this to me in farewell (at the Moskovsky Train Station in Leningrad): "Annushka (he had never called me that before), always remember that my home is your home." This was in 1938, just before his death.

Vladislav Khodasevich
GUMILEV AND BLOK

Vladislav Khodasevich (1876–1939), Russian poet and critic who emigrated in 1922.

Blok died on August 7, 1921. Gumilev on August 27 of the same year. But for me they both died on August 3. I will tell you why.

It is almost impossible to imagine two more different people. Only in age were they close, Blok being older by just six years.

Though they belonged to the same literary era, they represented different generations in poetry. Despite Blok's occasional rampages against symbolism, he was one of the purest symbolist poets. Gumilev, who remained under the influence of Bryusov his entire life, claimed to be a strong and consistent enemy of symbolism. Blok was a mystic, an admirer of the Beautiful Lady, and he wrote sacrilegious poems not only about her. Gumilev always made the sign of the cross in front of a church, but I have rarely known anyone so unaware of the meaning of religion. For Blok, his poetry was a real and primary spiritual deed, an integral part of life. For Gumilev poetry was a form of literary activity. Blok was a poet always, every minute of his life; Gumilev was a poet only when he was writing poems. To top all this, they loathed each other and never tried to conceal the fact. But in my memory I often see them together. I knew them only the last year of their lives. They died almost at the same time; and there was something contiguous in their demise and in the shock it evoked in Petersburg.

Gumilev and I were born the same year and were first published the same year. But we did not meet for a long time: I rarely visited Petersburg and he, it seemed, never came to Moscow. We became acquainted in Petersburg in the autumn of 1918, at a meeting of the World Literature board of directors.* Gumilev's gravity at this meeting reminded me of Bryusov.

---

* Gumilev was on the board of editors of Vsemirnaya Literatura, a publishing house.—ed.

Gumilev invited me to come see him, and our conversation was as formal as that of two kings. There was something so artificial about his ceremonious politeness that at first I thought he might be putting me on. Finally, I was compelled to adopt the same tone; any other would have seemed too familiar. There we sat in Petersburg—an empty, hungry city that smelled of salty, dried fish—two hungry, gaunt fellows dressed in worn-out coats and with holes in our boots conducting a conversation with preposterous gravity in his cold and untidy study. Knowing that I was a Muscovite, Gumilev felt it necessary to offer me tea. But his voice was so hesitating (he probably had no sugar) that I declined, apparently extricating him from a difficult situation. Meanwhile, I was growing increasingly interested in the furnishings of his study. His desk, bookshelf, pier-glass, armchair, etc., looked all too familiar to me. Finally, cautiously, I asked if he had been living there long.

"In actual fact, this is not my apartment," Gumilev answered. "It belongs to Makovsky." Then I understood: Gumilev and I were sitting in my former study! Approximately ten years before, some of this furniture had been mine. It had its own history. Admiral Fyodor Fyodorovich Matyushkin, who had attended the lyceum with Pushkin, took it off some boat or other and moved it into his lakeside estate near Bologoye. The estate was called Zaimka. There was a green morocco upholstered chair that, according to local legend, was a favorite of Pushkin. But it was only a legend; Pushkin never visited this area. As a matter of fact, Matyushkin bought the estate some thirty years after the poet's death. After Matyushkin died, the estate passed from one person to another and the name was changed to Lidino. But the furnishings remained the same. Even the special device in the pantry used for storing dishes in the event of strong waves was not replaced with ordinary shelves. In 1905 I came to be partial owner of this furniture and moved it to Moscow. Later it was moved to Petersburg. After the Revolution uprooted everything and everyone, I found Gumilev using it. The real owner was in the Crimea.

Having remained as long as was appropriate for such a stiff visit, I rose to leave. Gumilev accompanied me into the foyer. A thin, pale young boy wearing a dirty shirt and felt boots and with the same elongated face as Gumilev darted out of a side door. He had an Uhlan helmet on his head and was waving a toy sword and shouting something. Gumilev immediately sent him away in the manner of a king sending the dauphin back to his governess. But I had the feeling that only Gumilev and his son were living in the damp, dank apartment.

Two years later I moved to Petersburg, and we began to see each other more frequently. Gumilev had many good qualities. He had wonderful taste in literature, a little superficial but impeccable. His approach to poetry was formal, but here he was insightful and subtle. He understood poetic technique as few others did. In my opinion, he was more perspicacious than even Bryusov. He adored poetry and tried to be fair in his appraisals.

But for all that I rarely found the topics he discussed or his poetry to be "nourishing." He was incredibly young at heart and, perhaps, in intellect as well; I always thought of him as a child. There was something boy-like in his closely cropped head and in his carriage (more like that of a schoolboy than of an officer). This boy-like quality permeated his fascination with Africa and war and even the feigned gravity that so astonished me during our first meeting. Suddenly this gravity would disappear, until such time as he remembered it and once again ensheathed himself in it. Like all children, he liked to play at being a grown-up. He loved to play the role of a "master" among the "Gumilevites"; i.e., the little-known poets of his circle. The young poets were very fond of him. Sometimes, after giving a lecture on poetics, he would play blind man's bluff with them—literally, not figuratively. I saw this twice. Gumilev looked like a nice upperclassman playing with elementary pupils. It was amusing to see how half an hour later he would be gravely conversing with A. F. Koni, a man who was much more affable.

During the Christmas season in 1920 the Institute of History of Arts hosted a ball. I remember the large, cold halls of the Zubov residence on Isaac Square, the dim lighting and the frosty air. Damp firewood smoked and smoldered in the fireplaces. All of the Petersburg literary and artistic society was present. The music played: the people moved about in the semi-gloom and huddled near the fires. My God! How we were dressed! In felt boots, sweaters, and tattered fur coats. We couldn't take them off even on the dance floor. Then, appropriately late, Gumilev appeared with a woman on his arm. She was wearing a black decollete dress and was shivering with cold. Wearing an evening jacket, erect and arrogant, Gumilev walked about the hall. He was shivering, but majestically and politely bowed right and left. His appearance proclaimed: "Nothing has happened. The Revolution? Never heard of it."

• • •

Gumilev knew too much about poetry not to appreciate Blok at all. But this did not prevent him from personally disliking Blok. I don't know what their relationship was before, but when I moved to Petersburg I found them mutually hostile. I don't think the cause was insignificant, though it is possible that Gumilev, who cared a great deal about who occupied what place in the hierarchy of poets, was jealous of Blok. Probably, however, the reason was more serious. Their world outlooks and literary goals were antagonistic. The "concealed impulse," the spiritual message in Blok's poetry, must have been alien to Gumilev. He no doubt found the symbolic aspects of Blok's poetry to be clearly antagonistic and not quite understandable. It is no coincidence that the acmeists' manifesto was primarily directed against Blok and Bely.

On the other hand, Blok must have been irritated by the "fatuousness," "uselessness," and "superficiality" in Gumilev's poetry. Yet if the matter only concerned Gumilev's poetry, Blok could probably have accepted or at least tolerated it; there were two complicating factors. The student—Gumilev—became the object of years of Blok's accumulated hatred of the teacher—Bryusov. And the hatred was all the more intense because it grew out of the ruins of former love. Blok felt that acmeism and all that later came to be known as "Gumilevian" represented the corruption of "Bryusovism." Secondly, Gumilev was not alone. Each year his influence on young poets increased, and Blok believed this influence to be spiritually and poetically pernicious.

In early 1921 their enmity surfaced. In order to touch upon certain other events, I will go back further. About four years before the war a poetic society called the Poets' Guild was created. It included Blok, Sergei Gorodetsky, Georgy Chulkov, Yury Verkhovsky, Nikolai Klyuev, Gumilev, and also Aleksei Tolstoy, who was still writing verse at that time. The young poets were represented by Osip Mandelshtam, Georgy Narbut, and Anna Akhmatova, then Gumilev's wife. In a literary sense, the society was initially free of affiliation with one school of poetry or another.

Later the acmeists became dominant and those unsympathetic to acmeism, including Blok, gradually left. During the period of the war and military communism, acmeism died out and the Poets' Guild ceased to exist. In early 1921 Gumilev thought to resurrect the Guild and invited me to join. I asked if it would be the original Guild; i.e., unaffiliated, or the second—acmeist. Gumilev answered that it would be the first, and I agreed. It so happened that there was to be a meeting, the second so far, that evening. I was then living in the House of Arts, was frequently ill, and saw few people. Before the meeting I went to see my neighbor, Mandelshtam, and asked him why he had told me nothing about the resurrected Guild. He laughed:

"Because there is no Guild. Blok, Sologub, and Akhmatova refused to join. Gumilev just wants to head something. He loves to play soldier, and you fell for it. Only Gumilevites will be there."

"Well, tell me then, what are *you* doing in such a Guild?" I asked peevishly.

Mandelshtam made a serious face.

"I drink tea and eat sweets."

Aside from Mandelshtam and Gumilev, five other people were present at the meeting. We read poems and discussed them. To me the Guild was useless but harmless. Then an unpleasant surprise awaited me at the third meeting. A new member, a young poet by the name of Neldikhen, read his verse. Essentially, it was poetry in prose. But the poem was in a certain sense delightful: playfully ludicrous from the first line to the last. Neldikhen's poetic "persona" revealed a consummate fool; moreover, a happy, exultant, inveterate fool.

The neophyte read in a sing-song voice and in all seriousness. The listeners smiled. When Neldikhen had finished, Gumilev gave a short welcoming speech. First of all he noted that until that day stupidity had been on the wane; poets had unjustly shunned it. But it was time for stupidity to have its own voice in literature. Stupidity was as natural a trait as intelligence. It, too, could be developed and cultivated. Quoting Balmont's couplet about a fool,

> The image of a fool disgusts me
> Stupidity I cannot tolerate

Gumilev claimed that it was cruel and, in the person of Neldikhen, he welcomed blatant stupidity into the Guild.

After the meeting I asked Gumilev if he should have ridiculed Neldikhen, and why Neldikhen was even in the Guild. To my surprise, Gumilev claimed that there had been no ridicule. "It is not up to me," he said, "to figure out what the poets are thinking. I only judge how they present their thoughts or their stupidity. I myself would not want to be a fool, but I have no right to demand intelligence from Neldikhen. He expresses his stupidity with more skill than many intelligent people express their intelligence. And poetry is skill. Thus, Neldikhen is a poet, and it is my duty to accept him into the Guild."

A short time later there was to be a public Guild reading, and Neldikhen was scheduled to appear. I sent Gumilev a letter informing him that I was withdrawing from the Guild. It was not just because of Neldikhen. I had a much more serious reason.

Before I moved to Petersburg, a branch of the All-Russian Union of Poets—administered from Moscow and essentially headed by Lunacharsky himself—was being formed in the city. I don't recall the members of the administration, which was chaired by Blok; however, one night Mandelshtam came to me and announced that the "Blok administration" of the Union had been overturned an hour earlier and was replaced by another consisting solely of members of the Guild, including myself. Gumilev had been elected chairman. It happened in a strange manner, with notices being sent out only an hour or so before the meeting and many people not even receiving one. I didn't like it, and I said they shouldn't have elected me without asking me first. Mandelshtam tried to dissuade me from "raising a fuss," so as not to offend Gumilev. I understood from what he had to say that the "election" had been arranged by certain members of the Guild who needed the Union's printing press for commercial purposes. They were using Gumilev's name and position as a cover. And Gumilev, like a child, was seduced by the title of chairman. In the end, I promised not to resign officially from the administration but not to take part in any of the meetings or any Union activities. So this was another reason for leaving the Guild.

Blok, of course, did not care about being chairman of the Union. But he did not like the way the election was so obviously manipulated. Nor was he happy that Gumilev's literary influence would be strengthened by the Union administration. Blok decided to act.

It was at this time that permission was granted to publish a weekly called *Literaturnaya Gazeta*. A. N. Tikhonov, Ye. I. Zamyatin, and K. I. Chukovsky were on the board of editors. For the first issue Blok provided an article directed against Gumilev and the Guild. It was titled "Without Deity, Without Inspiration." *Literaturnaya Gazeta* ceased to exist before it began to be published: because of a Zamyatin story and my own editorial, Zinovyev ordered the issue confiscated while it was still being printed. I did not read Blok's article until many years later, in his collected works. I must confess that I found it vapid and vague, like many of his articles. But at that time it was rumored to be sharply critical. Blok told me the same thing at one of our meetings. He peevishly complained that Gumilev was making poets "out of nothing."

My leaving the Guild did not affect my personal relationship with Gumilev. It was around this time that he also moved into the House of Arts, and we began to see each other more frequently. He was busy and energetic. The beginning of his end occurred at approximately the same time as that of Blok.

One of our mutual friends returned from Moscow to Petersburg for Easter. He was a man of great talent and highly frivolous. He lived like a care-free bird; he spoke whatever he wished. Provocateurs and spies clung to him: he would tell them everything he knew about writers. He brought with him a new friend from Moscow. This was a young man with good manners who was generous with small gifts such as cigarettes and sweets. He claimed to be a beginning poet and hastened to meet everyone. Gumilev took a liking to him. The young man became a frequent guest. He helped to organize the House of Poets (an affiliate of the Union) and boasted about his connections in the high spheres of Soviet authority.

I was not the one to find him suspicious. Gumilev was warned, but he paid no heed. I cannot swear that this man was the sole or even major instigator of the reports that led to Gumilev's death. But after Gumilev was arrested, he disappeared without a trace. When I was abroad I learned from Maksim Gorky that this man had testified against Gumilev and that he had been a plant.

In late summer I made plans to go to the countryside for a vacation. I was supposed to leave on Wednesday, 3 August. The evening before my departure I went to say good-bye to some of my neighbors living in the

House of Arts. It was ten o'clock when I knocked on Gumilev's door. He was home, resting after giving a lecture.

We were on good terms, but we had never been really close. Yet on this occasion, just as two years before when he astonished me with his formal reception, he astonished me now with his pleasure at seeing me. He was especially and uncharacteristically friendly. I still had to go and see the Baroness Varvara Ivanovna Ikskul, who lived one floor down. But each time I got up to go, Gumilev begged me to stay a little longer. I stayed until two in the morning and never did make it to see the Baroness. He was in rare good spirits, talking a great deal about many topics. For some reason I only remember his telling about his stay in the Tsarskoye Selo infirmary, about Her Majesty Alexandra Feodorovna and the grand princes. Then Gumilev assured me that he was destined to live a long time, "at least until ninety." He kept repeating it:

"Positively until ninety. No less."

Until then he intended to write a number of books. He reproached me:

"We are the same age, but look at us. I seem to be ten years younger. This is because I love the young. I play blind man's bluff with my students; I even played today. That's why I'll definitely live to be ninety. But you'll turn sour in five years."

Laughing, he described what I would be like in five years—hunched over and dragging my feet, while he would be in fine form.

Saying good-bye, I asked if I could come the next day to leave some things in storage. The next morning I arrived with my things at the appointed hour, but no one answered my knock. In the cafeteria the servant Yefim informed me that Gumilev had been arrested that night. So I was the last of us to see him a free man. I believe that his exaggerated happiness at my visit was because he had a presentiment that I would be the last friend he saw.

I returned to my apartment and found the poet Nadezhda Pavlovich, a mutual friend of mine and Blok's. She had just seen him and had hurried to me. Her face was flushed with the heat and swollen from crying. She told me that Blok was in his death throes. I did what I could to calm and reassure her. She had run to me in despair. Gulping back her sobs, she said:

"You know nothing. . . . Don't tell anyone. . . . Over the past few days . . . he has lost his mind!"

Some days later, when I was in the countryside, Andrei Bely gave me the news of Blok's death. On the fourteenth, a Sunday, we attended a requiem service for him in the country church. In the evenings, young people would gather around campfires and sing. I wanted to remember Blok in my own secret way and asked them to sing "Peddlers," which he liked so much. Strangely, no one knew the song.

In early September we learned that Gumilev had been shot. Letters from Petersburg were somber, filled with veiled hints and supplication. When I returned to the city it had still not recovered from these deaths.

In early 1922 the theater Gumilev had tried to help before his arrest staged a rehearsal and then a premier performance of his play *Gondla*. The audience began to shout: "Author!"

Instructions came to remove the play from the theater's repertoire.

APPENDIX

Alphabetical Listing of
Names, Places, and Historical Events

The Academy of Poetry was the name given the Society of Zealots of Belles-lettres at *Apollo* magazine. The Society brought together writers affiliated with the Russian symbolists Vyacheslav Ivanov, Andrei Bely, and Alexandr Blok. *30, 33, 38, 236*

Adalis, Adelina (1900–1969), Soviet poet who in the early 1920s was a patron of Valery Bryusov. *28*

Adamovich-Vysotska, Tatyana (1892–1972), the sister of the poet Georgy Adamovich and the woman to whom Gumilev dedicated his collection of verse *Quiver*. *35*

Akhmadulina, Bella, Soviet poet. *191*

Aldanov, Mark (1889–1957), Russian writer, literary critic, and journalist who emigrated from the Soviet Union. *73*

Aliger, Margarita, Soviet poet and member of the board of editors for the collection *Literary Moscow.* The third edition of this book (which included some of Akhmatova's work) was not printed because, after the second edition came out in 1957, a political purge was conducted against the almanac's board of editors for printing ideologically "harmful" works. *159, 188, 203*

Alpatov, Mikhail (1902–1986), Soviet art critic. *206, 207*

Altman, Natan (1889–1970), artist and sculptor. He painted Anna Akhmatova's portrait (1914). *14, 42, 130*

Alya, Ariadna Efron, daughter of Marina Tsvetayeva. *117*

Alyansky, Samuel (1891–1974), owner of a publishing house. *26, 43, 45*

Andreyev, Leonid (1871–1919), Russian writer. *94, 96*

Andronikova, Salomeya (1888–1982), a Petersburg beauty who emigrated after the `Revolution. *66, 114, 144, 238*

Anikieva, Vera, friend of Akhmatova. *141*

Annenkov, Yury (1889–1974), artist who painted two portraits of Akhmatova in
    1921. *98*

Annensky, Innokenty (1855–1909), a Russian poet who was little known when alive
    but achieved fame after his death largely due to the acmeist literary movement,
    to which Akhmatova belonged. The acmeists considered Annensky to be their
    literary teacher. He was the director of the gymnasium in Tsarskoye Selo. *3,*
    35, 49, 222

Arbenina, Olga (1899–1980), actress and wife of the poet Yu. Yurkun. *238, 239*

Aseyev, Nikolai (1889–1963), Soviet Russian poet. *252*

Babel, Isaak (1894–1938), Russian writer, shot in 1938. *244*

Bagritsky, Eduard (1895–1934), Soviet poet. *47, 143*

Balmont, Konstantin (1867–1942), Russian poet. *39, 73, 258*

Baratynsky, Yevgeny (1800–1844), poet, a close friend of Pushkin. *xii*

Batalov, Nikolai (1899–1937), an actor with Moscow Art Theater. *174, 182, 196*

Bedny, Demyan (1883–1945), Soviet poet who gained official favor. *249*

Bely, Andrei (1880–1934), Russian writer and symbolist poet. *16, 32, 210, 257, 262*

Belyaev, Yury (1876–1917), playwright who wrote the vaudeville play *The Muddle of*
    1840 in which Olga Glebova-Sudeikina played the leading role. *231*

Berdyaev, Nikolai (1874–1948), Russian philosopher. Together with other eminent
    historians and philosophers, he was deported from Russia in 1922. *15, 39, 210*

Berkovsky, Naum (1901–1972), literary critic. *176, 178, 182*

Berlin, Isaiah, a British philospher who met Akhmatova in 1945 and later wrote his
    reminiscences of her. Many of her lyrical poems are addressed to him. *xiii, 16,*
    26, 205

Bestuzhev Institute, an institute of higher learning for women in pre-revolutionary
    Petersburg. *98*

Blok, Alexandr (1880–1921), Russian symbolist poet. Alexandr Blok was buried on
    10 August 1921. *1, 14, 15, 16, 29, 30, 31, 33, 39, 43, 49, 58, 59, 63, 66, 67, 68, 72,*
    93, 94, 97, 98, 120, 169, 172, 191, 200, 201, 205, 210, 214, 222, 230, 235, 239, 240,
    251, 254, 257, 258, 259, 260, 261, 262, 263

Blue Star. The reference is to Yelena Dyubushe, the object of Gumilev's attentions
    in Paris. He dedicated his cycle of poems *To the Blue Star. 55, 142*

Bobrov, Sergei (1889–1971), poet and literary critic. *40*

The Bolsheviks and the Mensheviks. The Russian Social-Democratic Party, the leader-
    ship of which for the most part lived outside of Russia in the 1910s, was split
    into two large factions. *3, 85, 227, 241*

Bondi, Sergei (1891–1983), philologist, Pushkin scholar. *140*

Borovikovsky, Vladimir (1757–1825), Russian artist. *232*

Bowra, S. M., British Slavic studies specialist and translator of Russian poetry. *16*

Brambeum, Baron. The pseudonym of the Russian writer Oleg Senkovsky (1800–1858). *13*

Brodsky, Joseph (1987 Nobel Prize winner for literature). In 1963 Joseph Brodsky was sentenced to exile from Leningrad. The formal charge was that of "sponging," or living on unearned money, for the judge refused to recognize the translation of poetic footnotes as work. In reality, Brodsky was persecuted by the Soviet authorities for his independence and unwillingness to cooperate with the regime. *x, xi, 74, 89, 112, 129, 160, 188, 189, 205, 208, 209, 210, 212*

Brodsky, Nikolai (1881–1951), writer, critic, and literary historian. *163*

Bryullov, Karl (1799–1852), Russian painter. *37*

Bryusov, Valery (1873–1924), one of the first Russian symbolist poets, was considered by Nikolai Gumilev to be his poetry teacher. *14, 28, 32, 38, 41, 254, 256, 257, 263*

Bukharin, Nikolai (1888–1938), was at the time of Mandelshtam's arrest editor-in-chief of the newspaper *Izvestiya*. *246, 249*

Bukhshtab, Boris (1904–1984), literary critic. *142, 244*

Bulgakova, Yelena Sergeyevna, wife of the writer Mikhail Bulgakov. *248*

Bunin, Ivan (1870–1953), Russian writer and winner of the Nobel Prize for literature (1933), in 1919 recited an epigram entitled "The Poetess." Opinion had it that the epigram was about Akhmatova. *28, 73, 74, 192, 193*

Bunina, Anna (1774–1829), a Russian poet and distant relative of Akhmatova's grandfather Erasm Stogov (1797–1880). *6*

Burenin, Viktor (1841–1926), a critic and a staff writer with the conservative newspaper *Novoye Vremya*, published a satirical article on Akhmatova in the paper on 29 April 1911. *28*

Byaka. Vera Shilling de Bosse (1888–1982). *238*

Chatskina, Sophia, publisher of the magazine *Severnye Zapiski*, belonged to the Socialist-Revolutionary Party (SRs). *42*

Chebotarevskaya, Aleksandra Nikolayevna (1869–1925), translator and writer. *38*

Chekhov, Mikhail (1891–1955), Russian director and nephew of the writer Anton Chekhov. He emigrated in 1928. *15*

Chinese Village. The summer pavilions in the Tsarskoye Selo palace, where, just as in the palace itself and on the premises of the former Tsarskoye Selo Lyceum (where Pushkin studied), sanatoria for the Academy of Sciences and the Commission for the Improvement of the Living Conditions of Scientists were later set up. *242*

Chukovsky, Kornei, wrote an article entitled "Two Russians: Akhmatova and
   Mayakovsky." He depicted Akhmatova as the personification of pre-
   revolutionary Russia and counterposed her to the revolutionary works of
   Vladimir Mayakovsky. Akhmatova believed this article was significant in the
   emergence of the official Soviet negative views on her works in the 1920s and
   later. (See his notes in this book.) *28, 34, 44, 45, 92, 260*

Chukovsky, Nikolai (1904–1965), Soviet poet and writer and son of Kornei
   Chukovsky. *94, 119, 244*

Chulkov, Georgy (1879–1939), Russian writer who favored the symbolists and friend
   of Akhmatova. He wrote one of the first critical reviews of her book *Evening.*
   30, 38, 45, 64, 138, 139, 246, 257

The Comedian's Stop-over replaced the Stray Dog cabaret as the meeting place of
   writers and artists. The Stop-over opened in 1916 in the same house in Mars
   Field in Petrograd where Nadezhda Dobychina kept her art studio (one of the
   places that continuously exhibited modern art and held other events pertaining
   to the literary and art world). Akhmatova chose Dobychina's art studio as the
   scene of action in the ballet libretto for *Poem Without a Hero. 68*

Culture and Life, the official Soviet paper, published a number of attacks against
   Akhmatova after the Central Committee resolution, and managed to publish
   the first such article as early as 10 August 1946, i.e., four days before the resolution was passed. *28*

Cypress Box, a collection of verse by Innokenty Annensky published posthumously.
   37, 40

A Day in the Life of Ivan Denisovich. A novella by Solzhenitsyn, it was the first work
   published in the USSR to describe the Stalin concentration camps. It was published in the magazine *Novy Mir* in 1962. *193*

D. and S. The reference is to Mikhail Sholokhov's speech at the Twenty-third
   Congress of the CPSU (1966) concerning the case of the writers Juli Daniel
   and Andrei Sinyavsky, who were arrested in 1965 and given five to seven years
   imprisonment for publishing their works outside the USSR. *107*

A Dead Woman in the House is a story by Mikhail Kuzmin containing veiled hints
   about Vyacheslav Ivanov's family life. *39*

Dekulakization. During the late 1920s and early 1930s, the practice of seizing the
   land and possessions of each and every more or less well-off peasant. The peasants themselves along with their families were deported to Siberia and the
   uninhabited regions of the North, as a result of which several million peasants
   died of starvation. *127*

Derzhavin, Gavriil (1743–1816), Russian poet. *2, 195*

Di Sarra, Dan Danino, publisher of Akhmatova's collection of verse in Florence (1951).
   25, 37, 45

Diaghilev, Sergei (1872–1929), Russian impresario who organized the World of Art artistic group and brought the Russian ballet to Paris in 1907. From 1911 to 1929 he headed the ballet troupe he created abroad—the Russian Ballet. *14, 94*

Doctor Zhivago. After Boris Pasternak (1890–1960) was awarded the Nobel Prize for literature in 1958, the Soviet press initiated a despicable campaign against the poet and this book, at that time published only outside the USSR. Pasternak was expelled from the Union of Soviet Writers and was threatened with the loss of his Soviet citizenship and exile. He was forced to refuse the Nobel Prize. *xi, 189*

Ehrenburg, Ilya (1891–1967), writer, poet, and journalist. *165, 205, 250*

Eikhenbaum, Boris. The author of *Anna Akhmatova, the Experience of Analysis* (Petrograd, 1923). *34, 45, 96, 164, 204, 244*

Engelgardt, Anna (1895–1942), Nikolai Gumilev's second wife. *142*

Erdman, Nikolai (1902–1970), playwright. Erdman and Mikhail Volpin came to Tashkent as members of the ensemble of the People's Commissariat of Internal Affairs where they were employed and thus wore uniforms. *109*

Fadeyev, Aleksander (1901–1956), Soviet writer who was a general secretary of the directorate of the Union of Soviet Writers from 1944. After the resolution of 1946 he often spoke to defend the accusations made against Zoshchenko and Akhmatova. *29, 157, 158*

Fedin, Konstantin (1892–1977), writer who at that time headed the Union of Soviet Writers. *208*

Flit, Aleksandr (1891–1954), Soviet writer and satirist. *170*

The Free Philosophical Association was a historical-philosophical and literary association functioning in Moscow and Petrograd from 1918 to 1925. *94*

Gaiduki. In 1923 the magazine *Na Postu* published an article by Marxist critic G. Lelevich. After quoting Akhmatova's poem "The Ghost," Lelevich wrote: " . . . drives with rotters and *gaiduki.* In other words we have a hot-house plant grown on a country estate." At that time such a conclusion carried the hint of a political accusation. After a number of such "critical" reviews, Akhmatova's poetry ceased to be published in the Soviet Union from 1925 until 1940. *97*

Galich, Aleksandr (1918–1977), poet and singer. *191*

Garshin, Vladimir (1887–1956), physician and close friend of Akhmatova. *149, 150, 151, 186*

Gessen, A. I., owner of the Petrograd Publishing House. In the latter half of the 1920s even private publishing houses in the USSR were required to obtain state permission to publish books. *34*

Gippius, Zinaida (1869–1945), Russian writer and poet. *38, 240*

Glebova-Sudeikina, actress and artist, wife of Sergei Sudeikin. *66, 93, 94, 95, 96, 97, 117, 152, 153, 230, 231, 264*

Glen, Nika, friend of Akhmotova in the 1950s and 1960s. *188*

Golden Cockerel. The reference is to Akhmatova's work "Pushkin's Last Story." The speaker is Mikhail Alekseyev, an academician. Nadezhda Mandelshtam is mistaken about Akhmatova's feelings concerning this work. She thought well of her first research article about Pushkin and continued to work on it up to the mid-1960s. *4, 140, 242*

Gollerbakh, Erich (1895–1942), art and literary critic who wrote the book *City of the Muses* about Tsarskoye Selo. His article "Petersburg Cameo" was published in the magazine *Novaya Rossiya* (1922, No. 1). *36, 95, 242*

Gorenko, Andrei (1848–1915), father of Anna, a naval officer and later a functionary of state control and a public figure. *9*

Gorodetsky, Sergei (1884–1967), Soviet poet who began his career as a symbolist in the 1900s and one of the organizers of the Poets' Guild. *26, 30, 32, 33, 38, 67, 239, 240, 247, 257*

Grin, Nina, widow of the writer Aleksandr Grin (1880–1932). *143*

Grossman, Vasily (1905–1964), Soviet writer. *177*

Grzhebin, Zinovy (1869–1920), artist and publisher. *93, 97*

Gukovsky, Grigory (1902–1950), literary critic and the husband of Akhmatova's close friend Natalia Rykova (1897–1928), who died in the camps after being arrested on false charges. *130, 132, 142, 244*

Gumilev, Lev, Akhmatova's son, he is a well-known historian and ethnographer today. *104, 146, 153, 157, 166, 168, 188, 239, 256*

Gumilev, Nikolai (1886–1921), Akhmatova's first husband, was one of the Russian poets to be sentenced and shot under the false charge of conspiring against Soviet power. Gumilev was arrested on 8 August 1921 and was, in all probability, killed on 25 August. *xi, xvi, 1, 3, 9, 12, 13, 15, 16, 29, 30, 31, 32, 33, 35, 36, 37, 38, 39, 40, 47, 49, 53, 54, 55, 56, 57, 59, 60, 62, 63, 66, 67, 68, 73, 86, 94, 97, 99, 104, 118, 121, 128, 142, 158, 172, 174, 175, 176, 183, 192, 199, 210, 212, 227, 235, 236, 237, 239, 242, 254, 255, 256, 257, 258, 259, 260, 261, 262, 263, 264, 265, 267*

Gungenburg, a resort on the Gulf of Finland. *47, 52*

Harkins. Author of the *Dictionary of Russian Literature* (New York, 1956). *30, 45*

Hertzen, Aleksandr (1812–1870), Russian writer. *126, 127*

Hertzen, Natalia, wife of the Russian writer and nineteenth-century critic Aleksandr Hertzen. *127, 196*

Khazin, Yevgeny, brother of Nadezhda Mandelshtam. *109, 143, 243, 246, 248*

Khlebnikov, Velimir (1885–1922), Russian poet, founder of Russian Futurism, known for his experimental verse. *14, 15, 16, 65, 66, 125, 204, 240*

Khodasevich, Vladislav (1886–1939), Russian poet and actor, he wrote a favorable article about Akhmatova's collection of verse *Rosary.* He emigrated in 1922. *15, 16, 42, 254*

Khrushchev, Nikita (1894–1971), as the leader of the Soviet state, he created a scandal at the exhibition of young artists held in the Manezh exhibition hall when he said that their works violated Soviet norms and concepts of morality. *177, 188*

Klychkov, Sergei (1889–1938), Russian poet who was arrested in 1937 and perished in prison. *116, 143*

Klyuev, Nikolai (1884–1937), Soviet Russian poet who joined the acmeists in 1911. He was deported from Moscow in 1934 and shot in 1937. *33, 115, 116, 244, 257*

Koktebel. A resort in the Crimea on the Black Sea. *156*

Kollontai, Aleksandra (1872–1952), member of the Central Committee of the CPSU(B), where she headed a women's section. From 1923 to 1945 she was a diplomat in Norway and Sweden. In her article about Akhmatova, published in the magazine *Molodaya Gvardiya,* Kollontai wrote that the poetic world of Akhmatova was close to the youth of the Revolution because it allegedly negated traditional family and marital relations. *47*

Koma. The family pet name for Vyacheslav Vsevolodovich Ivanov. *112, 198*

Komarovsky, Vasily (d. 1914), Russian poet. *204, 240*

Komissarzhevskaya, Vera (1864–1910), a famous Russian actress. *14*

Konev, Ivan (1897–1973), marshal of the Soviet Union. *178*

Koni, Anatoly (1844–1927), Russian lawyer and social activist. *256*

Kornilov, Vladimir, a modern poet. *209*

Krasnaya Konnitsa Street. Akhmatova lived on this street in Leningrad from 1952 until 1961. *158*

Kulbin, Nikolai (1868–1917), military doctor and amateur artist. He was one of the organizers of the avant-garde movement in Russian art in the early twentieth century. *231*

Kushner, Aleksandr, Soviet poet. *112*

Kuzin, Boris (1903–1973), biologist, friend of the Mandelshtams. *143*

Kuzmin, Mikhail (1875–1936), Russian poet, first a symbolist and then an acmeist, Kuzmin wrote the foreword to Akhmatova's first book of verse, *Evening. 16, 25, 26, 32, 39, 42, 64, 233, 266*

Kuzmina-Karavayeva, Yelizaveta (nee Pilenko, known in the convent as Mother Maria) (1891–1945), a poet who, after emigrating to France, served as one of the heads of the Russian Student Christian Movement. She was a hero of the French Resistance and died in a concentration camp in Germany. *13, 30, 239, 240*

Ladyzhenskaya, Olga, mathematician, candidate-member of the USSR Academy of Sciences, and friend of Akhmatova. *209*

Leonov, Leonid, Soviet writer. *244*

Leopardi, Giacomo (1798–1837), Italian poet whose work Akhmatova translated during the last years of her life. *76, 208*

Lerner, Nikolai (1877–1934), writer and journalist. *95*

Logatto. An Italian specialist in Slavic studies. *46*

Lomonosov, Mikhail (1711–1765), famous Russian scientist, naturalist, poet, artist, and historian. *236*

Lopatin, Herman (1845–1918), Russian revolutionary. He was a friend of Karl Marx and translated his works into Russian. He was a prisoner in Shlisselburg fortress from 1887 until 1905. *42*

Lozinsky, Mikhail (1886–1955), poet, translator, and close friend of Akhmatova. In the 1910s he published the magazine *Giberborei* which printed the works of acmeists. *30, 31, 40, 49, 50, 64, 89, 234, 237, 240*

Lunacharsky, Anatoly (1875–1938), people's commissar of education in the Soviet government, writer, and critic. He was appointed People's Commissar (minister) of Education of the Bolshevik Government in November 1917. *68, 259*

Lurye, Artur, composer and friend of Akhmatova (see his reminiscences in this book). *65, 72, 94, 153, 230, 251*

Makovsky, Sergei (1877–1962), artist and writer. From 1909 to 1917 he was the editor of the *Apollo* magazine. He emigrated and wrote a dubious account of Gumilev's life. *35, 38, 39, 251, 255*

Maksimov, Dmitry (1904–1987), poet and literary critic. *41*

Mandelshtam, Aleksandr, brother of Osip Mandelshtam. *143*

Mandelshtam, Osip (1891–1938), a Russian poet and friend of Akhmatova, was, together with Akhmatova, a member of the Poets' Guild (1911–14). The Guild attracted those poets affiliated with the acmeist movement in literature, who endeavored to oppose symbolism—at that time the dominant force in Russian poetry—with its own realistic understanding of the surrounding world in literature and art. *ix, x, xi, xvi, 1, 3, 14, 15, 22, 32, 35, 45, 47, 49, 64, 65, 67, 68, 89, 100, 104, 108, 110, 116, 117, 125, 126, 128, 137, 140, 141, 143, 144, 145, 146, 147,*

Marfa. Wife of the governor of the city-state of Novrogorod. In the fifteenth century she led the battle in Novgorod's fight for independence from the prince of Moscow. After Novgorod was captured, she was imprisoned under armed guard. *6*

Marina Roshcha, a region of Moscow. *123, 139*

Markish, Perets (1895–1952), Jewish poet accused in the "anti-fascist committee" case and shot. The "committee" was charged with actions against Soviet power during the period of anti-semitism that Stalin had stirred up, beginning in 1948. *247*

Marshak, Samuil (1887–1964), translator, children's poet. *140, 179*

Matveyeva, Novella, poet and singer. *191*

Mayakovsky, Vladimir (1893–1930), Russian poet, leader of the Futurist movement. *14, 34, 37, 44, 65, 66, 109, 115, 130, 132, 153, 207, 211, 237, 266*

Meierkhold, Vsevolod (1874–1940), Soviet Russian director, falsely accused and shot in 1940. *231*

Mikhalkov, Sergei, secretary of the Writers' Union Board. *113*

Modigliani, Amedea. Akhmatova's recollections of the artist, whom she met in Paris in 1912, were written in 1964. *49, 71, 152, 197, 204, 205, 208*

Modzalevsky, Lev (1902–1948), Pushkin scholar in Leningrad. *141*

Morozov, Nikolai (1854–1946), a writer and revolutionary with the People's Freedom. He was imprisoned in Shlisselburg fortress for twenty-five years. *98*

Motovilova, Anna, Akhmatova's grandmother on her mother's side. Motovilova (married name—Stogova, 1817–63) was in fact a descendant of the Akhmatov clan, which, according to family legend, descended from the Tatar Khan Akhmat (d. 1481). But the family never carried the title of prince. *6*

Na Postu and *Zhizn Iskusstva.* The article of G. Lelevich, "Anna Akhmatova," appeared in the magazine *Na Postu* (No. 192) and V. Pertsov's, "Along literary watersheds," in *Zhizn Iskusstva* (No. 43, 1925). Pertsov wrote that Akhmatova was so alien to contemporary readers it was as if "she were born too late or were unable to die in time." *26, 28, 267*

Naiman, Anatoly, Russian poet, Naiman became Akhmatova's secretary in her later years. *ix, 1, 129, 152, 160, 161*

Nappelbaum, Ida and *Frederika,* poetry students of Nikolai Gumilev. After he was shot his students organized a literary circle called "The Vibrating Shell." *94*

Narbut, Vladimir (1888–1940), member of the Poets' Guild. *3, 119, 143, 239, 257*

Nedobrovo, Nikolai (1882–1919), poet, critic, and friend of Akhmatova. Many of Akhmatova's lyrical poems were dedicated to him (see Boris Anrep's recollections about Nedobrovo in this book). Akhmatova considered the article by Nikolai Nedobrovo published in the magazine *Russkaya Mysl* (1915, No. 7) after her second book, *Rosary,* came out to be the best thing ever written about her. *16, 39, 40, 77, 78, 79, 86, 89, 90, 115, 121, 123, 153, 215, 216, 217, 218, 219, 220, 221, 222, 223, 224, 225, 226, 227, 228, 229, 241*

Nekrasov, Nikolai (1821–1877/78), Russian poet. *2, 97, 134, 153, 191*

Neldikhen, Sergei, poet. *258, 259*

Nevedomskaya, Vera, the Gumilevs' neighbor in Slepnyovo, Tver province. *35, 48*

The New Economic Policy. From 1917 until 1921 (the epoch of "war communism"), private property was essentially forbidden. In 1921 the Bolshevik government was forced to begin a "new policy" that permitted certain forms of private ownership and enterprise, including private publishers like Alkonost, Petrograd, and others. *34, 45, 68*

Nijinsky, Vatslav (1889–1950), Russian ballet dancer. Beginning in the early 1910s he danced primarily in Paris. Like Anna Pavlova, after 1917 he never returned to Russia. *15*

Novoye Vremya is a newspaper that was published in Petersburg by journalist and publisher Aleksei Suvorin (1834–1912). *41*

Odoevtseva, Irina, Russian poet and writer, student of Nikolai Gumilev and wife of Georgy Ivanov. *29, 45*

Oksman, Antonina Petrovna, wife of literary critic Yulian Oksman. *184, 196*

Oksman, Yulian (1895–1970), literary historian and Pushkin scholar. *141*

Okudzhava, Bulat, poet and singer. *191*

Orion carried Nikolai Gumilev's 1918 critical reviews of Akhmatova's poetry, praising the significance of her work. *37*

Osinsky, Valerian (1887–1938), a leading figure in the Bolshevik party. In 1922 he published an article about Akhmatova in the newspaper *Pravda.* Arguing that Akhmatova welcomed the Revolution, Osinsky pointed out as verification the fact that she had dedicated her poem "All is plundered, betrayed, and sold out . . ." to N. Rykova. Osinsky believed Akhmatova had in mind Nina Rykova, the wife of the head of the government of the USSR (in fact the poem was dedicated to her friend Natalia Rykova). *47*

Osmerkin, Aleksandr (1892–1953), an artist who painted Akhmatova's portrait in 1940, was married to Yelena Galperin-Osmerkina. *139, 140, 141*

Otsup, Nikolai (1894–1958), poet who wrote the foreword to Gumilev's *Selected Works* (Paris, 1959). *36, 45*

P.N.L. Pavel Luknitsky (1900–1973), poet who collected material on Gumilev in the 1920s. *240, 243*

Pavlova, Anna (1881–1921), Russian ballerina. *14, 15*

Pavlovich, Nadezhda (1895–1982), Soviet poet. *261*

Pavlovsk. A suburb of Leningrad near Tsarskoye Selo where one of the Tsar's palaces was located. *8, 9, 11, 21, 24*

Payne, Robert, author of *Les Trois Mondes de Boris Pasternak,* Paris, 1963. *30, 247, 248*

Pergam altar. The Altar of Zeus (180 B.C.), from the city of Pergam, now housed in a museum in Berlin. *25, 33, 44*

Petersburg Winters is Georgy Ivanov's book of memoirs (Paris, 1951). *29, 269*

Petrazhitsky, Lev (1867–1931), professor and lawyer who emigrated in 1918. *223, 224*

Petrovykh, Mariya (1908–1979), poet, translator, and friend of Akhmatova to whom Mandelshtam dedicated the poem "A Master of Guilty Glances." *188, 209, 238*

Pilnyak and *Zamyatin.* In 1929 an unprecedented campaign of persecution in all the Soviet papers was instigated against the writers Yevgeny Zamyatin (1884–1937) and Boris Pilnyak (1894–1938) because they allowed the works they could not have published in the USSR to be published abroad (until the mid-1920s such incidents were not noted). Pilnyak and Zamyatin were expelled from the All-Russia Writers' Union. As a sign of protest, Akhmatova, Mikhail Bulgakov, and others left the literary organization as well. *144*

Poletika, Idaliya (d. 1890) was a friend of the wife of Aleksander Pushkin and played an unpleasant role on the eve of the duel that killed Pushkin. *10*

Polonskaya, Nora, actress loved by Mayakovsky. *153, 154, 211*

Potemkin, Grigory (1739–1791), Russian Field Marshal and favorite of Empress Catherine II. *215*

Prokofiev, Sergei (1891–1953), Soviet composer, pianist, and conductor. *15, 49*

Punin, Nikolai (1888–1953), art critic and Akhmatova's third husband. He was Annensky's student at the Tsarskoye Selo gymnasium. Akhmatova divorced Punin in the late 1930s. He perished in the camps in 1952 after being arrested on a false charge in 1949. *36, 89, 96, 104, 125, 136, 138, 139, 141, 142, 148, 151, 152, 157, 158, 160, 269*

Punina, Irina, daughter of Akhmatova's husband, Nikolai Punin. *vii, 157, 160, 182*

Pushkarskaya, Nina, poet who befriended Akhmatova and Nadezhda Mandelshtam in Tashkent. *119*

Pyast, Vladimir (1886–1940), symbolist poet and author of the book of memoirs *Meetings* (1929). *38*

The Race of Time, Akhmatova's collection of verse published in 1965, contained many more of her later poems than the two books published in 1958 and 1961. These books, at the insistence of the publishers, mostly contained only her earlier work. *113, 146*

Radetsky, Ivan, journalist. *33*

Ranevskaya, Faina (1896–1984), actress and close friend of Akhmatova. *214*

Rasputin, Grigory (1872–1916), a peasant who gained the favor of Emperor Nicholas II and Empress Alexandra. He treated the throne's heir, Aleksei, for hemophilia and acquired great influence over the royal couple. He frequently interfered in matters of state and was killed by a conspiracy of monarchists. *13*

Rayevsky Courses were historical-philological classes of Rayev, one of the institutes of higher learning for women in Petersburg, where Akhmatova studied from 1910 to 1911. *38*

Remizov, Aleksei (1877–1957), Russian writer. He emigrated in 1921. *15, 16, 246, 268*

Repin, Ilya (1844–1930), Russian artist. *195*

Retsepter, Vladimir, actor, writer, and acquaintance of Akhmatova. *161*

Richter, Sviatoslav, Soviet pianist. *49*

Rostovtsev, Mikhail (1870–1952), Russian historian and archeologist. He emigrated after the Revolution. *14, 15*

Rozanov, Vasily (1856–1919), Russian religious philosopher, writer. *114, 116*

Rozhansky, Ivan and *Natalia,* Akhmatova's Moscow friends. Ivan Rozhansky was a physicist and philosophy historian. *30, 115, 122, 203*

Rozhdestvensky, Robert, Soviet poet. *191*

Rozhdestvensky, Vsevolod (1895–1977), a poet who was born and spent his childhood in Tsarskoye Selo. *36, 115, 242*

Rudakov, Sergei entrusted his papers and those of Osip Mandelshtam to his wife, who disposed of them after his death. Mandelshtam's papers had been given to Sergei Rudakov in the late 1930s by Akhmatova and Nadezhda Mandelshtam. *32*

Rybakova, Lydia, friend of Akhmatova. *150*

Ryleyev, Kondraty (1795–1826), Russian poet who was executed for taking part in the Decembrist uprising—a military action directed against the Tsarist government in December 1825. *145*

Samarin, Roman (1911–1974), Soviet literary critic. *35*

Savinkov, Boris (1879–1925), Russian revolutionary, member of the Socialist-Revolutionary Party, and writer. He was the head of the war ministry for the Provisional Government until the Bolsheviks seized power in 1917. *68*

Scriabin, Alexander (1877/78–1915), Russian composer. *14*

The Second Book, Nadezhda Mandelshtam's book of memoirs. *100, 165*

Selvinsky, Ilya (1899–1968), Soviet poet. *252*

Semashko, Nikolai (1874–1949), Soviet state and party official and minister of health. *61*

The Serapionov brothers. A group of writers who organized in Petrograd in the early 1920s. Members included Konstantin Fedin, Veniamin Kaverin, Mikhail Zoshchenko, Vsevolod Ivanov, and others. *68*

Sergeyev, Andrei, translator. *180*

Sergievsky, Ivan (1905–1954), Soviet literary critic. *29*

Serov, Valentin (1865–1911), a Russian artist who painted a portrait of the actress Mariya Yermolova (1853–1928). *70*

Serov, Vladimir (1910–1968), Soviet artist, from 1962 president of the USSR Academy of Arts. *177*

Severyanin, Igor (1887–1941), Russian poet. He emigrated after the Revolution. Leader of the "egofuturists," one of two poetry movements considered futurist in the 1910s. The other included Vladimir Mayakovsky, David Burlyuk, and Velimir Khlebnikov, who called themselves "cubofuturists." *14, 65, 94, 98*

Shaginyan, Marietta (1888–1982), Soviet writer. *46*

Shalamov, Varlam (1907–1982), writer and poet who spent almost twenty-five years in the camps and prisons. *102, 106, 120*

Shchegolev, Pavel (1877–1931), historian and Pushkin scholar. *94*

Shchegoleva, Valentina (1878–1931), philologist, Pushkin scholar. *140*

Shengeli, Georgy (1894–1956), Soviet poet. *35, 47, 179, 188*

Shervinsky, Sergei, poet and translator. *140*

Shileiko, Vladimir (1891–1930), Akhmatova's second husband, an orientalist, had an apartment in the official quarters of the Marble Palace in Petersburg on Mars Field. After the 1917 Revolution the palace was taken over by the Academy of Sciences. *31, 92, 93, 94, 178, 213, 237*

Shklovskaya, Vasilisa, and *Varvara*, wife and daughter of the writer *Viktor Shklovsky* (1893–1983). *253*

Shlisselburg fortress, a prison in Tsarist Russia. *271, 272*

Sholokhov, Mikhail (1905–1983), Soviet writer, winner of the Nobel Prize for literature (1965). *266*

Shostakovich, Dmitry (1906–1975), Soviet composer whom Akhmatova greatly admired. She inscribed a book of her verse that she presented to him with the words: "To Dmitry Shostakovich, in whose time I live. Akhmatova." *27*

Shvarts, Yevgeny (1896–1958), writer and playwright. *99*

Simonov, Konstantin (1915–1978), Soviet writer mentioned in Harkins' *Dictionary of Russian Literature*. *109, 136*

Sirena. A literary magazine published in 1918–19 in the city of Voronezh by the poet Vladimir Narbut—a member of the Poets' Guild from 1911 to 1914. *32*

Skabichevsky, Aleksandr (1838–1910/1911), Russian literary critic who based his criticism solely on his understanding of the progressive nature of a literary work. *62*

Slepnyovo. The estate of Nikolai Gumilev's mother in Tver. Akhmatova spent every summer from 1911 to 1917 in Slepnyovo. Today it is a museum to the poet. *7, 12, 13, 14, 47, 58, 81, 82, 83, 84, 270, 272*

The Snow Maiden, an opera by Nikolai Rimsky-Korsakov. *252*

Sobanskaya, Karolina, an acquaintance of Aleksandr Pushkin, who allegedly worked for the secret police. *212*

Sologub, Feodor (1863–1927), Russian writer and one of the first symbolist poets. *16, 41, 236, 258*

Sorin, Saveli, Russian artist. *231*

Spassky, Sergei (1898–1956), poet who was arrested in 1948 under false charges. He was freed in 1954 and later rehabilitated. *173*

Sreznevskaya, Valeria (1888–1964), Akhmatova's friend from the gymnasium (see her reminiscences in this book). *40, 51*

The Stalin Prize for literature was presented annually from 1940 until 1952 and, during that time, was the country's highest award (there were First, Second, and Third categories). Several writers could receive the award the same year. *278*

Stanislavsky, Konstantin (1863–1938), director, actor, and founder of the Moscow Art Theater. *174*

Stelletsky, Dmitry, painter and sculptor. *223, 224*

Stenich, Valentin (1898–1937), critic and translator who was shot under false charges. *207*

Stepun, Feodor (1884–1965), Russian philosopher. He describes his meeting with Akhmatova in his memoires *Gone but Not Forgotten* (New York, 1952). *42*

Strange Sky, Pearls, and *Bonfire*, titles of collections of verse by Nikolai Gumilev. *31*

Stravinsky, Igor (1882–1971), Russian composer who emigrated to the United States in 1939. *14, 15, 238*

Stray Dog. A Petersburg cafe that from 1912 to 1915 served as a gathering place for artists, poets, musicians, and actors. It was also the site of poetry recitation, ballet performances, and literary discussions. *64, 65, 66, 68, 237, 266*

Struve, Gleb (d. 1982), literary critic who published the collected works of Nikolai Gumilev in New York in the 1960s, published the authentic reminiscences of Boris Anrep, published excerpts from the letters of Nikolai Nedobrovo, and also fragments of Anrep's recollections of Nedobrovo in the third volume of Akhmatova's *Collected Works* (Paris, 1983). *32, 87, 89, 90, 215*

Sudeikin, Sergei, Russian avant-garde artist, husband of Olga Glebova-Sudeikina. *65, 96, 231, 232, 233, 238*

Suok, Serafima, widow of the poet Vladimir Narbut, who perished in the camps. In 1940 she married Khardzhiev and later, an evacuee in Alma Ata, she married Viktor Shklovsky. *124*

Surkov, Aleksei (1899–1963), Soviet poet, secretary of the board of the Writers' Union. His support helped in the publication of Akhmatova's books in 1958 and 1961. *105, 112, 156, 158, 195*

Suvorin, Aleksei (1834–1912), journalist, playwright, founder, and owner of the Maly Theater in Petersburg. *41, 231, 273*

Syndics. Sycophantic critics, especially Gumilev and Gorodetsky, who headed the Poets' Guild. *33, 94, 239, 247*

T., Vladimir Tatlin (1885–1953), artist and designer. *119, 120*

Talnikov, Sergei (Shpitalnikov), poet and critic. *40*

Tarkovsky, Arseny (1907–1989), Soviet poet, father of the film director Andrei Tarkovsky (1932–1986). *113, 191, 208, 209, 251*

Tashkent. In the 1940s Nadezhda Mandelshtam worked in the Central Asian University in Tashkent. From 1941 until 1944, Akhmatova and many other writers from Leningrad and Moscow lived there as evacuees. *5, 9, 20, 106, 109, 122, 125, 148, 149, 163, 186, 197, 213, 214, 267, 274*

Tata, nickname of Ekaterina Livshits (1902–1987), a ballerina and widow of the poet Benedikt Livshits, who was shot in 1938. She was arrested in 1939, released from camp in 1942, and lived in exile until 1953. Their son was killed during a bombing raid in 1942. *vii, 102*

Tikhonov, Aleksandr (1880–1956), writer. *260*

Tikhonov, Nikolai (1896–1979), Soviet poet. *47*

Tolstaya-Yesenina, Sofya (1900–1957), granddaughter of Lev Tolstoy and widow of the poet Sergei Yesenin. *139*

Tolstoy, Aleksei (1882/83–1945), Soviet Russian writer; one of the first to be awarded the Stalin Prize. *38, 145, 235, 246, 257*

Tolstoy, Petr (1645–1729), a diplomat, persuaded Aleksei, son of Peter the Great, to return to Russia in 1718. Immediately upon his return the prince was executed. *50*

Tomashevskaya, Irina, literary critic and friend of Akhmatova. *47, 157*

Tomashevskaya, Zoya, architect and daughter of Akhmatova's close friends. *112*

Vinogradov, Viktor (1894/95–1969), literary critic, philologist, and academician. *34, 45, 202*

Volpe, Tsezar (1904–1938), philologist who worked at the magazine *Zvezda*. He published an essay in 1933 in the magazine *Zvezda* (No. 5) by Mandelshtam entitled "Travels to Armenia," despite the censorship ban. Volpe was subsequently fired. In 1938 he was arrested and shot. *140, 244*

Volpin, Mikhail (1902–1988), writer. *109, 267*

Volynsky, Akim (1863–1926), art critic and ballet historian. *68*

Vsemirnaya Literatura (World Literature Publishers) was a publishing house where Aleksandr Blok, Kornei Chukovsky, Nikolai Gumilev, and others worked in the first years after the Revolution. *93*

Vyazemsky, Petr (1792–1878), Russian poet and critic. *130*

The Wolf. The title Akhmatova gave to Mandelshtam's poem in her *Poem Without a Hero. 246*

Yagoda, Genrikh (1891–1938), one of the major figures behind the Stalinist repressions, People's Commissar of Internal Affairs beginning in 1934. The fact that the warrant for the arrest of Osip Mandelshtam was signed by the head of the NKVD reflected the importance attached to the poet's case. *145, 246*

Yakobson, Roman (1896–1982), Russian and American literary critic. *204, 211*

Yakubovich, Dmitry (1907–1940), Pushkin scholar in Leningrad. *141*

Yegolin, Aleksandr (1896–1959), a high-ranking official of the Central Committee of the CPSU(B) in the 1940s. *29*

Yenukidze, Avel (1877–1937), at that time secretary of the All-Union Executive Committee. He was shot in 1937. *246*

Yesenin, Sergei (1895–1925), Soviet Russian poet. *109, 205, 244, 278*

Yesenina-Tolstaya, Sofya, a friend of Akhmatova. She was the widow of the poet Sergei Yesenin and granddaughter of Lev Tolstoy. *139*

Yevpatoria. A city on the Black Sea. In 1905, in many large cities of Russia, revolutionary actions (strikes, armed revolts) led to a number of political changes in the government, including the formation of a parliamentary body, the State Duma, which was to restrict the absolute power of the emperor, permit the creation of legal political parties, halt the preliminary censorship of published works, etc. *2*

Yevtushenko, Yevgeny, Soviet poet. *74, 191*

Yurkun, Yuri (1895–1938), poet. *233, 264*

Zabolotsky, Nikolai (1903–1958), Soviet poet. *141, 190, 191*

Zamoskvorechye, a region of Moscow where Akhmatova lived with her friends at Nina Ardova-Olshevskaya's apartment when she came to the city in the 1940s, 1950s, and 1960s. *20, 198*

Zamyatin, Yevgeny (1884–1937), writer and member of the board of editors of the magazine *Russky Sovremennik*. *44, 93, 260, 274*

Zamyatina, Mariya (1865–1919), Vyacheslav Ivanov's housekeeper and secretary. *39*

Zelmanova-Chudovskaya, Anna, artist who painted portraits of Akhmatova and Mandelshtam in the 1910s. *237*

Zenkevich, Mikhail (1901–1982), member of the Poets' Guild. *3, 31, 41, 143, 239, 248*

Zhdanov, Andrei (1896–1948), First Secretary of the Leningrad Regional and City Committee of the CPSU(B), reporting to meetings of Leningrad writers and the Party activists of the city of Leningrad, referred to Akhmatova's poetry as "mystical longings shared with eroticism." Akhmatova herself was called a "wanton and nun in whom lechery was mixed with prayer." *27, 29, 69, 137, 167, 212*

Zhirmunsky, Viktor (1891–1971), literary critic and scholar, and a student of Akhmatova's work. *32, 41, 42, 45, 207*

Zhukovsky, Vasily (1783–1852), Russian romantic poet, and Nikolai Karamzin (1766–1826), historian and writer, lived in the Tsarskoye Selo palace because both were at different times tutors to the Tsar's heirs. *243*

Zinovyev, Grigory (1883–1936), Soviet party official and member of the Central Committee of the Communist Party. From 1917 he was the chairman of the Petrograd Soviet of Workers' and Soldiers' Deputies. *260*

Znamya Truda. The Socialist-Revolutionary Party newspaper that was printed in Moscow from 1917 to 1918. *241*

Zoshchenko, Mikhail (1895–1958), like Akhmatova, was expelled from Soviet literary life after the 1946 Central Committee resolution. *5, 27, 28, 69, 99, 135, 156, 167, 173, 189, 194, 207, 244, 267, 275*